"To confront the challenges facing the Pentecostal and Charismatic movements in the future, we must wrestle with the implications of Pentecost through sustained reflection on Scripture and experience. The next hundred years demand a foundation in theology without lessening the focus on mission and experience. This is precisely what Macchia offers with this book. He blends both classical theology and global witness into one text, thereby providing a valuable contribution to the church's life and mission. I will use this book in my theology course!"

—**Terry L. Cross**, School of Theology & Ministry, Lee University

"Who better to declare the wonders of God than veteran theologian, sage, and theological statesman Frank Macchia. It wasn't that long ago that Pentecostal works of systematic theology were simply unavailable. Macchia leads the charge of a generation of Pentecostal and Charismatic scholars now working at the forefront of theological studies and inviting the rest of us in. This is an engaging, hospitable, informed, and deeply spiritual theology that rewards its readers. The final chapter on 'The Bottom Line' will form the start of my own lectures on theology. Students and teachers alike will appreciate this fresh and compelling work dedicated to the love of God in Christ made known by the Spirit."

—**Myk Habets**, Laidlaw College

"Macchia's book is the most readable, thorough, well-organized, historically interactive, and engaging introduction to systematic theology from a Pentecostal/Charismatic perspective that is available to us today! It covers every topic that one might expect and hope to find: the nature of global theology and its sources, God's perfections and triune being, the Son of God's incarnation and atoning sacrifice, the deity and person of the Holy Spirit who creates human beings and re-creates them through salvation, the community and mission of the church, and God's final purposes and our future hope. I cannot recommend this book highly enough!"

—**Gregg R. Allison**, The Southern Baptist Theological Seminary;
secretary, the Evangelical Theological Society

T0285652

Praise for the Foundations for Spirit-Filled Christianity Series

"I am amazed at how North American and European Christians continue to ignore the dramatic changes in global Christianity. These changes are not insignificant. They call for serious revisions in the Christian mission, ecumenism, and theological training. One of the most dramatic shifts has been the rapid rise of Pentecostal/Charismatic spirituality. It is safe to say that in all forms of the global church—Protestant, Roman Catholic, and Orthodox—people are increasingly seeing themselves as Spirit-filled believers. Unfortunately, colleges and seminaries often lack textbooks that address these changes. This series, Foundations for Spirit-Filled Christianity, is a timely intervention, one that will certainly help to fill this gap."

—**Cheryl Bridges Johns**, Global Pentecostal House of Study,
United Theological Seminary

"The Foundations for Spirit-Filled Christianity series rightly identifies the pivotal role of Pentecostal and Charismatic Christianity in shaping tomorrow's global Christianity and addresses the shortage of resources for training future leaders. The titles of the series will serve this Christian family's continuing growth by providing textbooks for its theological education."

—**Wonsuk Ma**, College of Theology and Ministry, Oral Roberts University

"The church and academy are finally ready for Foundations for Spirit-Filled Christianity, which relays the insights and perspectives of mature Pentecostal and Charismatic theologians and biblical scholars on a broad array of important theological topics, doctrinal loci, and practical realities. Pentecostal theologians from around the world are now ready to speak in their own accents in ways that will benefit the church catholic."

—**Amos Yong**, Fuller Theological Seminary

Introduction
to Theology

FOUNDATIONS FOR SPIRIT-FILLED CHRISTIANITY

SERIES EDITORS

Jerry Ireland, chaplain, US Navy

Paul W. Lewis, associate dean and professor of historical theology and intercultural studies, Assemblies of God Theological Seminary at Evangel University, Springfield, Missouri

Frank D. Macchia, professor of systematic theology, Vanguard University, and associate director of the Centre for Pentecostal and Charismatic Studies at Bangor University, Wales, United Kingdom

ADVISORY BOARD

Kim Alexander, director of academics and RSM online, Ramp School of Ministry

Roli Dela Cruz, Assemblies of God (USA) World Missions missionary serving as Greek and New Testament instructor at Asia Pacific Theological Seminary, Baguio, Philippines

Sarita Gallagher Edwards, practitioner-scholar and frequent speaker and writer on global Christianity, biblical theology of mission, and mission history

Robert L. Gallagher, professor of intercultural studies emeritus, Wheaton College Graduate School

Byron Klaus, professor of intercultural leadership studies, Assemblies of God Theological Seminary

Andy Lord, minister at All Saints' Didcot in the diocese of Oxford and visiting lecturer at the London School of Theology

Gary Tyra, professor of biblical and practical theology, Vanguard University

Nimi Wariboko, Walter G. Muelder Professor of Social Ethics, Boston University

Introduction *to* Theology

DECLARING THE WONDERS OF GOD

FRANK D. MACCHIA

Baker Academic
a division of Baker Publishing Group
Grand Rapids, Michigan

© 2023 by Frank D. Macchia

Published by Baker Academic
a division of Baker Publishing Group
Grand Rapids, Michigan
www.bakeracademic.com

Printed in the United States of America

Library of Congress Cataloging-in-Publication Data
Names: Macchia, Frank D., 1952– author.
Title: Introduction to theology : declaring the wonders of God / Frank D. Macchia.
Description: Grand Rapids, Michigan : Baker Academic, a division of Baker Publishing Group, [2023] | Series: Foundations for Spirit-filled Christianity | Includes bibliographical references and index.
Identifiers: LCCN 2022046585 | ISBN 9781540963376 (paperback) | ISBN 9781540966520 (casebound) | ISBN 9781493441617 (ebook) | ISBN 9781493441624 (pdf)
Subjects: LCSH: Theology, Doctrinal.
Classification: LCC BT75.3 .M26 2023 | DDC 230—dc23/eng/20221123
LC record available at https://lccn.loc.gov/2022046585

Baker Publishing Group publications use paper produced from sustainable forestry practices and post-consumer waste whenever possible.

23 24 25 26 27 28 29   7 6 5 4 3 2 1

In memory of my mother, Elizabeth

CONTENTS

SERIES PREFACE

The demographics of Christianity, along with those of the general world population, have changed and expanded significantly over the past few centuries. A key aspect of this expansion has been the influence and growth of the church internationally, especially in the Global South, which is largely composed of believers within Pentecostal and Charismatic streams of Christianity. Consequently, the changing face of global Christianity is becoming increasingly diverse and characterized by Pentecostal and Charismatic beliefs and praxis. Despite the massive increase in Pentecostal churches and educational institutions, there still exists a lacuna of textbooks that incorporate perspectives from Pentecostal and Charismatic streams of Christianity. The Foundations for Spirit-Filled Christianity series attempts to fill that void by offering high-quality introductory textbooks that include both global and Pentecostal streams of thought. These textbooks will explore primary topics of interest in the fields of biblical studies, church ministries and practical theology, church history, theology, and missions.

The global aspect of Christianity is reflected in the diversity and breadth of the series advisory board, and global perspectives have been intentionally highlighted by the series editors, who have been immersed in other cultural settings throughout their lives. Jerry Ireland and his wife, Paula, lived and worked in Africa, including in educational entities, for well over a decade; Paul Lewis and his wife, Eveline (a native Chinese Indonesian), lived and worked in East Asia, primarily in academic institutions, for almost two decades; and Frank Macchia and his wife, Verena (a native of Switzerland), lived in Europe while Frank studied at the University of Basel.

Each book in the series will also reflect the increasingly Pentecostal nature of global Christianity. The various authors will offer robust discussions and balanced appraisals of their topics while simultaneously situating Pentecostal perspectives alongside those traditionally showcased in introductory textbooks for evangelical Bible colleges and seminaries. These textbooks will also help students navigate the sometimes-controversial arguments surrounding some Pentecostal and Charismatic themes and concerns. Further, while remaining global in perspective, authors will locate their themes within a theologically conservative framework.

In summary, what distinguishes this series is, first, its primary focus on providing high-quality introductory college and seminary textbooks and, second, its resonance with contemporary students who are fully in tune with global Pentecostal and Charismatic theology and perspectives. Ultimately, the goal is to provide tools for the global church that represent the vast array of church expressions in order to set the stage for the next generation to continue to effectively and responsibly advance the good news of the gospel. To God be the glory!

ACKNOWLEDGMENTS

I sit at the conclusion of this project with a heart filled with gratitude. My wife, Verena, deserves the most honor for her patience and support as I took valuable time away from her to complete this book. I am also grateful to my fellow editors, Paul Lewis and Jerry Ireland, for graciously suggesting that I contribute in this way to the series that they did so much to bring together. I wish also to thank my colleagues at Vanguard University for their comradery during the difficult years of teaching that were marked by the COVID-19 pandemic. During this time (and for many years before that), my many students have never ceased to stimulate my thinking and to edify me with their kind encouragement. This book is in part the fruit of that interaction. And above all else, I wish to join my voice with countless others over the many centuries spanning church history to declare the wonders of God, to protect and explore them together with so many others. All glory goes to God for the fruit that this volume will bring.

INTRODUCTION

When the day of Pentecost came, they were all together in one place. Suddenly a sound like the blowing of a violent wind came from heaven and filled the whole house where they were sitting. They saw what seemed to be tongues of fire that separated and came to rest on each of them. All of them were filled with the Holy Spirit and began to speak in other tongues as the Spirit enabled them. . . . [Those in the crowd asked,] "How is it that each of us hears them in our native language? . . . We hear them declaring the wonders of God in our own tongues!" (Acts 2:1–4, 8, 11)

On the day of Pentecost, Jews from many nations were visiting Jerusalem to observe this feast day. In ancient Judaism, Pentecost celebrated the granting of the law at Mount Sinai. But the law was itself a witness to the new life that God grants by grace, especially in the coming of the Messiah. On this particular day of Pentecost, that fulfillment is announced as being accomplished. Behind the scenes of that Pentecost celebration, a grand fulfillment was occurring. It happened fifty days after Christ's resurrection. Christ had appeared to 120 of his followers to grant them a final discourse on the kingdom of God and to commission them for their mission "to the ends of the earth" (Acts 1:8; cf. vv. 1–8). He then ascended from their midst, took his place at the right hand of the heavenly Father, and poured forth the promised Holy Spirit to inaugurate his reign and to bring it to fulfillment in the world (2:32–35). When the first Spirit outpouring occurred on that day of Pentecost, there was a mighty sound of a rushing wind and flames of fire resting on Jesus's followers as together they declared the wonders of God in tongues that could be understood in the many languages of the world. Many in the audience were amazed that they heard the disciples declare the wonders of God in the native languages of the lands from which they came. Declaring the wonders of God—what a wonderfully diverse and expansive praise; what a wonderfully diverse and expansive witness!

Imagine this, the wonders of God being declared in multiple languages all at once. This was not just *any* prophetic communication of God's wonders: this was communication overload.[1] No one person could have taken it all in. No one community could have grasped it all. It required a large audience from many nations. This declaration of the wonders of God was implicitly global in scope, implying that theology will reflect on those wonders in many different contexts, languages, and cultures. As Amos Yong suggests, Pentecost opened up a cultural hospitality that was remarkably diverse.[2] Daniel Ramírez focuses on the fact that the "linguistic hospitality" revealed at Pentecost subverts the hegemony of dominant languages in the ancient Mediterranean world, such as Greek and Latin.[3] This event not only launched the birth of the global church; it also launched the task of theology along with it. Theology is one of the many wonderful gifts provided to us in the birth of the global church.

As we will note in the pages that follow, theology is "God talk." It is speech about the wonders of God that seeks to reflect on and guide the praise and witness of the church toward greater loyalty to the good news of Jesus Christ. The good news is the gospel of who God is and what God has done, is doing, and will do to fulfill the kingdom and to bring the new creation into being. The home base of theology is the church—its praise and its mission. The global tongues of Pentecost declaring the wonders of God are the larger chorus that theology joins and for which theology does its work. These tongues assume that through the redemptive work of Israel's Messiah, the barriers of sin and death that blocked the path to the new era of the Spirit and of the new creation have been overcome. The Spirit is now being poured out on all flesh! Israel's calling to bless the nations is being fulfilled! The renewing work of the Spirit is overflowing the boundaries of Israel and is now spilling out in the direction of the nations. God is transforming communication, turning it into a vast revelation of the Spirit and truth. Theology assumes this grand gift of divine

---

1. Michael Welker, *God the Spirit*, trans. John F. Hoffmeyer (Minneapolis: Fortress, 1994), 235.

2. Amos Yong, *Hospitality and the Other: Pentecost, Christian Practices, and the Neighbor* (Maryknoll, NY: Orbis Books, 2008), 99–128.

3. Daniel Ramírez, "Pentecostés Fronterizo: Hospitalidad Lingüística y Discurso Profético," online presentation, Facebook, August 22, 2020, https://www.facebook.com/watch/?v=9989 51217224099.

self-giving, of divine communication, that brings redemption and renewal. Theology is thus a *global* conversation. No single tongue or context can fully capture the wonderful diversity of the church's praise and witness. Yet there is a single point of reference in the work of the triune God that unites it all.

We should also bear in mind that the reach of theology is not only global but also eschatological, meaning that it points to the final and ultimate fulfillment of the new creation in Christ and the work of the Spirit. Not only do the transformed tongues of the church point beyond any one cultural context, they also point beyond all contexts. History itself is ultimately to be transcended. There is a grand mystery to which theology points that we could never bring adequately to expression. We study, reflect on, and speak theology with humility and stammering lips. We could never speak the final word on the wonders of God. We can only point meaningfully to that which is presently being revealed to us. What everyone saw and heard at the Spirit's arrival on the day of Pentecost implied as much. A sound of a rushing wind recalls the mighty Spirit that hovered over the deep to bring creation into being in Genesis 1:2. Except now at Pentecost, it is a new creation launched by the resurrection of Christ that is being depicted. The flames resting on the heads of Christ's early followers depicted the sanctified speech that had come forth from the mouths of those present. The abundance of the Spirit moves in conformity with the crucified and risen Christ so as to bear witness to a new world coming, the world of the kingdom of God that will bring mercy and justice to all. It will not be the dominant cultural and economic powers of this present world that govern the witness of the church, but rather the work of Christ and the new world that it ushers in. The church, in its praise and witness, seeks to share the good news of the coming new creation and its presence already in the Spirit being poured forth. Theology reflects on and joins with this praise and this witness so as to encourage and guide it.

In light of the above background, the following six chapters will take the reader through the major topics of theology. Chapter 1 will cover the norms that inform and govern theology—supremely Scripture but also tradition. It will also explore the creative task of theology as it seeks to be relevant to many cultural contexts and forms of living self-expression. Chapter 2 gets right to the chief subject matter of theology—namely, God. Chapter 3 explores the center of theology, which is Christ, and chapter 4 looks to the expansive and transcendent reach of theology in the Holy Spirit and in the reality of salvation. Chapter 5 then explores the doctrine of the church, which is the sign and instrument of the coming new creation. The concluding chapter covers eschatology, or final purposes. Bold type will be used to indicate key theological terms throughout the book.

Theology is not only a church discipline but also an academic area of study that presents us with an array of scholarly issues worthy of discussion. Readers who are expecting sermons or devotions in the pages that follow may be disappointed. Yet, while exploring the academic issues, I will also attempt to highlight and reflect on the fundamental issues that are of importance to the praise and worship that inform theology. Those in search of greater wisdom for their faith will have much to chew on as well. Theology seeks to provoke the mind, satisfy the heart, and guide one's steps. May the pages that follow bear witness, with stammering lips, to the wonders of God in a way that both encourages and guides the larger praise and witness of the church.

1

THEOLOGY, SCRIPTURE, AND CONTEXT

When I wrote in my introduction that theology is God talk, I referred primarily to the literal meaning of the term. "Theo" comes from the Greek word *theos* (θεός), which means "God," and "logy" comes from *logos* (λόγος), which means "word" or "discourse." Hence, theology is God talk! Typically, "logy" endings on words depict avenues of study and speech that have their own ways of gathering research and presenting it. So one could broaden the term "theology" to refer to an area of study that centers on God, especially on God's deeds and purposes. With this in mind, some would view theology as "faith seeking understanding." Theology would then be an area of study or research about God that involves disciplined research and reflection. Of course, theology is also communicated in a way that informs and guides other ways of thinking and communicating the faith of the church.

As I noted earlier, theology has its home base in the praise and mission of the church, but it is also open to various global contexts. In its loyalty to Scripture, theology joins the church in its ongoing praise and witness so as to encourage and to guide it. This means that theology also seeks to be relevant within many different cultural contexts. The encouragement and guidance that theology offers require both participation in the life of the church and a personal spiritual discipline to undergird it. After all, theology seeks to know its subject matter (i.e., the wonders of God) *from the inside*. Necessary for that task is a spiritual life that conforms to the love of Christ, which is where

God's wonders are most decisively revealed. "Whoever does not love does not know God" (1 John 4:8).

Yet academic study is important too, since theology uniquely reflects on the wonders of God as an academic field of study. This emphasis on academic study means that theology has a place in the university curriculum, especially in Christian universities and theological seminaries. The life of the church in loyalty to Scripture is the primary home base of theology, but the secondary place of work is the academy or academic world. Fields of academic study (the world of the academy), with all of the disciplined methods of study and reflection that go with them, play a role in theological reflection as well. Engaging these other disciplines helps theologians better understand Scripture and the history of theology in their original contexts. It also helps them understand how to relate the faith to their own contemporary contexts.

Theologians examine the Bible's original languages and changing historical-cultural contexts. They study the history of theology in light of the changing worldviews and social contexts that originally contextualized that theology. They attempt to express the contents of the Christian faith in a way that is sensitive to current trends of thinking about the world in relation to what may be termed ultimate reality. Theology as a distinctive gift to the body of Christ is academic in nature. It is an academic discipline that borrows insights from other areas of study, such as ancient languages, history, philosophy, psychology, and sociology. Amos Yong notes insightfully that different academic methods of study can be likened to different "languages" or modes of construing reality, meaning that to be multicontextual or multilingual in a way that is faithful to Pentecost requires one to appreciate other academic disciplines.[1]

There are, of course, potential risks involved when theology engages with other academic disciplines (e.g., the elements of the faith can be compromised), but that is why theology must be accountable first to the faith of the church, which it seeks to reflect upon and to guide. Risk is involved in any task worth doing, so that alone need not discourage the important work of theology in its interaction with other academic disciplines. The church may require further enlightenment and openness on some of these matters. Historically, some tension has existed between theology as a discipline of the church, seeking to be faithful to its worship and witness, and theology as an academic field of study that overlaps with other academic areas of interest. Theology is primarily accountable to the former and only secondarily accountable to the latter, yet it needs to be accountable to both. The task of history in particular

---

1. Amos Yong, *Renewing the Church by the Spirit: Theological Education after Pentecost* (Grand Rapids: Eerdmans, 2020), 100–104.

has shown theologians that all conceptions and expressions about God are conditioned and limited by a finite historical and cultural setting. Theology has to be contextualized in order to be faithful in its witness, in speaking to people where they live, move, and have their being. But that same contextuality exposes theology's limits. A contextual witness can always be questioned and to some extent transcended to meet the needs of a new time and place, but never in a way that abandons its core. This dynamic process of reinterpretation means that theology must be an ongoing task that learns from the past and is always faithful to its core in the gospel. But throughout, theology is also always open to a fresh formulation of the truth that strives for faithful contextual relevance.

Academic areas of study such as language, history, philosophy, and sociology have enhanced our understanding of the Bible. Many insights into the Bible and its relevance to the church have been gained from these secular areas of inquiry. For example, a study of ancient history and culture can show us how intertwined religion was with the culture and politics of ancient peoples mentioned in the Bible, including Israel. Religious idolatry was inseparable from a nation's quest for wealth and power. A people's gods were thought to guarantee their hold on power over others. Erecting and worshiping the idols devoted to these gods was thought to make them "user friendly" toward that end. Idolatry was not limited to bowing before statues on pedestals! And Israel was not immune to this temptation, as the Old Testament abundantly shows. A knowledge of our own history as a nation, including our global economics and politics, can help us discern how the biblical condemnation of idolatry relates to our context today. How have we as a nation attempted to make God user friendly in our own quest for power? How have we misused the Bible to justify the unjust cases of war or the unjust exclusion of people who were viewed as undesirable by a dominant culture?

The overall goal of theology is faithfulness to the biblical message; the desire to search for the message's relevance in our time and place serves that faithfulness. We will use other academic disciplines to help us better understand our Scriptures and our context, and we will do so freely, yet with our faithfulness to the foundation of the gospel securely in place.

One may use the analogy of ancient statues to illustrate what I mean. Many ancient statues have a base leg, which is straight and bears the weight of the statue, and a free leg, which is bent and serves a more creative though still necessary function. The base leg is foundational and thus stands for the theologian's devotion to the faith and witness of the church, especially as found in the witness of Scripture. The free leg is the theologian's involvement in secular academic methods and insights, especially as a help in relating the faith to the church's secular context, in service to the mercy and justice of the kingdom of God. The theologian is free to engage and to be enlightened by the academy, but not in a way that departs from the foundational faith of the church. As I mentioned above, there are many forms of God talk in the church. What distinguishes them from academic theology is, in part, the latter's involvement in related academic areas of inquiry, which grant theology its direction as a critical discipline. I often remind the students who join me in my introductory theology course that this study is not like what goes on in Sunday school or discipleship training. We will indeed pursue theology in a way that seeks to be faithful to Scripture and to the faith and witness of the church, but we will also go about our study as an academic discipline that has a history and draws from other academic methods of inquiry.

Systematic Theology

"Theology," as it is used in this introduction, can be more broadly referred to as **systematic theology**, since it follows the major doctrines of the faith in systematic fashion. These doctrines are sometimes called **loci**. The term comes from the Latin word *locus* (plural: *loci*), which can mean "area," such as an area of study. The standard areas or doctrines of study for systematic theologians are taken from those that have been most discussed in the history of theology:

- theology proper (the study of God's nature and existence)
- Christology (the study of Christ)
- pneumatology (the study of the Holy Spirit—*pneuma* being the Greek term for "Spirit")
- soteriology (the study of salvation—*sōtēria* being the Greek term for "salvation")
- ecclesiology (the study of the church—*ekklēsia* being the Greek term for "church")
- eschatology (the study of final purposes—*eschaton* being the Greek term for "end" or "final")

Notice how the top three loci concern God and the three loci that follow deal with God's purposes and deeds in the world. Theology is still all about *God*—more specifically, the triune God: the Father as source, the Son as mediator, and the Spirit as perfector of the divine work mediated through and in the Son. The doctrine of the Trinity may thus be regarded as the flowering of doctrine, the overall framework in which all theological concerns are discussed. The theologian can study and discuss any one of these areas of concern in its own right. The study would still be systematic in the sense that the theologian attempts to construct a coherent presentation of this area of concern, showing how all the various elements of their discussion follow a logical sequence and fit together into a consistent whole. If systematic theologians investigate and discuss all of the loci together, they do not do so in a way that treats each one in isolation from the others. The effort is to show how they all fit together into a logical sequence and a coherent whole. The work also seeks to be contextually sensitive and relevant. Theology is scientific in that it is accountable to the revelation given objectively in Christ and in the Scriptures. But there is also an artistic quality about theology, since it seeks a unique presentation of theology's coherence, one that is open to a particular context. This leaves room for different systematic theologies to grace the landscape of the church's life and to both inspire and guide the life and work of the church.

Theology as systematic theology is sometimes called **dogmatics**, especially in Europe. The word "dogma" has a negative connotation in common English usage today, usually referring to a narrow-minded or overly biased viewpoint. But the term has a positive meaning in theology, referring to doctrines that are vital to the gospel, such as salvation by grace, the deity of Christ, and atonement through Christ alone. Dogmatics, like systematic theology, addresses key doctrines with an eye toward coherence and relevance to culture. Karl Barth's multivolume *Church Dogmatics* is a massive treatment of key doctrines of the faith from a Reformed perspective (the second branch of the Protestant Reformation, next to the Lutheran movement). It is a favorite place to turn for theological stimulation among advanced students and accomplished theologians. Systematic theology is doctrinal, but it is not doctrine per se. Doctrinal statements are formulated by *churches*; they tend to be brief, and they are erected as guardrails to keep the speech of a church faithful to orthodox or biblically established guidelines. Systematic theology, though doctrinal, reflects and elaborates on the concerns of the church in a way that expands upon, illuminates, and critically probes these areas. It is done by *individuals*, not by churches.

Systematic theology is different from biblical studies. Biblical studies tend to focus on biblical texts or a biblical book, with an emphasis on what these texts meant at the time they were written and how they would have been received and understood by their original audiences. We don't always know much about such things. Of course, the Bible contains stories. There are indeed times when narrative and other literary analyses of the biblical texts will play as much, if not more, of a role as historical research into the original setting in which the Scripture was written. Be that as it may, it is still important to note that the Bible was written to audiences in another time and place. The Bible was thus written to express God's will *for* us, but it was not written directly *to* us. As Paul wrote about the earlier stories of the Old Testament, "These things happened to [the Israelites] as examples and were written down as warnings for us, on whom the culmination of the ages has come" (1 Cor. 10:11). This is not to say that the ancient Scriptures cannot speak to us with a sense of immediacy in the power of the Spirit. They do! The world of the biblical narrative draws us in as we identify with its characters and view our world in a fresh light from the vantage point of their challenges, failures, and successes—and, most of all, in the light of how God pursues people by grace. God will indeed speak to our hearts through this text. But if one wishes for an in-depth study of Scripture that avoids reading our own thoughts into it, contrary to the original meaning of the text, we need to be attentive to the results of biblical scholarship. We need to include what the ancient texts were written to say to their original audiences.

Exegesis is the science of methodically extracting the meaning of Scripture *out of* the text in light of its original context. **Eisegesis** is wrongly reading our own thoughts *into* the text, contrary to its original meaning. We want to be exegetical rather than eisegetical! **Hermeneutics** is the *theory* of biblical interpretation, and exegesis is the method and *practice* of it. For example, interpreting the parables of Jesus in light of their original time and place and their literary form is exegesis. But the more philosophical question of what parables are generally crafted to do or how they function belongs to hermeneutics. Hermeneutical questions might ask whether there is more than one meaning to a parable and whether in this light some incidental elements in the story do not require interpretation. Hermeneuts can also ask broader questions, such as those relating to the role of narrative in the Bible or how language functions in the process of interpretation.

The field of biblical studies is also concerned with theology, but it focuses on the theological implications of a certain text or biblical book. Biblical scholars are bound to the text: they tend to be cautious about grand, sweeping theological conclusions, a caution that systematicians need to consider in their important work of grander theological construction. However, biblical scholars who are theologically inclined sometimes write volumes describing the theology of a biblical book or author, even the diverse theology of an entire Testament (Old or New). Though biblical theologians will sometimes draw general conclusions about a book, author, or Testament, they are especially attuned to the uniqueness or diversity of voices in the Bible. Systematicians who construct broad theological visions need to be attentive to the results of biblical scholarship. Systematic theology needs to be biblically based and should seek to be accountable to Scripture in all that it says.

Church history deals with the history of churches, movements, and key theologians in the light of their historical settings. **Historical theology** focuses on theological developments rather than historical and institutional realities involved in the diverse journey of the churches over the centuries. Systematic theologians study historical theology because the doctrinal issues discussed by systematicians have a history, offering insights that may be useful when discussing what these doctrinal concerns mean for us today. A storehouse of wisdom is accumulated in the tradition of the church and can be helpful in dealing with challenges to the faith today. Grand liturgical texts, creeds, confessions, and works of significant theologians can speak to us today in our own efforts to be faithful to the biblical message in our time.

Although not devoid of internal conflicts, the church was a unified entity for its first thousand years. During this time, the Latin-speaking West and the Greek-speaking East were taking somewhat different paths theologically—and deep cracks were forming in their relationship—but they were still one church. The Great Schism between these two streams began in the eleventh century and extended to the fourteenth century. Eastern Orthodox churches (East) and the Catholic Church (West) trace their histories to this divide and to the roots of each tradition before that. Theologically, the churches of the East emphasize the problem of mortality or death: salvation is primarily viewed as mortal beings partaking in Christ's immortal life. Christ's death and resurrection mediate that victory to us. There is a strong accent on the gift of the Spirit and *theōsis*, or participation by the Spirit in God's life. Forgiveness of sins is viewed as a subordinate element of salvation. In the Catholic West, however, the problem of sin is stressed: salvation comes primarily through atonement, by which the guilt and condemnation of sin are removed. Forgiveness of sins is key. Immortal life is the more subordinate point, a consequence of the forgiveness of sins. The gift of the Spirit thus tends to play a more subordinate role in the West. Although their approaches are different, these two traditions are still rooted in the same gospel message.

In the West, Protestants broke from the Catholic Church in the sixteenth century in order to stress salvation *by grace through faith alone* (rather than by grace through faith working in love), *by Christ alone* (rather than Christ and the church), and *according to Scripture alone*, as the supreme standard of truth (rather than Scripture and tradition). Martin Luther, in Germany, was arguably the major figure in the Reformation, though he had forerunners. His emphasis was on justification by grace (by Christ) through faith alone. Reformers from other places in Europe (like John Calvin and Huldrych Zwingli) joined the nascent Protestant movement even though they had some theological beliefs (besides those just mentioned) that were not exactly the same as Luther's (such as differing views on the Lord's Supper). They began what is called the Reformed tradition, as distinct from the Lutheran tradition. Presbyterian churches, for example, locate themselves in the Reformed tradition. The Anglican Church (the Church of England, called the Episcopal Church in the US) is also a branch of the Protestant churches, though one could argue that it had its own distinct identity within the Catholic Church even before it joined the Protestant movement in the sixteenth century. The Anglican tradition cherishes theological diversity, viewing the church as a many-branched reality. Wesleyan and Methodist churches trace their heritage to that Anglican root as well. The Wesleyan tradition elevates sanctification, or our consecration by God to the holy life, as a point of emphasis (as does the Reformed tradition to some extent). There were also so-called radical Reformers (called Anabaptists), who pushed for the separation of the church from the state, which the mainstream Reformers in the sixteenth century rejected since they relied on the state (or rulers within it) to resist the power of the Catholic Church. This radical Reformation tradition is sometimes called the "free church" tradition. Their focus is on faithful discipleship above all else. Mennonite churches trace their heritage to this root. Baptist churches are influenced by Reformed and Anabaptist traditions. Pentecostals reflect Wesleyan and Reformed influence. And so the list goes on. One may view the different church families as gifted with unique points of emphasis. In the same way that individuals within a local congregation possess different gifts, so also can church families edify the people of God on a global scale with their unique points of emphasis.[2]

Most of the many church denominations that splintered from one another did so in the modern era and mostly on American soil. But the trend over the last half century has been in the direction of uniting splintered churches under larger umbrellas. The **ecumenical movement**, which strives for the visible unity of the churches (not necessarily or even typically conceived of as a world church), has influenced this development. It was inspired by the modern emphasis on missions. The diversification of churches is not necessarily negative in and of itself. This is a good thing, so long as the churches maintain a sense of common faith and practice that the world can see. It's the toxicity of divisiveness and the thought that one's church is the only true church (denying any sense that other churches or communities of faith participate

---

2. See Oscar Cullmann, *Unity through Diversity* (Philadelphia: Fortress, 1988).

in Christ) that are to be avoided. Here is where one must balance a passion for truth with a tolerance for difference of viewpoint and practice. Certain essentials—such as salvation by grace, the deity of Christ, and the exclusivity of salvation through Christ's death and resurrection alone—cannot be compromised and may thus be cause for division if denied. Theologians can help us discern whether newer formulations concerning these doctrines are faithful to Scripture.

But not all doctrinal issues are important enough to be church dividing. Truth is always important, but different truths carry different weight. For example, whether or not a person can fall or backslide from grace is a family squabble among evangelical Christians, an argument that can feasibly exist within a church denomination or at least among Christian churches that maintain a sense of joint mission and purpose. But whether Christ is divine is not a family squabble. Those who disagree with this point have separated from the Christian tradition in an important way, giving a cause for division. One must never celebrate or relish division. It is painful and grievous. But some differences are serious enough to require it.

Of most importance to theology are the ancient creeds and theological works, especially those formulated before the church divided. The **church fathers** of the early centuries, such as Irenaeus of the second century, Athanasius and the Cappadocians (Gregory of Nyssa, Gregory of Nazianzus, and Basil) of the fourth century, and Augustine and Cyril of Alexandria of the fourth and fifth centuries, offer theologians of all traditions gold mines of theological insight. The **Nicene Creed** of the fourth century, which affirmed the deity of Christ (true God from true God; begotten, not made; of one nature, or *homoousios*, with the heavenly Father), is widely regarded as *the* creed of all creeds. The statement at Constantinople later in the century, which affirmed the equal deity of the Spirit (who is to be glorified with the Father and the Son), brought to creedal expression the doctrine of the Trinity. Great treatises on the Trinity by the Cappadocians and Augustine offer theologians a deep dive into the issues surrounding the Godhead. The famous **Chalcedonian Definition** of the fifth century affirmed the true humanity of Christ, which existed in distinct but inseparable union with his deity, allowing the church to confess that Christ was *one person*, fully divine and fully human, and thus fully involved in all that he did, including his suffering and death. It was not merely Christ's humanity that experienced death, while Christ's deity (or divine self) looked on. The church fathers commonly stated that Christ, as the God-man, suffered death in the flesh "impassibly," or in a way that did not adversely diminish the infinite power of his deity. Christ's divine and human natures could not act as separate subjects and independent of each other. The God-man participated in all that Christ did.

Modern movements of importance to theology include the following:

- the Pentecostal and Charismatic movements (stressing the Holy Spirit and the church's diverse giftedness and missional life)
- the ecumenical movement for the visible unity of the churches (which also raised to prominence the church's missional life)
- the Second Vatican Council of the Catholic Church (which produced documents stating, in renewed form, key areas of Christian doctrine)
- the social witness of the churches (on behalf of the poor and marginalized people of the world)
- new global thinking during the demise of colonialism (concerning how to do theology in ways that reject normalizing Western culture as universal and implicitly superior to other cultures)

Historical theology climaxes with the global challenges from many different contexts facing the church in our time. Theology as God talk is involved in a vastly diverse conversation today.

Systematic theology also relates to **practical theology**, which deals with theoretical issues and strategies for embodying the gospel among church congregations. Systematic theologians do have an eye on the practical life of the church. After all, God talk is not only done with the mouth but also, in a sense, with one's life. The same is true for the church as a whole. Theology as a special (disciplined and trained) form of God talk will be done in continuity with a life dedicated to the gospel, to the larger worship and witness of the church. Systematic theology itself could be called a church "practice." Yet there is still a difference of method and concern within systematic theology as compared with practical theology. Systematics moves methodically through the various doctrinal loci; practical theology does not. Practical theology deals rather with areas of church practice other than reflection on doctrine. It may deal with preaching (**homiletics**), teaching (**pedagogics**), counseling, worship, mission, administration, or organizational leadership. For example, the two-volume work titled *Leading the Congregation*, by Roger Heuser and Norman Shawchuck, is an example of practical theology.[3] We see both ministerial and academic (research-oriented) sides to these concerns, but they all exist under the category of practical theology.

3. Roger Heuser and Norman Shawchuck, *Leading the Congregation: Caring for Yourself While Serving the People*, rev. ed. (Nashville: Abingdon, 2010).

It is important to note that there are some theologians who reflect on doctrinal concerns and are fully involved in the constructive work of systematic theology but who would not use the label "systematic" to describe their work. To them, our grasp of biblical and dogmatic truth is not final or exhaustive enough to conform to a "system." Such efforts, they fear, bear the risk of denying or adjusting elements of truth to make them "fit" into the theologian's overarching vision. Moreover, these theologians may be more concerned with how theological truth engages the cultural or social context than how neatly or aesthetically it all fits coherently into a creative pattern. Or they may be oriented more toward reflecting on the truths that arise within a narrative framework (that of the Bible or the testimonies of the church) than within an abstract, systematic presentation of doctrinal truth. Theology can be a disciplined and constructive (even doctrinal) task without being intentionally "systematic." In presenting theology as systematic theology, I am indeed sensitive to these concerns. In fact, I welcome them and the creative versions of theology that they produce. They add insight to systematic theology. I do hold that it is possible to incorporate their concerns into systematic theology. For example, one can write an "open" system that allows for alternate ideas not favored by the theologian, emphases that do not quite fit the theologian's constructive vision, or loose ends that are not fully or neatly tied up. But systematic theologians still see value in coherent reflection on the doctrinal areas of gospel truth as a legitimate gift to the body of Christ. After all, biblical truths are not to be viewed as a fragmented collection of ideas; there is a unity and coherence to truth.

Theological Method

Theological methods, or the approaches to theology in the modern era, are typically discussed under the following labels.

Liberal (or progressive) theology. The name most commonly attached to this approach to theology is the towering theologian of the nineteenth century, the German Reformed theologian Friedrich Schleiermacher (1768–1834). Schleiermacher came from a Moravian background, which was pietistic. Pietists placed a strong emphasis on religious experience. From them, Schleiermacher gained an intense interest in the reach of the soul for God, what he came to call "absolute dependence" on God, or "feeling," which was deeper than a mere emotion. He was taken with the Romantic movement, which emphasized the role of human imagination in unifying various elements of culture and areas of academic study. Those belonging to this movement reached implicitly for transcendence, for that which brings unity and meaning to all things. But those who identified with this movement were convinced that the institutional church was irrelevant to their spiritual quest. Schleiermacher wanted to show them that Christian spirituality, rightly understood, was indeed relevant to their spiritual journey. What thus became important about Christianity for Schleiermacher was the "God consciousness," or experience of God, that it offers. He connects the fleeting consciousness of God in the world with the more profound God consciousness in the church, and he asks why the church has such a spiritual awareness.

The answer for Schleiermacher was Jesus Christ. Christ's consciousness of God was the ideal; it was entirely at one with divine love in action, to the point where Christ's entire being manifested God. Christ's redemptive power or influence was entirely in his perfect manifestation of God, which he communicates to the church through the presence of the Spirit, by which the church fellowships with Christ. Schleiermacher did not locate Christ's redemptive work decisively at the cross; he recognized no substitutionary atonement; and he did not believe in the resurrection, only in the belief that Christ was alive after death as a spiritual influence. But Christ, for Schleiermacher, did represent humanity before God; in this role, Christ offers forgiveness and the power of his perfect unity with God. Since Schleiermacher, liberal theologians have continued to place most of their emphasis on the cultural relevance of Christianity, even if it means radically revising biblical and historically cherished doctrines. It also tends to bypass the need for atonement or resurrection, locating Christ's redemptive influence in his life of perfect unity with divine love. Overall, Schleiermacher made a culturally relevant view of humanity's spiritual or religious journey the dominant force in his theology. He interpreted Christ's significance through that lens. Christ became the ideal manifestation of that quest. It was not revelation that shaped experience as much as it was a culturally relevant experience that shaped revelation.

Neoorthodox theology. The evangelical response to Schleiermacher came most powerfully through the theology of the Swiss Reformed theologian Karl Barth (1886–1968). Barth taught for the bulk of his career at the University of Basel in Switzerland. His approach to theology was commonly called neoorthodox (labeling a rediscovery of the orthodox, or doctrinally true, theology of the Reformation), though Barth himself did not prefer this term. Barth dominated theology for most of the twentieth century, much as Schleiermacher dominated theology in the nineteenth. Although Barth was trained in Germany under the liberal theology of his day, he became disillusioned with it early on. He soon formed the opinion that liberal theology was too concerned with the human spiritual or religious quest, interpreted in a way that seemed culturally relevant. This theology was not nearly concerned enough with what the divine revelation given in Scripture says about what God has done to save us—what *God* has done to reveal Godself to us in Christ. Liberal theology read the Bible as a guide to the spiritual or religious life, as a way of understanding what the spiritual quest tells us about God in light of the larger cultural quest for meaning. Barth wanted to shift our understanding of the biblical message to *God and God's quest for us*. We are to view human religion and cultural context in *that* light. The Bible is not about what human religion tells us about Christ, but rather about what Christ tells us about human religion, its idolatry, and the only thing that can free us from it and for it. In Barth's revolution, the atoning death and resurrection of Christ took center stage once more as the interpretive lens through which to view the Bible. We interpret the Bible primarily through the lens of Christ, rather than through the lens of a culturally relevant view of the human religious quest.

Since the cross and the resurrection interpret the significance of Christ for us, Christ's meaning is ultimately transcendent, never entirely graspable by human spirituality. Though we can know Christ and know profound truths about Christ, we should always be humble in what we claim to know, always cognizant that we can never have Christ or God at our disposal as the mere element of *our* quest for meaning. There continues to be a dialectic, or ongoing tension, between *our* knowledge of Christ and the mystery of *his* ongoing transcendence—a transcendence beyond the reach of human reason and religion, beyond the reach of human idolatry or self-serving agendas. His theology was thus called "dialectical" in the early decades of its prominence. The power of the Barthian revolution was in making revelation in Christ, especially his atoning death and resurrection, the center and chief standard of theology. This defines religious experience, rather than the other way around. Relating such revelation to our cultural context is still important, but never in a way that forsakes biblical faithfulness.

Correlation theology. The German Lutheran theologian Paul Tillich (1886–1965) lived at the same time as Barth. He immigrated to America to escape Nazi Germany and spent most of his career at Union Theological Seminary in New York. Tillich called his approach to theology "correlation theology." He was convinced that we need a way beyond the dominant alternatives of his day, between the liberal theology of Schleiermacher (which sought above all else a culturally relevant view of the spiritual quest) and Barthian neoorthodox theology (which highlighted our primary devotion to divine revelation in Christ). *Tillich's correlation theology was thus a revision of older liberal theology, but with greater emphasis on faithfulness to divine revelation.* He stressed the fact that faith is always correlating revelation and cultural context.

This was the case even in the Bible. The biblical authors were at least implicitly sharing revelation from God in a way that was relevant to their cultural context. And as we read the Bible, we are correlating its revelatory symbols with meanings that are culturally relevant. Yet Tillich's concern for correlation never entirely escaped liberalism's overarching concern with the religious quest of the soul's reach *for God*, which for him was our ultimate concern. Barth would have defined faith as shaped by God's reach *for us* or the revelation of God *to us* in Christ. Tillich noted that faith as ultimate concern is to be "existentially" relevant, following the popular philosophical quest of his day for the meaning of human existence in the world. In a way not very different from Schleiermacher, Tillich viewed Christ as the ideal human manifestation of divine love, calling him the "New Being" in the world. But Tillich gave more weight than Schleiermacher did to the cross, holding that Christ, on the cross, overcame human alienation from God for us. Yet Tillich's view of the Bible as containing mere "symbols" of the transcendent God, which can bear different meanings, allowed him to deem some of them as irrelevant or susceptible to radical revision in the light of cultural demands. For example, he ended up denying any realistic sense of the divine Son's incarnation in human flesh. Christ becomes the mere manifestation of new Being in God. Tillich also exaggerated the charge that Barth did not pay enough attention to cultural context, perhaps to highlight the need for his own approach.

Liberation theology. In a post-Barthian theological situation, theology began to take a secular turn, with greater attention than ever before placed on the significance of secular context. Inspiration was taken from the attention paid earlier by biblical theologians to God's self-disclosure in *history* (rather than in the life of the church).[4] Another source was Dietrich Bonhoeffer (1906–45), a German Lutheran theologian who escaped Nazi Germany in the 1930s to study and then briefly teach at Union Theological Seminary in New York, only to return to Germany to serve as a force for change during Nazi rule. He ended up being martyred for his efforts. While he was imprisoned, he wondered in his writings how the church was to make sense of its faith in a world that had "come of age" or come to believe that it had outgrown the need for faith in God as the door to hope in the present situation. In response, Bonhoeffer turned to the cross as the place where God enters the secular world, the place of the absence of faith, in order to make God freshly relevant in a world that might come to feel it no longer needs God. Inspired by these trends, Harvey Cox (b. 1929) of Harvard Divinity School wrote *The Secular City* in an effort to show the relevance of biblical revelation to an increasingly secular

4. Brevard S. Childs, *Biblical Theology in Crisis* (Philadelphia: Westminster, 1970), 39.

world seeking to extricate itself from the narrow and irrelevant ideas of reli-gion.[5] Liberation theology was born from the conviction that, from the start, such secular theologies need to focus on human suffering. In particular, the focus needs to be on the *liberation* of people who are being dehumanized by the oppression of social injustice. The Latin American liberation theology of the 1970s emphasized economic injustice and poverty. The primary text here, *A Theology of Liberation*, was written by the Peruvian theologian Gustavo Gutiérrez (b. 1928).[6] Gutiérrez was inspired by the trend, supported by Latin American bishops, to move beyond merely preaching and distributing sacra-ments in the hope for life after death in heaven. He stressed God's will to realize the mercy and justice of the kingdom of God in the world *in history*, and he also viewed the church as an instrument in that fulfillment. Black theology in the US was popularized by James Cone (1938–2018) of Union Theological Seminary in New York. His classic work, *The God of the Oppressed*, is the book to read in this area.[7] He focused more on liberation from the dehumanization caused by racism. God's saving presence is revealed in the liberation of the oppressed in history. Liberation theology also took on issues of liberation from sexism (as in feminist or, among women of color, womanist theologies). Though God transcends sex distinction, the Bible naturally uses images that are implicitly gender related. Though those images are mostly masculine, some feminist or womanist theologians point to the fact that the Bible sometimes uses feminine images to describe God in relation to God's people (e.g., Isa. 66:13). Some will also note that male and female are, in partnership, created in God's image (Gen. 1:26–27) and that Eve's subordination is not mentioned until the curse of sin is described (Gen. 3:16). After Christ undoes the curse (Gal. 3:13), the new humanity in Christ is "neither Jew nor Gentile, neither slave nor free, nor is there male and female" (v. 28). Though distinct, humans all have equal access to the privileges and responsibilities of the Spirit's calling and gifting.

Liberation theologians are deeply pained by the failure of the church, espe-cially its socially privileged members, to address the issue of social oppression when discussing sin and redemption. Liberation theologians have stressed the need for the church to define itself as the instrument of the mercy and justice of the kingdom of God in the world. Some liberation theologians are quite orthodox in their support of the authority of the Bible, the incarnation of the divine Son in Christ, and the atoning death and resurrection of Christ. They do not deny the promise of eternal life. Others, however, are more liberal in their

5. Harvey Cox, *The Secular City* (New York: Macmillan, 1965).

6. Gustavo Gutiérrez, *A Theology of Liberation: History, Politics, and Salvation* (Maryknoll, NY: Orbis Books, 1973).

7. James H. Cone, *The God of the Oppressed* (Maryknoll, NY: Orbis Books, 1975).

theology. Yet all stress that sin and redemption are not just personal realities but much more profoundly social realities. They speak of redemption prominently as applied to humanity in the liberation of the oppressed in history. In my view, we are not to deny the secular implications of the gospel for social liberation; nor are we to deny the need for the church, in its witness to Christ, to address such issues in favor of divine mercy and justice. But we also need to locate the social meaning of the gospel first and most prominently in the life of the church. The church is to be the society that signifies social mercy and justice in history. But if any of the churches ignore the cries of injustice and suffering in the world, they undercut their witness, their very reason for being.

Contextual theologies. After the waning of colonialism in the twentieth century, many nations and cultures outside the West, in places like Africa and Asia, began to think about how theology can be done in ways that are culturally relevant *to them*. They brought emphases to the theological table that were not typical for dominant theological trends in the West. Kosuke Koyama, of Union Theological Seminary in New York, wrote *Water Buffalo Theology* as a classic example of this theological method.[8] Koyama starts with the tension between the ancient Hebrew (and biblical) emphasis on God's mighty acts of salvation in history and the celebration of the cycles of nature in certain Asian cultures. The biblical picture of salvation history is linear, moving from the past into the present, constantly being challenged by the future coming of the kingdom of God. As we will note, the culturally-relevant emphasis on the cycles of nature is different.

According to Koyama, key biblical events culminate in Christ and have once-and-for-all significance over the entire biblical narrative. Protest against evil is implied in the story and in the crisis decision to accept salvation, which the key salvation-historical event offers us. The Asian cycles of nature are by contrast cyclical, moving in repeated cycles without any once-and-for-all significance granted to any one of them. There is no protest against evil, only a peace that nature will faithfully sustain us, no matter what happens. Koyama notes that the latter is not sufficient to meet the needs of a person's deepest yearning for salvation. Human beings need to protest evil and to be ushered into the salvation that Christ offers us. Yet there is also room within the Bible's salvation-historical framework for nature, in all its faithful cycles, to be part of a linear, salvation-historical narrative fulfilled by Christ. Indeed, all of nature is to be redeemed in Christ.

On the African continent, theologians like Esther Acolatse from Ghana (now at the University of Toronto) write of the unfortunate tendency for

---

8. Kosuke Koyama, *Water Buffalo Theology* (Maryknoll, NY: Orbis Books, 1974).

theologians in the West to reject or largely ignore the victory of Christ over evil spirits, even though this victory plays an important role in the New Testament. The Bible cautions us not to exaggerate the significance of evil spirits, as is often done in African cultures. But neither are the real existence of such spirits and the assurance of victory in Christ over them to be ignored.[9]

Postliberal theology. Postliberal theology was birthed in the 1980s and beyond at Yale Divinity School, with such scholars as Hans Frei (1922–88) and George Lindbeck (1923–2018).[10] Postliberalism takes a stand against liberalism's assumption that there is a general experience of God in the world that is symbolized and expressed in different ways. Postliberalism rather assumes that the Scriptures and the broader communicative practices of the church (e.g., preaching, sacraments, forms of ministry, and moral behavior) actually shape our experiences of God. The language and communication of faith do not *express* experience: they *shape* it. This means that the church's primary task, according to postliberalism, is not to be relevant to a general experience of God in the world (since such a thing does not exist), but rather to be the communicative instrument that brings people into an experience of God. The practices of the church guide the interpretation of Scripture, not cultural context. In this approach it is possible for secular language to indirectly influence the church's language and experience of God. It is, then, the role of doctrine to guide this influence so that the church remains faithful to its Scriptures and general life practices. Postliberalism is correct to grant the Scriptures the formative role in people's experience of God. But granting church practices the means of interpreting Scripture tends to blur the line between the voice of Scripture and the voice of the church. Evangelical theologian Kevin Vanhoozer has noted that Scripture has its own historical context and its own voice, both of which are distinct from the church's interpretive practices—a point not always clear in postliberal theologies.[11] Plus, granting Scripture and church witness the formative role in people's experience of God does not force us to deny that humans have a capacity to experience God in the world, even in a way that leads to salvation and even though Scripture and the witness of the church are granted by God to guide humanity.

9. Esther Acolatse, *Powers, Principalities, and the Spirit: Biblical Realism in Africa and the West* (Grand Rapids: Eerdmans, 2018).

10. See Hans W. Frei, *The Eclipse of Biblical Narrative: A Study in Eighteenth and Nineteenth Century Hermeneutics* (New Haven: Yale University Press, 1980); George A. Lindbeck, *The Nature of Doctrine: Religion and Theology in a Postliberal Age* (Louisville: Westminster John Knox, 1984).

11. Kevin J. Vanhoozer, *The Drama of Doctrine: A Canonical-Linguistic Approach to Christian Theology* (Louisville: Westminster John Knox, 2005), 16–24.

Norms: Scripture and Tradition

Systematic theology has norms or standards that fundamentally guide it. Scripture is the privileged norm of the church; it is not the only norm, but it is the privileged or supreme norm or standard. The Reformation principle that informs this conviction is *sola Scriptura*, or Scripture alone. I do not mean by this term that *only* Scripture guides theology. Such an idea is called **biblicism**. Biblicists think that it is wrong to draw insight from anything but the Bible. They imagine that all their beliefs are in accordance with the Bible, which tends to foster in them a sense of spiritual superiority over others. Biblicism is unrealistic, though, since no one is a blank slate, interpreting the Bible with no theological or cultural influences from outside of the Bible. It is helpful to become aware of our theological influences so we can be grateful for those that are helpful and rightly critical of those that are not. Moreover, biblicism denigrates all sources of guidance except Scripture, granting Scripture a role it was never meant to have. At no point in the church's history did the church ever rely *only* on Scripture for guidance. The church received the Scriptures from the beginning as their chief or *supreme* source of guidance but never as their *only* source. *Sola Scriptura* thus refers to the Scriptures *alone* as the *supreme* measure of the church's practices, the final court of appeal in the church's discernment of truth.

The role of Scripture as the supreme norm in the church has its explanation in the belief that God has not been silent but has self-disclosed in history—for all time fully and decisively in the person and work of Jesus Christ. Hebrews 1:1 tells us that God was revealed in Israel's past "at many times and in various ways," through a prophetic witness; but more recently God has been revealed with finality, by way of fulfillment, through his Son, who mediated creation and is heir to all things willed by God for it (v. 2). Hebrews goes further to note that in distinction to the prophetic witness of Scripture, "the Son is the radiance of God's glory and the exact representation of his being" (v. 3). Scripture is the inspired witness to the Word of the Father; Christ *is* that Word. Scripture in this context is *inspired* (i.e., God-breathed) to be the privileged witness to Christ and his gospel in the church and in these latter days. Note what Paul writes to Timothy: "All Scripture is God-breathed and is useful for teaching, rebuking, correcting and training in righteousness, so that the servant of God may be thoroughly equipped for every good work" (2 Tim. 3:16). The metaphor in play here is that of breath and word. All words that are spoken require breath. Placing one's hand near one's mouth when speaking will reveal that breath is required to speak. By way of comparison, the word of Scripture is pictured here as coming forth from the biblical authors on the breath of God, the Holy Spirit. And the word of the Scriptures that penetrates our hearts and minds continues to come to us in the power of the Spirit as well.

Timothy was a young pastor who needed to hear this. He was beginning to neglect his gift of preaching and teaching the Scriptures because of his inexperience. Perhaps he was being criticized for his lack of maturity at the task. One can read between the lines of the following encouragement from Paul to the young pastor. Paul writes: "Don't let anyone look down on you because you are young. . . . Until I come, devote yourself to the public reading of Scripture, to preaching and to teaching. Do not neglect your gift, which was given you through prophecy when the body of elders laid their hands on you. Be diligent in these matters; give yourself wholly to them, so that everyone may see your progress" (1 Tim. 4:12–15).

Timothy was young and inexperienced. But he was not to allow anyone to reject him for this. Paul tells him to stick with his gift of preaching and teaching; if he does so, everyone will see his "progress." Unfortunately, Timothy did not heed Paul's advice, for in the first chapter of 2 Timothy, Paul continues to implore Timothy not to neglect his gift but rather to stoke it into flame. He was not to be timid in the matter of asserting himself in the exercise of his gift of preaching and teaching (vv. 6–7). Then, in 2 Timothy 3, Paul reminds Timothy of the powerful and formative role that the Scriptures played in his own life in leading him to Christ—as if to say that God will be faithful to do the same in the lives of others through him (v. 15). Then comes our key text about the Scriptures being "God-breathed" and useful for all that a minister will do in serving a congregation. The message is clear: the inspired Scriptures were to be the strength of Timothy's ministry. He was to learn to lean on the Scriptures as the strong arm of his ministry—in all that he does to motivate, build up, reprove, and guide others.

The inspiration of Scripture is *verbal* and not only conceptual. All of Scripture is involved. One may thus refer to the **verbal-plenary view** of biblical inspiration (plenary referring to all of Scripture). But this does not mean that God dictated word for word what the authors were to write. The biblical authors have different writing styles, and Peter concedes that Paul wrote in ways that were sometimes "hard to understand" (2 Pet. 3:16). One would think that the Spirit could be clearer than that! It might help to view the inspiration of Scripture as its *sanctification*, its being set apart and consecrated for a sacred task among the churches. It is set apart eventually as a canon or supreme standard for the church's faithfulness to the gospel of Jesus Christ. The Scriptures were sanctified themselves as the faithful witness par excellence to Christ and his gospel.[12] Peter writes that we have the prophetic message in Scripture "as something completely reliable" (2 Pet. 1:19). The Bible's witness to truth will not mislead or deceive. Its witness is faithful and true.

The Scriptures in their entirety bear witness to Christ and are all fulfilled (i.e., summed up) in him, as Hebrews 1:1–3 implies. Jesus states, "Do not think that I have come to abolish the Law or the Prophets; I have not come to abolish them but to fulfill them" (Matt. 5:17). Hebrews 10:7 elaborates that Christ says to the heavenly Father, "Here I am—it is written about me in the scroll—I have come to do your will, my God." Reconciliation with creation could not be achieved by Israelite religion or a sacrificial system; only the incarnation of the Son in flesh can accomplish this. "Sacrifice and offering you did not desire, but a body you prepared for me" (v. 5). Christ overcomes sin and death so as to redeem creation and make it worthy of the Holy Spirit ("He redeemed us . . . so that by faith we may receive the promise of the Spirit," Gal. 3:14). He pours forth the Spirit so as to make all things new as the temple of God's dwelling. When all things foreshadowed and taught in the Scriptures are fulfilled by him, when the new creation fully comes, the Scriptures will be once and for all fulfilled, vindicated as the Word of God for history. After claiming that he has come to fulfill the Law and the Prophets, Jesus continues concerning the entirety of the Jewish Scriptures (which would apply to the New Testament as well): "For truly I tell you, until heaven and earth disappear, not the smallest letter, not the least stroke of a pen, will by any means disappear from the Law until everything is accomplished" (Matt. 5:18).

Christ comes to us wrapped in the Scriptures of the Old and New Testaments. These Scriptures, in the power of the Spirit, point to him and vindicate him as the Chosen One sent by the Father in the Spirit to fulfill their witness. But his redemption and renewal of creation in the Holy Spirit fulfill these Scriptures and show them to be true, vindicating them. Christ and the Scriptures are mutually vindicating because they are both brought to material expression by the Spirit. But they are not equals; Christ is the Lord of Scripture. Only Christ is divine, and only he is in essence (ontologically)—and not only by sanctification—the revelation of the Father. Christ alone is for all eternity the divine Word of the Father (John 1:1, 14). The Scriptures are his primary and authoritative witness; they function to reveal God in witness to Christ. As it was said of John the Baptist, so it may be said of Scripture: "He came as a witness to testify concerning that light, so that through him all might believe. He himself was not the light; he came only as a witness to the light"

---

12. John Webster, "Dogmatic Location of the Canon," *Neue Zeitschrift für systematische Theologie und Religionsphilosophie* 43, no. 1 (2001): 33.

(John 1:7–8). The Scripture is a light, but only as a reflection of Christ, for Christ alone is "the radiance of God's glory and the exact representation of his being" (Heb. 1:3).

In this context, we can best understand 2 Peter 1:19: "We also have the prophetic message as something completely reliable, and you will do well to pay attention to it, as to a light shining in a dark place, until the day dawns and the morning star rises in your hearts." Notice that the lights here are heavenly bodies. The light that shines in the darkness is contrasted with the sun rising at the dawn. One is tempted to view the light in the darkness as the moon. When the sun rises, the light of the moon is no longer needed. When the great light, which is Christ, appears, the lesser light of the Scripture is outshined. "For now we see only a reflection as in a mirror; then we shall see face to face. Now I know in part; then I shall know fully, even as I am fully known" (1 Cor. 13:12). Notice that when Christ as the great light returns, the morning star also rises in our hearts, perhaps poetically describing our rising in resurrection in Christ's image. When Christ, the great light, appears to fulfill the Scriptures once and for all time, we fulfill them, too, in our rising. From our perspective, the Scripture as the moon is such a fitting metaphor since it reflects the light of the sun. So also, the Scriptures reflect the light of Christ and the glory of the Father, which shines forth from him, transforming us more and more into his image. "And we all, who with unveiled faces contemplate the Lord's glory, are being transformed into his image with ever-increasing glory, which comes from the Lord" (2 Cor. 3:18). We currently hold this treasure in vessels of clay, but the day is coming in which we will hold it in bodies shaped into the image of the exalted Christ. Until then, the strength of the risen Lord sustains us (4:7–11).

For all their faithfulness and power in the hands of the Spirit, the Scriptures are still a finite witness, using human conceptuality and language. God must stoop low to accommodate such a witness as this. "To whom will you compare me?" says the Lord (Isa. 40:25). Even the noblest images and descriptions of God in Scripture, though as faithful as a human witness can be, fall short of God's infinite glory. Theologians call Scripture anthropomorphic, describing God by using language and concepts drawn from the realm of finite human life. This doesn't mean that the Bible fails to realistically depict who God is and what God is like. But that is the point. The Bible shows what God is *like*, the Scripture being at best *analogous* to the transcendent divine reality. Jesus is God's way of self-imaging in the world; the Scriptures give us the best presentation available to us of his impact and glory. Since Christ is the Lord of Scripture and all Scripture is fulfilled in him, he should be viewed as the chief subject matter of all Scripture, the "canon within the canon" (or standard within the standard), by which the overarching sense of Scripture (its central message or the gospel) is understood. Any interpretation of Scripture must pass the test of Jesus Christ to be legitimate. It must conform to Christ to be valid.

Scripture is a **canon**, which means "standard," as noted earlier, or "supreme standard." The boundaries of the Old Testament canon were uncertain at the time of Jesus. About three hundred years before Christ, the Jewish Scriptures (our Old Testament) were translated from Hebrew into Greek, because many Jews were living in gentile lands where Greek was a known language. The translation came to be called the **Septuagint**. Added to the translation were books that came to be called the **Apocrypha**. The Apocrypha was more accepted outside of Palestine among Greek-speaking Jews than within Palestine. Eventually, Judaism came to reject these books as part of its canon. In the Christian church, their reception was more favorable, but even then, acceptance was never universal. Some in the early centuries considered them of devotional value, but not on the same level as Scripture.[13] This was Luther's stance on the matter as well. Most Protestants came to reject them, whereas Catholics accepted them. The fact that Catholic Bibles contain the Apocrypha as part of their Old Testament is the only substantial difference between Catholic and Protestant Bibles today. That the Apocrypha never gained the kind of universal acceptance enjoyed by other canonical books speaks against its canonicity.

The New Testament canon was in formation very early, and its formation was inevitable. At the end of the Gospel of Matthew, Jesus tells his disciples to make disciples of all nations, baptizing them in the name of the Father, Son, and Holy Spirit (28:19). Here one is reminded of the many tongues at Pentecost signaling the rise of the global church—except that at the end of Matthew, Jesus says that converts should be taught all that he had commanded and that he would be with his church as they undertook this task to the very end of the age (28:20). How was the church to teach all that Jesus taught until the end of the age unless his teachings were written and preserved in the form of a canon, or standard of instruction? Christ's presence with his church until the end of the age would surely guide the process of forming such a canon. Accordingly, the New Testament canon was formed.

Paul, the earliest writer of the New Testament, refers to the Jewish Scriptures (our Old Testament) as the *palaias diathēkēs* (παλαιᾶς διαθήκης), or **old covenant** (one might say, Old Testament; 2 Cor. 3:14). The new covenant that Paul had in mind was Christ's covenant with his church, but the fact that

---

13. J. N. D. Kelly, *Early Christian Doctrines* (New York: Harper & Row, 1959), 52–56.

Paul's reference to the "old covenant" in this verse was recorded in a body of Scripture, the door was wide open for a new-covenant canon of Scripture, built on Christ and completing the Scriptures. The first one to mention a New Testament canon that we know of was the church father Irenaeus, in the second century.[14] Some have taught that the New Testament canon was formed to correct the inadequate canon put together by the heretic Marcion, which was a truncated New Testament canon consisting of an expurgated version of Luke's Gospel and some of Paul's letters.[15] Evidence exists that Paul, the earliest author of the New Testament, wrote with the authority of Scripture, as though he knew that his writings would gain that status. Notice what he writes to the Corinthian prophets: "If anyone thinks they are a prophet or otherwise gifted by the Spirit, let them acknowledge that what I am writing to you is the Lord's command. But if anyone ignores this, they will themselves be ignored" (1 Cor. 14:37–38). The gift of prophecy in the churches, even if seemingly spoken by the power of the Spirit, must be tested in the light of Scripture to be accepted as valid. Scripture is the privileged standard of truth. We should not be surprised that 2 Peter 3:16 refers to Paul's writings as Scripture already within the first century.

Yet Paul's Letters alone were not sufficient to complete the New Testament canon. There is very little in his letters about the conception, birth, life, or teachings of Christ, or even about the drama of his death and resurrection as it actually transpired. The church was indeed to be taught *all* that Christ had commanded, according to Matthew 28:20. The Gospels were needed to fill in this background. Mark was the first Gospel written (ca. 70 CE): a dependence on it is evident in Matthew and Luke. Luke informs us that many accounts have been drawn up of what transpired in the life and mission of Christ, but he also tells us that he did thorough research as he wrote his Gospel, even consulting eyewitness testimonies, "that you may know the certainty of the things you have been taught" (Luke 1:4; see vv. 1–3). John was most likely written after Luke.

The fact is that the bulk of Paul's Letters, the four Gospels, and Acts were most likely accepted as authoritative very early. That Irenaeus quotes 206 times from Paul's Letters and the Gospels, prefaced by the phrase "the Scripture says," implies that they were already a collection.[16] In the so-called Muratorian Canon of the late second century, we find a list of New Testament books that contains all of the New Testament books familiar to us except Titus,

---

14. Irenaeus, *Against Heresies* 4.9.1; Kelly, *Early Christian Doctrines*, 56.

15. Michael J. Kruger, *Christianity at the Crossroads: How the Second Century Shaped the Future of the Church* (Downers Grove, IL: IVP Academic, 2018), 202–26.

16. Kelly, *Early Christian Doctrines*, 58.

Hebrews, 1 and 2 Peter, and 3 John. The canon listed by the church father Origen in the third century omits Titus, Hebrews, 2 Peter, 2 and 3 John, and Jude. Eusebius, at the end of the third century, omits Hebrews, James, 2 Peter, 2 and 3 John, and Jude (he includes Titus). In the fourth century (367 CE), the church father Athanasius in his Easter Letter includes all the New Testament books familiar to us.[17]

A few conclusions can be drawn from this evidence. First, among Paul's Letters, only Titus is disputed. The Gospels and Acts, the narrative foundation of the New Testament, are never doubted. What this means is that from early on the four Gospels, Acts, and Paul's Letters represented the undisputed backbone of the New Testament canon. They are never omitted in second-to-fourth-century canon lists. Unless one wishes to believe that the list of New Testament books from the late second-century Muratorian canon and mentioned decades earlier by Irenaeus was composed out of thin air, the implication is that the backbone of the Gospels, Acts, and Paul's Letters goes back to the early second century, perhaps within one or two generations of the time these books were composed. Second, most of the books that were typically omitted in the second and third centuries (Titus, 2 Peter, 2 and 3 John, Jude) were widely known and accepted by parts of the church at that time. The very fact that the canonical lists mentioned above include "1 John" without 2 and 3 John or "1 Peter" without 2 Peter is proof that their writers were aware that 2 and 3 John and 2 Peter were widely known. Why list a Johannine letter as "first" if there is not at least a second? Third, Hebrews had difficulty gaining acceptance because its authorship was unknown (meaning that it did not carry the name of an apostle or someone known by an apostle). But its stunningly rich and insightful theological content almost guaranteed its eventual acceptance.[18] The edges of the New Testament canon were in dispute, but the bulk of it seems to have been in place from early on. Popular in some circles today is the idea that the New Testament canon was wide open until the **Council of Nicaea** in the fourth century composed a list to keep out writings thought to be heretical, but this is pure fiction.

John Webster rightly points out that the Holy Spirit guided not only the writing but the canonization of the inspired New Testament writings. The churches may be said to have "received" and approved these books rather than selected them.[19] As the early leaders of the church said of the acceptance of gentile converts by grace alone, so may we also say of the Spirit's leading

17. Kelly, *Early Christian Doctrines*, 60.
18. See Kelly, *Early Christian Doctrines*, 60.
19. John Webster, *Holy Scripture: A Dogmatic Sketch*, Current Issues in Theology (Cambridge: Cambridge University Press, 2003), 61–62.

concerning the formation of the canon: "It seemed good to the Holy Spirit and to us" (Acts 15:28). As we noted above, Christ asked the church to hand down all that he had commanded, and he followed this request by promising that, to help his followers do this, he would remain with the believers until the end of the age (Matt. 28:20). Surely his presence with the church guided it in preserving the canon that contains all those commands. One has good grounds for believing that Christ is fulfilling that promise.

The relationship between Scripture and **tradition** needs to be addressed as well, since spiritual discernment in the church surely involves the rise of tradition that serves and illuminates Scripture. But such illumination is not simply to be assumed in every case. Just as prophecy and other charismatic gifts in the church need to be tested in the light of Scripture to be accepted as valid, so must tradition in the history of the church be tested in that light. However, tradition should not be viewed as in itself a negative term (as in the worn-out statement, "We accept Scripture, not the traditions of men"). Not all traditions are nonbiblical! There is much in the traditions of the church that serves to illuminate Scripture and apply it to new situations. In fact, very early church traditions (i.e., confessions, hymns, prayers) exist within the Bible itself. Note the hymn in Philippians 2:6–11 and the creedal statement implied in 1 Corinthians 15:3–4. Prior to Christ, the book of Psalms is a collection of Israel's hymns. But postcanonical tradition, as valuable as it may be, is still subordinate to the Bible and must prove its worth in service to it, which is the point being made here. As noted above, when the Protestant Reformation affirmed *sola Scriptura* (Scripture alone), it did not mean that tradition is not a source of truth and a norm of faith. It is! Creeds, confessions, liturgies, and great theological works have helped the church at key moments of its history to understand more deeply the meaning of Scripture for its time and place. The Reformers just meant that Scripture is alone the final court of appeal and that tradition, in its use in illuminating Scripture, must show that this is indeed what it's doing.

The Catholic Church of today does indeed affirm the notion that tradition serves Scripture. The Second Vatican Council helpfully notes that the teaching office behind much of the postcanonical traditions of the church "is not above the word of God, but serves it, teaching only what has been handed on, listening to it devoutly, guarding it scrupulously and explaining it faithfully in accord with a divine commission and with the help of the Holy Spirit."[20] The difference with Protestantism is the Catholic confidence that such tradition *will* serve Scripture faithfully and should therefore be revered

---

20. Second Vatican Council, *Dei verbum* (Rome: The Holy See, 1965), chap. 2, sec. 10.

in a way that is equal to our reverence for Scripture. Protestants do not share this confidence—for good reason. Their very origin as a movement was due to a failure of Catholic tradition to live up to Scripture at that point in time. They, of course, were not the only ones who failed. That failure was shared in some ways by Protestants too! But that is precisely the point. The greatness of the Protestant movement is in its conviction that all churches throughout the world, in all of their diversity, must return to the Scriptures again and again with a fresh ear to hear what may be neglected or betrayed in the current moment. Theology, in its faithfulness to Scripture, must help the church to do this again and again.

FINAL REFLECTIONS

The term "theology" literally means God talk. It is speech about God that informs and guides how the church speaks about God. Theology is not the only speech about God in the church that does this. There are preachers, teachers, and prophets who do this too. But theologians are trained in specialized ways to speak about God in a way that even informs and guides *them*. Theology in this volume is systematic theology, which proceeds systematically through the major doctrinal loci (areas of doctrine) in a way that shows their coherence and faithfulness to the gospel. Systematic theology is sometimes called dogmatics. It differs from doctrine in that the latter represents brief statements of belief crafted by churches or denominations to regulate their practices. Systematic theology is done by individuals who reflect on and explain these doctrinal statements (or doctrines in general) in an appreciative and critical way and in the light of Scripture. Systematic theology is to be done in humility and openness to diverse voices, especially those that cry out for the mercy and justice of the kingdom of God, voices from the margins of society. To do so is to participate in the cultural hospitality of Pentecost. It is to be based in the faith, worship, and witness of the church—loyal especially to the Scripture's witness to Christ—and, in being faithful, to also remain intimately engaged in the contexts of its time and place.

Biblical scholars are more or less interested in theology, too, but their theological concern is focused much more narrowly on a given biblical text or book in terms of the theological issues at play in the book's formation and message to its original audience (or in the formation of a biblical tradition that spans more than one book). Biblical theology may have a wider and more prominent theological concern, even covering an entire testament. But even here, the effort is not so much a systematic statement of truth as it is an attendance to the diverse voices that come to expression throughout the span of the biblical material being examined. Church historians are also more or less interested in theology. But they, too, have a more focused concern that is less constructive. They wish to understand the theological issues at stake in a given time period, movement, church, or thinker. Historical theology has a more prominent and broader theological interest, but it is, again, focused on the theological developments at work in the history of the church. Systematic theology learns much from these other theological disciplines, but its interest is in standing back and asking what the church is to believe today in the various areas of doctrine most important to the Bible and the history of the church. And the theologian seeks to explore and discuss these areas while constructing a systematic presentation of the church's faith—the big picture of truth, so to speak—in a way that shows its inner coherence, its biblical faithfulness, and its contextual relevance.

Modern theological method has struggled with the issue of Scripture and context. Liberalism has allowed for a radical redefinition of Scripture and doctrine, aiming to be relevant to a general cultural understanding of the world in relation to the ultimate. Liberal theologians dismiss doctrines like the atonement and the resurrection of Christ in order to make the influence of his life the key to his redemptive work. Karl Barth's neoorthodoxy sought to make faithfulness to the biblical witness to revelation the church's supreme loyalty. It is not just Christ's influence on us that interprets the significance of his life, but his death and resurrection. Tillich's correlation theology sought to revise liberalism so as to grant both revelation and contextual relevance their due, but he ended up with a similar radical revisionism of scriptural revelation in order to be relevant to his contemporary context.

Liberation theology has represented a secular turn to the world in order to bring theology into serving the mercy and justice of the kingdom of God in society. Though the gospel is relevant to matters of social justice, social salvation is to be realized first in the church. Yet the church denies its own witness if it does not, in its witness to Christ, raise a voice against social injustice. Contextual theologies have focused on the relevance of the biblical message to cultures outside of the West and the issues that they raise. More recently, postliberalism represents a turn back to the church from the conviction that there is no general experience of God in the world to which the church must seek to be relevant. The church's communicative practices that interpret Scripture shape our experience of God. Though postliberalism is correct to grant Scripture the formative role in our experience of God, it needs to include an emphasis on the corrective function of Scripture over against the church's witness. And it is still possible within this emphasis to allow for an experience of God that is in need of the church's guidance to find fulfillment. Cultural context is still important, having a secondary influence on the church's interpretation of the gospel.

Scripture is inspired by God (i.e., God-breathed) and thus is the privileged voice of the Spirit (or witness to Christ) in the church. Yet Scripture is not the only voice of the Spirit in the church. The Spirit uses testimony, prophecy, confession, worship, and various other means of communication, not all of which are verbal. Preaching, baptism, and the Lord's Supper are the communicative means that Christ has instituted to bring the church together around his presence and, in a definitive way, to celebrate the gift of Christ and commit to following him again and again.

To sum up, in the midst of all these communicative means, the Scripture is the privileged voice of the Spirit in the church; it is the medium of the Spirit that functions as the supreme standard, the only final court of appeal in theological discussion and debate. Such is the meaning of *sola Scriptura* (Scripture alone). Scripture is reliable in its witness to Christ. Christ is indeed its chief subject matter, its inner standard of meaning (the canon within the canon). In its faithful and authoritative witness to Christ, Scripture is the canon or standard of the church. The Spirit inspired not only the writing of Scripture but also its canonization process. The Spirit continues to speak through the Scriptures in conforming the church to Christ. Not only understanding the Scripture but also obeying and embodying its message is the goal.

Christian leadership has this encouraging embodiment as its calling. Since the meaning of Scripture will only be fully revealed when Christ accomplishes all to which the Scripture bears witness in the new creation (Matt. 5:17–18), no individual or church grasps it all. We need the many tongues and insights of the global church, and even then, the Bible's full meaning is still not fully in reach. But we are on a path of discovery that represents the grandest adventure of all, one that gives all in self-crucifixion and receives all in the risen life. If only we will have the courage to yield and commit to it.

TOPICS FOR REVIEW

1. What does the term "theology" literally mean? Discuss the issue of theology as an academic field of study.
2. Distinguish systematic theology from biblical studies (and exegesis).

3. Distinguish systematic theology from church history (and historical theology).
4. Distinguish systematic theology from practical theology.
5. Discuss the verbal-plenary inspiration of Scripture in relation to 2 Timothy 3:16 and 2 Peter 1:19.
6. Relate the Scriptures to the revelation of Christ, according to Matthew 5:17–18; Hebrews 1:1–3; and 2 Peter 1:19.

2

GOD

The diverse tongues of Pentecost declared the wonders of God. The wonders of God! God is the chief and all-encompassing point of reference. All the loci of theology are God based, God intoxicated, God directed. The overarching declaration refers above all else to the divine perfection and glory. Saying that *God exists* cannot be a neutral or abstract idea but is always a gospel of redemption and a call to discipleship. Knowing and loving God makes life purposeful and worthwhile. This faith confession is essential to the human quest, and testimonials to its truth abound. Still, the emphasis of theology among the many tongues of Pentecost is not with the rewards of faith, but rather with doxology or worship. Theology begins and ends with the *wonders of God*.

If Pentecost teaches us anything, it teaches us that the words "God exists" call us way beyond what our minds and tongues can grasp. The ecstasy of divine love revealed in the outpouring of the Spirit makes faith ecstatic, causing us to rise above our limitations to reach for something transcendent, global, and ultimate. So one must exercise care in saying "God exists," since human nature is so prone to idolatry. When we say "God exists," we tend to think of God as one existing being among others, just a larger and more powerful version of ourselves. But this understanding of God is anthropomorphic (stated in human terms and concepts), as are all thoughts and statements about God. Humans with authentic thoughts and statements are aware of this limitation and seek to be careful to respect God's *transcendence*. God is personal. We can pray to God, and God answers. God loves and shows mercy. Even though God is personal, God is not personal in exactly the same way that we are. God is the source of all personhood; we aren't. God is personal not only as the existent One but also as the One who is the ground and ongoing possibility of the existence of all else. God's existence is not dependent on anything else. We are dependent. Acts 17:28 notes that all the various peoples of the world "live and move and *have [their] being*" in God (emphasis added).

Interestingly, the exact wording of Hebrews 11:6 concerning faith in God is this: "Anyone who comes to him must believe that *he is* and that he rewards those who earnestly seek him" (emphasis added). The phrase "God is" perhaps is the preferred way of saying God *exists*, though the latter way of saying this is acceptable as long as the theologian bears the above-stated qualifications in mind. Moreover, saying that seeking and knowing God makes life purposeful and rewarding ("he rewards those who earnestly seek him") must also be declared with caution, since we can all too easily define the divine purpose according to our own self-serving wish list. This is why the gospel of Christ and the totality of the scriptural witness surrounding it must remain the criteria for how we define the divine purpose and fulfillment.

God and Creation

The conviction that God exists causes us to view *nature* as *creation*. Nature does not contain within itself an adequate explanation for its existence. Nature is thus to be viewed as created. All things have their origin in God. Hebrews 11:3 notes, "By faith we understand that the universe was formed at God's command, so that what is seen was not made out of what was visible." Genesis 1:3 has God speaking into the emptiness and darkness of the deep: "Let there be light." In the mighty storm of the Spirit, God brings light in the midst of the darkness, order from chaos, and beautiful form from emptiness (Gen. 1:1–3). Genesis starts with creation already in progress. The voidness and formlessness do not lack substance but rather lack order and purpose.[1] God does not command the light into existence as a tyrant might: "Light, *appear*!" Rather, God says, "*Let* there be light." God creates the light and immediately enables its flourishing in a way that allows it to participate in the divine purpose. God is the God of the possible, granting all that exists its being, yet in a way that immediately invites its own participation in the creative process.

---

1. John H. Walton, *The Lost World of Adam and Eve: Genesis 2–3 and the Human Origins Debate* (Downers Grove, IL: IVP Academic, 2015), 28.

Hebrews 11:3 implies an *absolute beginning* to all things by pointing to the origin of all things by the command of God *alone*, not from things that already exist: "What is seen was not made out of what was visible." Romans 4:17 is more to the point by referring to Abraham's faith this way: "He is our father in the sight of God, in whom he believed—the God who gives life to the dead and calls into being things that were not." Notice that God brings into being "things that were *not*." God creates *out of nothing*—in Latin, *ex nihilo*. This miracle of creation is connected to the grand miracle of raising the dead. All of creation is called into being miraculously, *out of nothing*, by the Word and Spirit of God, which points to the fact that God will call the new creation forth by that same Word and Spirit, from the clutches of death unto life. And that new creation will be the final vindication of the truth of faith in God as Creator. God as Redeemer assumes God as Creator, and vice versa.

Creation out of nothing means creation out of *absolutely* nothing, which is impossible to imagine. If one tries to imagine it, included in the mental image will be something like light or empty space. But physicists inform us that even light or empty space is *something*. It's not nothing in the absolute sense of the term. So saying that God creates from absolutely nothing is an unimaginable confession of faith. But it is a confession that makes sense in another way. If there were no absolute beginning to all things, nature would extend infinitely into the past. Yet that idea is arguably absurd, since all things are caused by something else. If nature lacked an absolute beginning, a series of causes would extend infinitely into the past. According to that view, it would take an infinity to reach the present state of affairs! This would be so even if infinity were a frozen block rather than a flowing stream of events, for even a block requires a sequence of some sort if the reality of which we speak is nature.[2]

Let's imagine infinite time as a hotel with an infinite number of rooms, each one occupied by a different phase of natural history. But that perspective does not omit the fact that nature still moves from phase to phase (room to room) to be that nature at that phase. One cannot deny that there is such a thing as an arrow of time, a sequence of sorts, that moves in only one direction, forward. One can anticipate and experience the rising sun of the next day, but one cannot anticipate and experience the dawn of the previous day. Within this "block" version of time, an infinite sequence of *any* sort would make reaching the present state of affairs impossible, since it would take moving through an infinite number of "rooms" to get to the one of which we are

2. A point brilliantly defended by Curtis J. Metcalfe, "A Defense of the Kalam Cosmological Argument and the B-Theory of Time" (master's thesis, University of Missouri, 2013). See also Peter J. Bussey, "God as First Cause—A Review of the Kalam Argument," *Science and Christian Belief* 25, no. 1 (April 2013): 22.

currently aware. Even if an infinity of "rooms" into the past were possible in mathematical reasoning, that doesn't mean it would make sense in actual physical reality. Thus, it stands to reason that there must be a "first cause" of all things, a first cause that is *uncaused*. Creation would then be *finite* into that past. Now that makes sense. The above discussion is an argument for God's existence based on *causality*.

In making this argument from causality, we must note that God is not a cause like any other cause. Saying that God is the "first cause" means that God is the *uncaused cause*. That makes God unique. Being the uncaused cause means that in God—and in God alone—are the conditions necessary for existence and that these conditions and the existence that they explain are *essential* to God. Because we are contingent, dependent on conditions other than ourselves to exist, it is possible for us not to exist. For example, my parents were necessary to my existence. If they had never met, I would not have existed. This means that it is possible that I might not have existed. But God is not contingent. God is not dependent on anything beyond God to exist. Thus, there is no possible way, no possible lack or barrier, that would prevent God from existing. God does not just *happen* to exist: God *must* exist because it is God's very essence to exist, meaning that God has within Godself all that is necessary to exist as God. *God's infinite perfection means that the conditions necessary for God to exist could not have possibly been absent.* For God not to exist is a theological absurdity. This is the **argument from contingence**. Even if nature is thought to have within itself the conditions necessary for its existence, we could imagine such conditions lacking. Such a lack is impossible regarding God.

The above argument from God's perfection is also called the **ontological argument** for God's existence. It was advocated in the eleventh century by Anselm of Canterbury (1033–1109). Anselm noted that God is "that than which nothing greater can be thought," meaning that God is perfect in every way, lacking nothing, including existence.[3] Nature is different. According to this argument, even if nature *had* existed eternally into the past, it may still be said that it just *happened* to have existed eternally. If the conditions for such eternal existence had been lacking, nature would not have existed. This means that the thought we have of an infinitely perfect being who is not contingent in any way must correspond to a divine reality: it must be ontological rather than merely notional (or an idea that might or might not exist). The inherent reach of the soul for transcendence points to One who is by definition existent.

3. Anselm, *Proslogium* (chap. 3), Internet Medieval Sourcebook, Fordham University, January 20, 2021, https://sourcebooks.fordham.edu/basis/anselm-proslogium.asp.

God's creating everything "out of nothing" (*ex nihilo*) means that creation does not emanate out of God's essence in a way that shares that essence, as pantheists assume. The term **"pantheism"** literally means "everything is divine" (*pan* means "everything," and *theism* refers to "God"). To assume that the cosmos and humans share the divine nature is to deify nature or to treat it as if it warranted the reverence and adoration that belongs to God alone. Pantheism also tends to strip God of personhood, which is why meditation rather than prayer tends to be the preferred response to the divine mystery in pantheism. Pantheists are in awe of the universe, but they tend not to ask God for mercy, nor do they seek answers to prayer. Lastly, imagining a pantheistic universe assumes a unity between human nature and the divine nature. The human soul is considered to be divine by nature. There is thus no need for atonement or reconciliation with God. Sin is often viewed as essentially a lack of consciousness of God—meaning a lack of consciousness of our true selves in continuity with God. In light of all of these theological missteps, it is important to reject the notion of emanation and instead to affirm creation *ex nihilo* (out of nothing). God creates by the power of the divine Word and the Holy Spirit *alone*.

The creation of the world is restated in John 1:1–5, placing Christ in the place of "the Word." This christological focus means that the divine fiat (i.e., decree) "Let there be . . . ," which brought the creation into being in the power of the Spirit, was spoken by and even in *Christ*. Christ mediated creation from the heavenly Father and in the power of the Holy Spirit. All things were created *through* and *for* Christ (Col. 1:16). Not only is Christ eternally God's gift to creation; creation was eternally chosen by God to be a gift to Christ! Creation was made as a tabernacle in which God would dwell and in which humanity would dwell in God's image. "He stretches out the heavens like a canopy, and spreads them out like a tent to live in" (Isa. 40:22). But this creation was also to be analogous to a kingdom in which the God-man, Jesus Christ, would reign. Creation was thus meant to be Christ's dwelling place, Christ's kingdom in the presence of the Spirit. The Spirit created all things in order to bring into being a creation that is obedient to the command represented and expressed in the divine Son of the Father. The Son mediates the Spirit at creation to sanctify it as the receptive vessel of the divine indwelling that will be shaped into Christ's glorious image one day. The Spirit was to make creation into a mirror of Christ's glory directed to the heavenly Father; indeed, all things were made to eventually be offered up by Christ in glory to the Father. "Then the end will come, when he hands over the kingdom to God the Father after he has destroyed all dominion, authority and power" (1 Cor. 15:24).

The new creation, in the sanctity of the Spirit, fulfills the old creation that fell under the curse of sin and death. The glory offered to God in the old creation (Ps. 19:1–4) is dimmed by the curse of chaos, decay, and death. God's glory will shine with unfathomable purity, beauty, and strength in the new creation ruled by Christ and sanctified and glorified by the Spirit. "I did not see a temple in the city, because the Lord God Almighty and the Lamb are its temple. The city does not need the sun or the moon to shine on it, for the glory of God gives it light, and the Lamb is its lamp" (Rev. 21:22–23). God pervades creation even now to sustain and renew it in the natural sphere. The Spirit works in the natural realm in talented human endeavors, in social justice, and to alleviate suffering. But such flourishing is limited by the curse of evil, decay, and death. Christ conquered this curse and broke through those barriers in his death and resurrection: "You will not abandon me to the realm of the dead, you will not let your holy one see decay" (Acts 2:27). Creation can now be sanctified and glorified supernaturally through Christ and in the Spirit, who is poured forth through Christ's redeeming work. That which is mortal will be "swallowed up" in God's immortal life (2 Cor. 5:4). The mercy, righteousness, and justice of the kingdom of God will reign on earth as they do in heaven (cf. Matt. 6:9–10). We are now to seek signs of the kingdom in the life of the church and, beyond this, analogous signs in the world.

The Problem of Suffering

The text from Hebrews 11 quoted above deserves another look: "Anyone who comes to him must believe that he exists and that he rewards those who earnestly seek him" (v. 6). Faith in God is not an abstract idea. It is forged in the context of real-life challenges, especially those that give rise to human suffering, in which reward is attached to believing. Suffering is often the occasion in which faith in God arises. However, the very same suffering that occasions the rise of faith can also give rise to questioning God's existence. Faith requires courage in the face of doubt, and we can trust in God to renew and sustain our faith. As Paul writes in 2 Corinthians 4:8, we are "perplexed, but not in despair." According to the text above from Hebrews, faith involves the conviction that God rewards those who seek him. In other words, the person who seeks after God in faith is driven by the conviction that faith will be vindicated as worthwhile; it will bring the reward that it promises. The evil and suffering of this age will not gain the upper hand, nor will they have the final word.

Despite suffering and loss, God makes it all worthwhile. The glory that will one day define creation will so overwhelm the former suffering in both depth and extent that the suffering will not be worth mentioning. The entire passage of Romans 8:18–21 is worth including here:

> I [Paul] consider that our present sufferings are not worth comparing with the glory that will be revealed in us. For the creation waits in eager expectation for the children of God to be revealed. For the creation was subjected to frustration, not by its own choice, but by the will of the one who subjected it, in hope that the creation itself will be liberated from its bondage to decay and brought into the freedom and glory of the children of God.

Paul's topic is the resurrection of the saints in glory. He calls it a great "revelation" of the children of God. The audience of this event is all of creation, which implicitly waits "in eager expectation" of the glorification of the new humanity. The phrase "eager expectation" implies that creation is straining to see that glorification, desperately wanting it, needing it. Why? The reason Paul gives is that creation was "subjected to frustration" with humanity, not by its own choice but because of what humanity had done and what God did in response. What is frustrated is life—frustrated because it cannot itself attain what God had intended for it—life abundant, life immortal, life in the full liberty and sanctity of the Spirit. But God subjected creation along with humanity to this frustration "in hope."

In other words, judgment had redemption as its goal. When humanity failed God, then God could have destroyed it all, even more thoroughly than was the case during the flood in the time of Noah. God could have brought an end to it all. But what God did instead was subject humanity and all of creation to a path of suffering "in hope," with redemption as its intended conclusion. In that conclusion, all of creation "will be liberated from its bondage to decay and brought into the freedom and glory of the children of God." Those who believe will indeed hold that God exists and that a life of seeking God will be rewarded or vindicated as worthwhile. Since **theodicy** is the challenge of justifying faith in God in the context of suffering, there can be no theodicy that does not have at its core this conviction that the coming glory will make life with God worthwhile despite the suffering that one may endure.[4]

The very fact that God would bring humans toward redemption on a path of suffering does not mean that they are expected to work their way there by their own resources. God joins them on that path, bearing them up under their pain. "Surely he took up our pain and bore our suffering" (Isa. 53:4).

---

4. See Stewart Goetz, "The Argument from Evil," in *The Blackwell Companion to Natural Theology*, ed. William Lane Craig and J. P. Moreland (Malden, MA: Wiley-Blackwell, 2012), 455.

In doing so, God makes this journey possible, opening a path to redemption that would not otherwise be attainable. God did not watch us suffer from a distance but rather took up our problem and carried us on the path to redemption and to the renewal of life. God calls us to a path of faith and repentance and enables our participation in the divine life. Yet God does not repent and believe for us. Our path to redemption involves us entirely. The solution to the problem of suffering for humanity has involved the history of trial and redemption because God wants humanity's involvement in the defeat of evil, the overcoming of suffering, and the victory of redemption. Just imagine how far and wide the gospel of salvation would go if the entirety of the church were involved in communicating it with their very lives. Imagine what would happen to social injustice, poverty, and disease if humanity were to prioritize the defeat of such ills. Many ask what God is doing about such things. The cross, the resurrection, and the divine presence by the Spirit are the answer. However, what *we* are doing to alleviate these things is an equally important question to ask ourselves.

I have no intention of trivializing the problem of evil and suffering. All of creation suffers greatly. Humanity shares in this suffering too. The most difficult problem to understand and to bear is the suffering of children. Why does God allow it? That humanity can fall into depths of evil is not hard to understand. God did not create automatons that are preprogrammed to always obey. God created persons who can choose otherwise. Their evil choices affect a broader circle of people, especially as corporate groups institutionalize those choices (as with racism). Augustine (354–430) noted that humanity was made for God. But humanity was also made *from nothing*. In that process, God spoke light and order into being from the emptiness and the chaos. Made for God, humanity implicitly reaches for God; made from nothing, humanity is threatened by the emptiness and the chaos into which they can descend by parting from God. Augustine writes of humanity: "that it is a nature, this is because it is made by God; but that it falls away from Him, this is because it is made out of nothing."[5]

The Eastern tradition adds the point that humanity was not made as perfect but rather as innocent. Perfection would come with human involvement. Humans were made in the divine image and after the divine likeness as an ongoing process. The *image* was thought to consist of natural propensities from God, like procreation and the care of creation (Gen. 1:27–28). But the *likeness* is a supernatural destiny of regeneration, sanctification, and immortality in

---

5. Augustine, *City of God* 14.13, as quoted in John Hick, *Evil and the God of Love* (New York: Palgrave Macmillan, 1966), 46.

Christ. The human journey to immortality, by the grace of God, was tragically interrupted by the human fall, requiring redemption (the cross and the resurrection) as the bridge. Following this tradition, John Hick writes, "And so man, created as a personal being in the *image* of God, is only the raw material for a further and more difficult stage of God's creative work," which is the *likeness* of God revealed in Jesus Christ and taken on through the work of the Spirit.[6] So, for Hick, humanity is in the process of "soul making" on this path of suffering, from emptiness and chaos to beauty and fulfillment.[7] The cross and the resurrection mediate the journey from natural image to supernatural (immortal) likeness.

What about cases of suffering so terrible that they baffle the mind? We should seek to do what we can to protest and change such terror. But the question remains: Why does God allow it? Such questions often bring us to the outer limits of theological knowledge. The book of Job addresses this issue. When God points out to Satan how faithful Job is, Satan plays the role of the quintessential cynic. He points out that Job is faithful only because God protects him from all harm and cares for all his needs. Satan states his protest: "Have you not put a hedge around him and his household and everything he has? You have blessed the work of his hands, so that his flocks and herds are spread throughout the land. But now stretch out your hand and strike everything he has, and he will surely curse you to your face" (1:10–11). God has protected Job from all the tragedies of life that normally affect others. Why *wouldn't* he be faithful? He knows it is in his interest to obey! Satan implies that God is deluded in thinking that Job's faith is genuine. God is being used, and faith is a joke. One hears this criticism today too. Religion is a farce; it is used by those who are only interested in what they can get out of it, and the rest are fools.

So God allows Satan to remove the protective hedge and expose Job and his family to the full brunt of life in this cursed, suffering-filled world. Satan strikes a blow to every area of Job's happiness. His herds, wealth, and servants are ravaged by outside invaders. A tornado strikes the home where his children are feasting, causing it to crash down upon them. Chapter 1 ends with a testimonial to Job's continued faithfulness despite the unbelievable sorrow that has overtaken him. At this point, Satan's argument is losing credibility. His back is against the wall. He has one card left to play. It seems, Satan supposes, that Job is so self-centered that all he really cares about is his own skin. "'Skin for skin!' Satan replied. 'A man will give all he

6. Hick, *Evil and the God of Love*, 254 (emphasis added).
7. Hick, *Evil and the God of Love*, 279–400.

has for his own life'" (2:4). So Satan gains permission from God to strike Job with a dreadful disease. But even then, Job remains faithful. "Shall we accept good from God, and not trouble?" he asks (2:10). At this point, Satan is silenced. Job has vindicated the possibility of genuine faith and has shown what it looks like under fire. It was to this end that God allowed Job's suffering.

But Job does not know this. He knows nothing of the background of the trial to which we as the readers are made privy. After Satan exits the drama, Job's comforters enter. A lengthy discussion ensues in which Job defends his innocence. Contrary to his comforters' views, Job argues that he does not deserve this trial. Job says of God, "If only I knew where to find him; if only I could go to his dwelling! I would state my case before him and fill my mouth with arguments" (23:3–4). Job wrestles with God, but he does not denounce his faith. This becomes another purpose of Job's life. As Gustavo Gutiérrez points out, Job illustrates the language of protest that is possible before God when faced with the horrors of life.[8]

At the end of the book, God appears before Job in a storm. God basically reminds Job that there is much he does not know, a higher purpose of which he is not aware. Job sees the light.

> Then Job replied to the LORD:
>
> > "I know that you can do all things;
> >   no purpose of yours can be thwarted.
> > You asked, 'Who is this that obscures my plans without knowledge?'
> >   Surely I spoke of things I did not understand,
> >   things too wonderful for me to know." (42:1–3)

What is interesting about this statement is that God has a redemptive purpose that will be fulfilled in the midst of every hardship, sometimes much more in spite of than because of it. And best of all, this purpose cannot be thwarted; the hardship cannot be the all-defining reality. Second, Job confesses that he does not know what this purpose is. "Surely I spoke of things I did not understand, things too wonderful for me to know." Even after meeting God, Job *still* does not know, *but he trusts God*. He does not know what purpose could ever make his life worthwhile in spite of it all. His demonstration of genuine faithfulness, what it looks like under fire and how one can respond to God as a result, is fulfilled by Christ while hanging on the cross: "My God, my God,

---

8. Gustavo Gutiérrez, *On Job: God-Talk and the Suffering of the Innocent* (Maryknoll, NY: Orbis Books, 1985), 101–3.

why have you forsaken me?" (Mark 15:34). And as for Christ's resurrection, this is indeed the ultimate purpose that cannot be thwarted and that makes life worthwhile despite the suffering. Job seems to have caught a glimpse of it:

> I know that my redeemer lives,
>   and that in the end he will stand on the earth.
> And after my skin has been destroyed,
>   yet in my flesh I will see God;
> I myself will see him
>   with my own eyes—I, and not another.
> How my heart yearns within me! (19:25–27)

Job's hardship cannot thwart this purpose, dim its glory, or destroy its place of supremacy over the meaning of his life, over the meaning of history. The reason for that is because we are made for God's glory. Despite unimaginably grievous suffering, life in God proves to be worthwhile after all. The glory of resurrection fulfills us so deeply and so fully that not even tragedy on Job's scale can nullify it. Not even suffering on that scale can cut deeper or reach further when it comes to the meaning of life. As Paul says, "I consider that our present sufferings are not worth comparing with the glory that will be revealed in us" (Rom. 8:18). Paul did not write this from an ivory tower. Just read 2 Corinthians 11!

Divine Perfections

Divine attributes (characteristics that are considered divine) may best be called **perfections**. God is infinitely perfect. Such perfection is unimaginable to us. Essential to God is divine love; God is infinitely perfect love. First John 4:8–10 is key to this insight: "Whoever does not love does not know God, because God is love. This is how God showed his love among us: He sent his one and only Son into the world that we might live through him. This is love: not that we loved God, but that he loved us and sent his Son as an atoning sacrifice for our sins." Notice how the text assumes that "like knows like." The more we become *like* God by participating in divine love, the more we *know* God, since God *is* love. Then the text focuses on the cross as the major place where God reveals divine love.

It is significant that God would define Godself at the cross, at the deepest pit of human despair and condemnation. God has chosen to meet us precisely there, where we need God the most. Pointing to the cross, the text says, "This is love," and then follows this identification with the words "not that we loved God, but that he loved us." This cross is where it all begins for the Christian—not where *we* reach for God but where *God* reaches for us. Of course, we by God's grace must reach for God, but all things begin and are sustained by God's prior movement. God's grace always takes the first and all-defining step. The love that binds God to us and enables us to respond does not arise with us. We do not define it. We do not initiate it. We do not account for its ongoing and all-sustaining power. This love comes from God—it *is* God! In this light, Romans 5:5 is also significant: "And hope does not put us to shame, because God's love has been poured out into our hearts through the Holy Spirit, who has been given to us." The love of God that is revealed and that conquers at the cross and in the resurrection is poured forth through Jesus Christ at Pentecost. The Spirit fills our lives and transforms us at the moment we become Christians by faith in the gospel. This love is the path to knowing God. One who does not love does *not* know God. We should let that thought sink in.

The classical view of God that informed theology in the modern era tended to contrast creaturely and divine attributes. To be creaturely is to be finite, limited, subject to change, corrupt, suffering, and dying. To be divine is to be infinite, unlimited, unchanging (immutable), unaffected by evil, impassible (invulnerable to suffering), and eternal. Though such contrasts do exist (with needed qualifications), stressing them could eclipse the *relationality* of God with creation and the engaging involvement of God in creation, especially through the life, suffering, death, and resurrection of Jesus Christ. The key is to qualify the above-mentioned contrasts by what is actually revealed of God in the Christ event, in the context of the biblical narrative as a whole. Though no easy connections should be made between the God revealed and active in history and God's life in Godself throughout eternity, a correspondence certainly does exist. Otherwise, the God revealed in history would not authentically be *God*.

When exploring the divine perfections, it helps to be reminded that we speak here centrally of the perfection of divine love. Arguably, love is both free and for the one who is loved. From the fullness of the triune communion, God is indeed both—free and totally involved in our reality. The divine freedom is not only apart from us (meaning that it is not dependent on us) but also *for us*. But divine love is indeed still not dependent on us. God does not need humanity to be God. As Paul preaches in Athens concerning our gracious God, "And he is not served by human hands, as if he needed anything. Rather, he himself gives everyone life and breath and everything else" (Acts 17:25). But God does love and long for humanity. The question obviously arises: Can God suffer? This has been a difficult question to answer in the history of theology. The God of Scripture is presented as passionate. Though anthropomorphic, this perfection shows how intensely God longs for us. God, to be God, does not need us, but this does not mean that God has no desire for us.

As an example, Genesis 6:6 notes that God's "heart was deeply troubled" when observing how much sin there was in the world at the time of Noah. Moreover, God "so loved the world that he gave his one and only Son" in the power of the Spirit to save us (John 3:16). The divine Son took on flesh and went to a cross to bear our suffering, condemnation, and death, so that we may know life everlasting. Surely, God can be said to have borne suffering for us. The problem here is that suffering implies a need or a lack; the one who suffers needs relief or a desired fulfillment. But God is infinitely perfect and has no need of anything. For this reason, the church in the early centuries regarded God as **impassible** (essentially invulnerable to suffering). But how can a God who is impassible suffer?

Perhaps it would help if we were to say that God can suffer in bearing our suffering, but without having a damaging effect on the divine essence or life. There can be no need or lack in God. God "suffers" without creating a lack within God's perfect fullness of life, meaning that God does not suffer in the way we do, nor in a way that involves any lack or that reaches for personal fulfillment. And yet God *still* suffers! The prominent theologians of the first several centuries of Christian history (the church fathers) maintained that God "suffers impassibly," in a way that does not involve any lack in God's perfection. God's perfection is revealed precisely in loving freely and fully. Indeed, if God cannot give in a way that enters unimaginably fully into the suffering of others, would that not in itself reveal a lack in God? So lacking nothing, God does indeed reveal the fullness and perfection of divine love by entering fully into our suffering and need so as to bear it for us to redeem and heal us. Yet we should still maintain that God loves in a way that does not reveal a lack of divine perfection, a loss of divine fullness; his bearing our suffering fully reveals his fullness! But God suffers no lack in bearing our suffering. God does not lose any divine perfection. As Karl Barth writes, "God gives Himself, but he does not give Himself away."[9] God is perfect love, but out of grace, God overflows onto others to bring them into that fulfillment so that they may be blessed by it. God bears their suffering without being essentially and adversely changed by it, for God is **immutable** (he cannot change essentially). God has freely determined from all eternity to be the God who

---

9. Karl Barth, *Church Dogmatics*, vol. IV/1, *The Doctrine of Reconciliation*, trans. G. W. Bromiley, ed. G. W. Bromiley and T. F. Torrance (Edinburgh: T&T Clark, 1956), 185.

loves others fully and unconditionally—so much so, in fact, that God takes on their burdens so that they can be free.

I say this knowing full well that some modern theologians, like Kazoh Kitamori (1916–98) and Jürgen Moltmann (b. 1926), go so far as to reject divine impassibility. In their view, God so longs for humanity as to experience suffering at the very core of God's being. God's very wholeness or self-reconciliation depends in some sense on the history of salvation. Writing from postwar Japan, Kitamori maintains that God responds to a sinful and suffering world by being deeply divided or in conflict. God's justice requires wrath for sinners, but God's love requires embracing them. God is in conflict! God resolves the conflict in favor of love. At the cross especially, God overcomes wrath to extend love and grace to sinners. In providing for reconciliation with sinners, God reconciles with Godself. In taking on our suffering and overcoming it, God's own turmoil is resolved.[10] In a similar vein, Moltmann maintains that by committing the Son to human flesh, the Father longs for the Son in longing for humanity. Reconciling with humanity involves the reconciliation of the Father and the Son in the Spirit.[11]

I respond to this rejection of divine impassibility with both gratitude and hesitance. There is no question that creation *matters* to God and that God desires it, willing grace rather than wrath for it. As Daniel Castelo has shown, God's impassibility does not mean divine *apathy*. It just means that God does not lose any divine perfection and fullness in desiring humanity and bearing their suffering. That fact helps to explain how God's love conquers wrath and suffering to save us.[12] But I regard Kitamori and Moltmann as going too far in rejecting the classical doctrine of divine impassibility. I agree with Kitamori that God overcomes wrath to reach out to humanity in grace. I am grateful to him for rhetorically driving this point home to me. Yet this overcoming love cannot literally involve an inner conflict in God that requires resolution. God does not require inner wholeness by loving others. God is perfect love and loves others in the abundant overflow of that love. Likewise, I agree with Moltmann that the incarnation binds God to humanity in eternal covenant relation. Due to the incarnation, God will never be known as God again without us. Jesus will forever be the God-man. This is a covenantal marriage without

---

10. Kazoh Kitamori, *Theology of the Pain of God: The First Original Theology from Japan* (1965; repr., Eugene, OR: Wipf & Stock, 2005), 19–42.

11. Jürgen Moltmann, *The Trinity and the Kingdom: The Doctrine of God*, trans. Margaret Kohl (Minneapolis: Fortress, 1993), 75–90.

12. Daniel Castelo, *The Apathetic God: Exploring the Contemporary Relevance of Divine Impassibility*, Paternoster Theological Monographs (Milton Keynes, UK: Paternoster, 2009), 14–18.

the possibility of divorce. How God loves us! I am grateful to Moltmann for rhetorically driving home the unfathomable depth of divine love and longing for humanity. Yet, again, God is not in need of reconciliation with humanity in order to be self-reconciled. There is no need or lack in God.

What would help is for us to distinguish between God's eternal, inner communion as Father, Son, and Spirit (the **immanent Trinity**) and God's involvement in history to save us as an overflow of divine perfection and love (the **economic Trinity**). Though there is only one Trinity, there are these two distinct dimensions. The former (i.e., God as God in God's inner being) does not require the latter (i.e., God's self-giving in history) for fulfillment. Rather, the latter is the overflow of the former. So God suffers, but not as we do. God bears our suffering without ceasing to be fully and perfectly God. In fact, God's perfection is revealed in this overflow of gracious love to sinners, thus entering with unimaginable depth into our suffering to save us. God loses no power in taking on our weakness; otherwise, our hope would rest on a limited foundation.

To explain God's wrath, one needs to take God's infinite **holiness** into consideration. God's love is holy love, love that is infinitely pure, not vulnerable to evil or seduction, not tainted by darkness and corruption. God is infinitely powerful and has invulnerable purity. For this reason, evil cannot conquer God; it cannot be the final word of history. God in infinite holiness is a consuming fire (Heb. 12:29). Holy love conquers all. This means that God rejects evil so intensely because God loves us so intensely and knows what evil does to us. All of this means that divine wrath is not simply anger, though God rejects evil and is displeased with the path we have chosen in our flight from God. Theologically, wrath is an objective state, alienation from divine love. Equating divine wrath simply with anger is reductionistic and leads to distortions in our image of God. Wrath is ultimately alienation from divine love, which God overcomes on the cross. It is impossible to understand wrath apart from the cross.

More to the point theologically, God's wrath consists of God's handing us over to the destructive alienation of sin and death that we have chosen for ourselves. Note Isaiah 53:4–6:

> Surely he took up our pain
>   and bore our suffering,
> yet we considered him punished by God,
>   stricken by him, and afflicted.
>
> But he was pierced for our transgressions,
>   he was crushed for our iniquities;

the punishment that brought us peace was on him,
  and by his wounds we are healed.

We all, like sheep, have gone astray,
  each of us has turned to our own way;
and the LORD has laid on him
  the iniquity of us all.

Notice that God's Messiah, the suffering servant, is said to "take up" our pain and suffering by having the punishment of our iniquity laid upon him. Looking at this event in light of the cross, Christ was no victim involved in events that had spun out of his control. He freely took up our suffering to save us. We considered *him* stricken by God, but it was *our* suffering that he took on himself and not that which *he* deserved. He suffered *vicariously*, in our place. His taking on our suffering and judgment resulted in our healing. But notice especially the nature of our sin, the source of our judgment, sorrow, and despair: "We all, like sheep, have gone astray, each of us has turned to our own way" (v. 6). This is the "iniquity" that was laid on him. The sin is our straying from God, and the judgment is the condemnation and death that we endure in alienation from God and to which God hands us over in our fleeing from God (Rom. 1:24–28). God also handed over the divine Son to a cross so that we can be justified in his rising from the dead (4:25). "For God did not send his Son into the world to condemn the world, but to save the world through him" (John 3:17). Christ as God's Son was predestined to be condemned in our place so that we may all share in his predestination to glory. Divine love and holiness are thus not different perfections that can be played off against each other or placed in tension with one another.

The idea of divine **simplicity** assumes that God's perfections are one. God's perfections cannot be dissected into separate parts. God's perfection is simple in the sense that it is indivisibly one. All of God's perfections are unique lenses through which to view the God who loves in freedom. God is also faithful and true, the loving God who is the rock of our salvation. "If we are faithless, he remains faithful, for he cannot disown himself" (2 Tim. 2:13). God is the great "I AM WHO I AM," which can be translated to say that God *always* "is what God is," unchangeably faithful (Exod. 3:14). God is the one who will make good on the promises that God made with "uplifted hand," as if swearing an oath (6:8). The author of Hebrews elaborates that "since there was no one greater for him to swear by, he swore by himself" (6:13). God swore to Godself to always be faithful and true! So also Christ is the "same yesterday and today and forever" (13:8). God's faithfulness "continues through all generations" (Ps. 119:90), for it has no expiration date; this is who God *is*, faithful and true, for God's "compassions never fail" (Lam. 3:22). God's faithfulness changes us into its image. Faith in God endures as well, being sustained by divine faithfulness: "Let us hold unswervingly to the hope we profess, for he who promised is faithful" (Heb. 10:23). Indeed, "for your steadfast love is before my eyes, and I walk in your faithfulness" (Ps. 26:3 ESV). God's occasional change of mind in Scripture never has God betraying a divine promise or contradicting the divine nature or purpose. In changing circumstances, the perceived change in course is caused by God's enduring faithfulness to the divine purposes.

God is not limited by anything external to God. God is **omnipotent**, or all-powerful love, for "with God all things are possible" (Matt. 19:26). God's limitless power is not naked or raw power but rather the power of divine love. Our hope is based on this very point; at the end of history, all will learn that divine love wins. Nothing can separate us from that love. "For I am convinced that neither death nor life, neither angels nor demons, neither the present nor the future, nor any powers, neither height nor depth, nor anything else in all creation, will be able to separate us from the love of God that is in Christ Jesus our Lord" (Rom. 8:38–39). God's limitless power liberates and empowers toward the fulfillment of the good; it does not oppress. It is not tyrannical. Thus, divine omnipotence does not mean that God can do just *anything*. There are things that God cannot do because they are outside of the divine nature and will. For example, "it is impossible for God to lie" (Heb. 6:18). God cannot sin. God cannot engage in foolish tasks. This popular riddle is a good example: "Can God make a rock too heavy for God to lift?" The answer is obviously no. God cannot contradict Godself or even attempt such a senseless act. Omnipotence means, rather, that God can do whatever is within God's nature and will to do in service to divine love. The cross highlights the nature of divine love; the resurrection and its fulfillment in the future kingdom of God reveal divine omnipotence.

God as loving is also all knowing or **omniscient**. "I make known the end from the beginning, from ancient times, what is still to come. I say, 'My purpose will stand, and I will do all that I please'" (Isa. 46:10). All that God pleases to do is known by God in all of eternity. As with God's other perfections, God's omniscience serves the purposes of divine love; it is a property of this love. God's all-seeing eye does not show any hint of evil or oppression as its purpose. In his effort to flee from God, the psalmist writes that "surely the darkness will hide me," but he quickly adds, "even the darkness will not be dark to you" (Ps. 139:11–12). God sees and knows all, and we can thank God that this is so. Given our idolatrous ways, if we could hide something from God, the temptation to do so would at times seem irresistible. But God will not allow us to rest comfortably in our effort to hide behind our sin and self-justification. "Nothing in all creation is hidden from God's sight. Everything is uncovered and laid bare before the eyes of him to whom we must give account" (Heb. 4:13). I am deeply grateful that God knows all.

But does God's limitless knowledge imply that humans do not have any free will? Does the fact that God knows all that will happen in human history mean that history is determined by God down to the minutest detail? There are theologians called "open theists" (or "freewill theists") who hold that God's omniscience does indeed eliminate human free will. All of history ends up as a script written in advance, which God knows from beginning to end. Nothing can happen outside of what is known by God. To avoid determinism and the elimination of human freedom, open theists reject divine omniscience. Some open theists say that God knows all *possibilities* of what could happen as well as the major salvation-historical events that are vital to the victory of divine love in history, such as fulfilled prophecy. But God chose not to know history in every detail so as to grant space for history to be "open" to unforeseen and divinely graced human accomplishments.[13] Biblical statements that reveal God "regretting" a former action in the light of new developments (e.g., Gen. 6:7), changing the divine intention (2 Kings 20:1–6), or showing surprise at an event (Jer. 7:31) indicate that God does not know exactly which among numerous possibilities will occur in many instances.

The major problem with this view of God is that it allows human history to limit God. If God moves through time discovering things along with the rest of us, God is limited by time. How far can this limitation hem God in? History can be a powerful force. Many fear that in open theism the rock upon which our hope is built would end up frighteningly weak. God would arguably resemble a finite god more than the Lord of history, who declares the end from the beginning. Moreover, the idea that omniscience eliminates human free will can indeed be challenged. Knowledge is not the same as determination. God can be said to know something because it happens rather than saying that it happens because God knows it. This is not to say that God is not Lord of history or that he is not at work guiding and influencing. God's involvement in human history can leave space for human input, quite apart from the fact that God knows all things. Moreover, statements in the Bible that show God as regretting, changing course, or showing surprise are anthropomorphic and have other points to make besides the issue of God's knowledge. For example, God's showing shock at Israel's behavior is rhetorically meant to

13. See, e.g., Gregory A. Boyd, *The God of the Possible: A Biblical Introduction to the Open View of God* (Grand Rapids: Baker Books, 2000).

be a commentary on the magnitude of Israel's disobedience in that moment rather than on the nature or extent of divine knowledge.

God is also all present or **omnipresent**. There are no boundaries to the loving God. God is not bounded; rather, God bounds all else. God in essence has no bodily form, nor is God spatially limited, for "God is spirit," or incorporeal (John 4:24). Old Testament stories of God appearing in human form (such as God's walking in the garden and calling for Adam and Eve, Gen. 3:8–9) may be termed "theophanies" of God. A **theophany** is a visible manifestation of the transcendent, incorporeal God. Theophanies foreshadow the incarnation of the Word of the Father in flesh, but they are still not incarnations, only manifestations that reserve the incarnation as a unique, once and for all time event: "The Word became flesh and made his dwelling among us" (John 1:14). This Word reveals the Father, who has never been seen: "No one has ever seen God, but the one and only Son, who is himself God and is in closest relationship with the Father, has made him known" (John 1:18). That the Word or Son reveals the Father who has never been seen implies that Old Testament theophanies of God may perhaps best be termed "Christophanies" (i.e., preincarnate manifestations of the Son of God), since Christ has always been (from before the beginning of all things) the Word or revelation of the Father (John 1:1). An example is Isaiah's beholding a theophany of the Lord in the temple in Isaiah 6, which John tells us was a Christophany: "he saw Jesus' glory and spoke about him" (John 12:41).

As omnipresent, God not only acts in creation: creation exists in God. Not only does God act in time: time exists in God. No matter how the psalmist might try to flee, God confronted him at every turn.

> Where can I go from your Spirit?
>   Where can I flee from your presence?
> If I go up to the heavens, you are there;
>   if I make my bed in the depths, you are there.
> If I rise on the wings of the dawn,
>   if I settle on the far side of the sea,
> even there your hand will guide me,
>   your right hand will hold me fast. (Ps. 139:7–10)

No matter where the psalmist might go, he never ceases to say to God, "You hem me in behind and before, and you lay your hand upon me" (139:5). How can we evade God? "Do I not fill the heavens and the earth?" declares the Lord (Jer. 23:24 NASB). Nor can any place of worship contain the infinitely transcendent God. "But will God indeed dwell on the earth? Behold, heaven and the highest heaven cannot contain you; how much less this house that I have built!" (1 Kings 8:27 ESV). God is always present but not always in the same way; his omnipresence, though, is always consistent with divine love. In evil situations, God is the power of resistance; in resistance to grace, God is convicting and patient; in praise, God is inviting. When worship leaders invite God to be present, they are actually inviting a mode of presence appropriate to that setting.

The Triune God

God is one, the one incomparable God who loves in freedom. God's oneness is God's absolute uniqueness, for God *alone* is God. "To whom will you compare me? Or who is my equal?" (Isa. 40:25). As Katherine Sonderegger notes, "Radical Oneness, radical uniqueness, demands thought beyond any class, any universal, any likeness."[14] God's oneness also demands undivided loyalty. The great Shema (a declaration to "hear") makes this point clear: "Hear, O Israel: The LORD our God, the LORD is one. Love the LORD your God with all your heart and with all your soul and with all your strength" (Deut. 6:4–5). In this text, God's oneness means that God alone is God and worthy of absolute loyalty. There is no pantheon from which we can choose one god over against the others; neither can we divide our loyalty among more than one. If deity is shared among separate deities, no single one would be infinite or omnipotent since they would border and limit one another. Idols are indeed finite, but that is not true of the one and only incomparable God. We were made for God, so giving loyalty to anything but God causes us to slip into bondage and a distorted version of ourselves. Only faith in God frees and fulfills us.

In the light of the New Testament, it seems clear that the one God exists as Father, Son, and Holy Spirit. Every step in the story of Jesus presents the accomplishment of salvation as a shared action of three. The Holy Spirit of "the Most High" overshadows Mary so that she will conceive in her womb the holy Son of God (Luke 1:35). At Christ's baptism, the Spirit descends from the heavenly Father upon him as the beloved Son of the Father (3:22). At the cross, Christ offers himself "through the eternal Spirit" to the heavenly Father on our behalf (Heb. 9:14), and the Father raises Christ from the dead "according to the Spirit of holiness" to save us (Rom. 1:4 ESV). Before his ascension, Christ instructs the church to baptize in the name of the Father,

---

14. Katherine Sonderegger, *The Doctrine of God*, vol. 1 of *Systematic Theology* (Minneapolis: Fortress, 2015), 25.

the Son, and the Holy Spirit (Matt. 28:19), indicating that the God into whom we are incorporated at salvation is the triune God, the one incomparable God who is eternally three. At Pentecost, Christ receives the Spirit from the Father and pours forth the Spirit onto all flesh, diversely throughout the peoples of the world, as expressed in many tongues and contexts (Acts 2:4, 33). Indeed, only *God* can save us: "You shall acknowledge . . . no Savior except me" (Hosea 13:4). In this light, the fact that the Father, the Son, and the Spirit are all involved in obtaining salvation for us means, without question, that all three are the one incomparable God.[15] In the Spirit and in truth, the church glorifies Christ as Lord to the glory of the Father (John 4:24; 1 Cor. 12:3; Phil. 2:11).

Father, Son, and Holy Spirit are the one God who loves in freedom. To be free means, in part, that one does not do something out of need but purely from want and choice. That God loves in freedom means that God does not need creation to know perfect love because, in all eternity, God is perfect love as a communion of three. God did not need to create to be God; in loving us, he does not do so under the threat that our lack of reciprocation would in any way create a lack of fulfillment in the divine life. Perfectly fulfilled as a communion of love, God loves us in freedom, which means out of grace and not necessity. Jesus's reception of the Spirit at his baptism beautifully illustrates the communion of love that is God. Looking again at Christ's baptism, we notice that the Father declares to him, "You are my Son, whom I love; with you I am well pleased" (Luke 3:22). At that moment, the Spirit is poured forth from the Father upon him as if bearing free and abundant witness to the Father's love for the Son. The Son moves forth in the power of the Spirit and in devotion to the Father. The meaning seems clear. In this text, God is a communion of love in which the Father loves the Son, the Son loves the Father, and the Spirit is the bond of and overflowing witness to that love.

God is, in fact, a communion of love throughout eternity. The Father has loved the Son "before the creation of the world" (John 17:24), and the Son has loved the Father, sharing glory with the Father "before the world began" (v. 5). The communion between them is eternally and unfathomably penetrating and intimate; as Christ says to the Father, "You are in me and I am in you" (17:21). This interpenetrating communion has historically been called **perichoresis** (Greek *perichōrēsis*). The Holy Spirit has commonly been viewed as essentially the freedom and "ecstasy" (or overflowing abundance) of divine love that the Father and Son share eternally with each other. The Spirit plays

15. I develop this point in Frank D. Macchia, *The Trinity, Practically Speaking* (Downers Grove, IL: IVP Books, 2010).

this role intentionally, interpenetrating the Father and the Son, who interpenetrate the Spirit as well. They delight in the Spirit and the Spirit in them, as the three delight eternally in their communion of love. This communion has been called an eternal "dance" of interpenetrating love.[16]

Let's look more deeply into the eternal or immanent life of the triune God. Though we cannot penetrate the inner mystery of God, we do have some clues from Scripture about this divine inner life that allow us to say something about it. A guiding light for probing the inner life of God is Christ's statement that "as the Father has life in himself, so he has granted the Son also to have life in himself" (John 5:26). Since this statement starts with the very divine life inherent in the Father, it points to an eternal reality beyond time. Notice that the Son has the divine life "in himself" *as the Father does*. This is not a reference to the incarnation, since the comparison is between the life of the Son and the life essential to the Father, who is not incarnate. Notice that the divine essence or life of the Father and the essence or life of the Son are shared equally; the Son "has" divine life in himself as the Father does. Notice also that the Father grants this, meaning that the Father is its eternal source (without beginning). From this, we can surmise that in eternity the Father shares the divine essence or life with the Son; but this does not make the Son essentially inferior to the Father, for the Son is granted to have life in himself *as the Father does*. The same could naturally be said of the Spirit, who proceeds or "goes out" from the Father (John 15:26).

The facts that all three persons obtain salvation for us and that only God can save (Hosea 13:4) deny the possibility that the Son and the Spirit are not truly divine. The heresy of **subordinationism**—the notion that the Son and the Spirit are different from the Father in nature and are not equal to the Father in deity—is disputed by the biblical attribution of full deity to the Son and the Spirit, as I will defend further in my chapters on Christology and pneumatology. On the other hand, neither are the three divine persons mere modes of operation, as **modalism** has maintained. Some today inadvertently support this heresy when they liken the Trinity to a man who plays three roles—father, son, and friend. To discover the error in this comparison, notice the fact that the Father loved the Son before the worlds were made and created all things through the Son (cf. John 1:1–5; 17:5, 24). Love cannot be shared between *roles* or *modes* of operation. Love is shared between *persons*! There is no question that all three divine persons share the same divine essence and yet enjoy eternal communion as persons.

16. Richard Rohr, *The Divine Dance: The Trinity and Your Transformation* (New Kensington, PA: Whitaker House, 2016), 27.

Yet there is an order to the divine persons that does not imply any difference in rank or value. Historically, the church has recognized the Father as the *source* of deity and the Son as eternally *begotten* (or generated) from the Father without beginning. The term "begotten" is mysterious in meaning. We only know that it results in a filial (Son-like) relationship of the begotten to the Father. The Son reveals the Father and has enjoyed a communion of love and glory with the Father from eternity (John 17:5, 24). The Spirit is obviously not "begotten" of the Father since the Spirit is not a Son. The Spirit "proceeds" from the Father from all eternity, without beginning: "the Spirit of truth who *goes out* from the Father" (John 15:26). In the history of theology, the Spirit is also said to be spirated, or breathed forth, from the Father, for the Spirit is figuratively designated as the breath or wind of God; indeed, the wind blows where it pleases (John 3:8). The Spirit also has the divine life *as the Father and the Son do*; the Spirit *is* the divine life. Historically, the Spirit as the breath of God has been regarded as the bond, freedom, and ecstasy (overflowing delight) of divine love shared between the Father and the Son. But there is no hierarchy of essence or value here. It is just as fully divine to be the beloved Son and the Spirit as it is to be the Father, who is the fount or source of the divine life. "Only by virtue of the particularity and relatedness of all three is God God."[17] Interestingly, the divine life shared without beginning between the Father and the Son and the Spirit accounts for the unity of God. But the fact that this divine life is shared differently among the three (the Father as source, the Son through begetting, and the Spirit through procession or spiration) refers to the diversity of the three. God is one, but diversely so.

In its early centuries, the church struggled to find the language to describe God's oneness and God's threeness. Thanks to the Eastern Cappadocian theologians of the fourth century (who came from Cappadocia in modern-day Turkey)—Gregory of Nyssa (ca. 335–ca. 395), Gregory of Nazianzus (330–390), and Basil of Caesarea (330–379)—the church settled on the language of *essence* (*ousia*) for the oneness or unity of God and *persons* (*hypostases*) for the diverse relations of the three. When this language was first introduced in the fourth century, there was some pushback. The Western theologian Jerome (ca. 347–419) balked at the "newfangled" language of *ousia* and *hypostases*.[18] This language is now fairly common among theologians. These terms, however, need to be used with caution.

17. Colin Gunton, *The Promise of Trinitarian Theology* (New York: T&T Clark, 1991), 197.
18. Jerome, "Letter 15," in *The Letters of St. Jerome*, vol. 1, *Letters 1–22*, trans. Charles Christopher Mierow, Ancient Christian Writers 33 (New York: Newman, 1963), 71.

When we speak of the one divine essence that the Father, Son, and Spirit share in common, we are not talking about something abstract or impersonal that can exist somehow apart from them as if it were a fourth reality. No, the divine essence is living and personal, arising from the Father and shared diversely by the Son and the Spirit. It depicts the shared life of the three. Moreover, when using the term "persons," we do not refer to three separate "people," each with their own "ego" (as in three separate people who act in unison today). That idea would be tritheism (three gods) and would even imply finite gods since, as separate beings, they would border and limit each other. We refer to divine persons in a way unlike our normal use of this term. Though the three persons are eternally "conscious" of each other, they still share fully in one divine mind and will. The three persons are interactive subjects of the one divine mind in God's eternal self-relation. Walter Kasper thus notes "that in the Trinity we are dealing with three subjects who are reciprocally conscious of each other by reason of one and the same consciousness which the three subjects 'possess,' each in his own proper way.[19] The divine persons are thus distinct but not separable. And they are not people! God's fullness is shown in the shared life of the three, though also in each person in a way appropriate to each. So the Father is not one-third (or a "part") of God but is rather the fullness of God as the source of the divine life. The Son is not one-third (a part) of God but is rather the fullness of God as the Son begotten of the Father. And the Spirit is not one-third (a part) of God but is rather the fullness of God as proceeding forth in ecstatic delight from the Father.

It may be said that Western theologians stress the oneness of God and those of the Eastern tradition emphasize the threeness of God, but this point can be exaggerated. More recently, the so-called social doctrine of the Trinity has become popular globally. This newer trinitarian doctrine views God as three seats of consciousness that share life through perichoresis, or interpenetration. Social trinitarians do not anchor the oneness of God in the person of the Father (referred to as the divine monarchy), as did the tradition of the ancient church. Contrary to the developing orthodoxy of the early centuries, they tend to think that the monarchy of the Father as the eternal source of deity implies the essential inferiority of the Son and the Spirit. But this conviction can lead to an overreliance on perichoresis for understanding the shared triune life. One can wonder whether this understanding of divine unity is adequate to anchor the oneness of God.

Social trinitarians also follow the method of reasoning from the life of Jesus to the triune life. The incarnate life of Jesus will naturally lead to a stress on

---

19. Walter Kasper, *The God of Jesus Christ* (New York: Crossroad, 2002), 289.

the distinction and relationality of the divine persons. Moltmann connects the social doctrine of the Trinity to an egalitarian church fellowship and an egalitarian social and political ethic.[20] Brazilian theologian Leonardo Boff is a strong supporter of the social doctrine of the Trinity, using it to anchor the quest for a just and loving society in the Trinity as its chief image or icon.[21] Korean theologian Jung Young Lee finds in the concept of *yin* and *yang* an illustration of the Trinity, since they are contrasting ultimate principles that may also be said to comprise each other, as do the Father and the Son. The comprising, or the "in-ness," of the two in one another is the third, which is symbolic of the Spirit.[22] Lee also finds his Asian family to be a symbol of the Trinity—the father, the son, and the mother, the latter as the link of intimate relation between the former two, uniting them in her empathetic love. The feminine figure, symbolic of the Spirit, unites the two masculine figures of father and son.[23] So also Adonijah Okechukwu Ogbonnaya develops an African trinitarian theology that rejects monotheism as unable to grant the relation of persons equal weight in the community of the triune God, especially as the anchor to a just community on earth.[24] These social understandings of the Trinity are intriguing, but in my view they require an adequate anchoring of the oneness of God in the monarchy of the Father. They should also seek to understand the three persons as agents of consciousness of the one divine mind in communal self-interaction.

The Father as the sole source of the Son and the Spirit was a contentious topic of debate between the East and the West in the ancient and medieval church. Both traditions honored the Father as the source of the Spirit, but the West added that the Son was the source of the Spirit too, the Spirit proceeding eternally from the Father *and the Son* (*filioque* in Latin). In the Middle Ages Western theologians added the term "*filioque*" (and the Son) to the Nicene Creed so as to bolster belief in Christ's deity. (If the Spirit proceeds from both the Father *and* the Son, it would be clear that the Son's deity is equal to the Father's.) Though the Eastern churches also defended the full deity of the Son, they rejected the Western addition, believing that the Father is the *only* source of deity, a property unique to the Father as the person who anchors the unity of God. In 1054 CE, this difference was the major

20. Moltmann, *Trinity and the Kingdom*, 10–20.

21. Leonardo Boff, *Holy Trinity, Perfect Community*, trans. Phillip Berryman (Maryknoll, NY: Orbis Books, 2000).

22. Jung Young Lee, *The Trinity in Asian Perspective* (Nashville: Abingdon, 1996), 212–19.

23. Lee, *The Trinity in Asian Perspective*, 92.

24. A. Okechukwu Ogbonnaya, *On Communitarian Divinity: An African Interpretation of the Trinity* (St. Paul: Paragon House, 1998), 89–90.

reason for the onset of division between the church of the West (the Catholic Church) and the churches of the East (now called the Eastern Orthodox churches). There are compromise positions that have historical precedent in the Eastern tradition, such as the view that the Spirit proceeds eternally from the Father *through* the Son. Catholic theologian Thomas Weinandy has recently suggested that the Son is also eternally begotten from the Father *through the Spirit*.[25] The Son is begotten eternally from the Father through the Spirit, who bears abundant witness of the Father's love for the Son in eternally begetting him, and the Spirit proceeds through the Son back to the Father, abundantly expressing in procession the Son's love for the Father. Through it all, there is an intimate communion of love involving the three. In the perfect abundance and intimacy of the Spirit, the Father is in the Son and the Son is in the Father in perfect communion, a perichoresis of perfect love.

Besides the immanent Trinity in eternity described above, there is also the economic Trinity revealed in time through the triune missions. The circle of love that exists eternally in God by way of the processions of the Son and the Spirit from the Father is not meant by God to forever be a closed circle. It was God's eternal will to be an *open and overflowing* circle that involves creation. Jesus's prayer to the Father for his followers in John 17 reveals the goal of God's opening of the triune life to creation. Jesus prays "that all of them may be one, Father, just as you are in me and I am in you. May they also be in us so that the world may believe that you have sent me" (v. 21). And we are in the triune communion through the Spirit (1 John 4:13). Such is the triune mission of God: *may they be in us that the world may believe!* The church bears witness to the world of divine love in their communion together in God. Just as the Father is in the Son and the Son is in the Father in intimate communion, may humanity be in them to share in that circle of love, to let it transform them and shape their witness. The Father creates the world through the Son in the power and presence of the Spirit; later, he sends the Son and the Spirit into the world to incorporate humanity as participants in the divine communion. The Spirit mediates both Christ's coming into flesh (Luke 1:35) and the Son's victory over sin and death at the cross and in the resurrection (Rom. 1:4; Heb. 9:14). Then the Son mediates the Spirit to all flesh at his exaltation so that those who are redeemed might gain passage to the life of the Spirit (Gal. 3:14). In the Spirit, we are united to Christ (Rom. 8:9) so that we may have communion with his heavenly Father.

25. Thomas Weinandy, *The Father's Spirit of Sonship: Reconceiving the Trinity* (Eugene, OR: Wipf & Stock, 1995), esp. 17–23.

There is a *correspondence* between the immanent Trinity in eternity and the Trinity present and revealed in time. As the Father is the eternal source of deity for the Son and the Spirit, so the Father sends the Son and the Spirit into the world (John 3:16; 15:26). The Father is never sent. Likewise, as the Son is eternally begotten as the Son, so is the Son begotten in flesh. As the Spirit binds the Father and the Son in communion in free and abundant (ecstatic) witness, so the Spirit, poured forth from the Father, overflows the life of the Son in free and ecstatic witness at Pentecost, giving rise to the many tongues that declare the wonders of God. In the end, creation is transformed by the Spirit in the image of the glorious Son so that the Son may offer it up in glory to the Father, so that God may be all in all (1 Cor. 15:23–28).

FINAL REFLECTIONS

"God is," and God rewards those who seek him above all else. On this path, we learn that all of the hardships of this age—though sometimes hard, if not impossible, to understand—will be so outshined by the coming glory of the resurrection and the new creation that they cannot nullify its significance. Life will be shown to be worth it all because of God. We were made for God, body and soul; therefore, there is no evil that will prove to be insurmountable. And in Christ, nothing can separate us from the love of God. As we participate in the divine love, the reward of knowing God will be vindicated as worth it all.

God exists necessarily. Since God is absolutely perfect in every way, there is no imaginable accounting of reality that might explain why God *would not exist* as the ultimate ground and telos (ultimate purpose) of all else. I can well imagine scenarios in which *I* would not come to be. My parents might not have decided to have me. Physicists might well imagine why the universe might not have been. I, along with the rest of creation, am contingent, dependent on the right conditions or the will of God to be. But God is not contingent. There is no condition that might explain why God would not exist. This means that God exists necessarily as the ultimate ground and explanation of all else. God creates out of nothing (*ex nihilo*) so as to make creation the divine dwelling place. Created out of nothing, creation does not emanate out from God, sharing the divine essence. Though God pervades all things, God is not the essence of all things. Only God is God.

God loves in freedom. God is perfect love, as Father, Son, and Holy Spirit. Thus, God did not need to create or have fellowship with others to be God, to know perfect love. Neither does the refusal of humanity to love God cause a lack in God that requires healing or fulfillment. God creates and loves others freely, out of grace. Divine simplicity implies that God's perfections are one. Thus, all of God's attributes are properties of divine love. Holiness is infinitely holy love. Since God is infinitely pure, evil cannot seduce God and therefore cannot win. Wrath is a holy God's response to evil, a rejection of evil driven by holy love for the very creation that evil is bent on destroying. Passionate, divine wrath is more than anger; it is God's handing humanity over to the wayward path that they have chosen for themselves. But God does so with a larger goal. God bears with sinners on their wayward path with the goal of drawing them to repentance and redeeming them. God hands the divine Son over to alienation and death in order to save sinners. Wrath has redemptive love as its goal. God reigns as Lord so as to free creation from the oppressive reign of evil. Divine sovereignty is thus not tyrannical; it is reigning love. Omnipotence is all-powerful love; omnipresence is a boundlessly present love; and omniscience is the loving God knowing all things while loving all things.

God is one as the one and only incomparable God. God's oneness explains why absolute loyalty belongs to God alone. The one God is also three, which means that our loyalty to the incomparable God occurs in the context of loving communion in the divine embrace. God is one in essence but three in person. The Father is the ultimate source of deity as the one who loves, the Son is begotten from the Father eternally as the beloved, and the Spirit proceeds eternally from the Father as the freedom and ecstatic delight of divine love. The divine persons enjoy communion in interpenetrating perichoresis. This immanent Trinity is revealed in time as the economic Trinity, whereby the Father sends the Son to redeem and the Spirit is sent through the Son to perfect creation in the image of the Son. The goal is that God is all and in all and that the knowledge of the glory of God covers the earth as the waters cover the seas (Hab. 2:14).

TOPICS FOR REVIEW

1. What does it mean to say that God creates *ex nihilo*? Explain it also in relation to the belief in emanation.

2. In what sense can God suffer? And toward what end has God handed us over to suffering, joining us on this path?

3. What is the central divine perfection? Describe it in relation to 1 John 4:7–10.

4. What is divine wrath? Describe it.

5. Briefly explain divine omnipotence, omniscience, and omnipresence.

6. How is John 5:26 the guiding light for understanding the deity of the three persons in the inner life of the Trinity? Explain.

7. Is the shared essence of God something impersonal and abstract? Are the three persons of God three separate parts or people? Explain both answers.

3

JESUS CHRIST

The many tongues of Pentecost that speak in the Spirit assume a mediator, Jesus Christ. Peter's sermon on that day makes this point clear. Speaking of David, Peter declares: "Seeing what was to come, he spoke of the resurrection of the Messiah, that he was not abandoned to the realm of the dead, nor did his body see decay. God has raised this Jesus to life, and we are all witnesses of it. Exalted to the right hand of God, he has received from the Father the promised Holy Spirit and has poured out what you now see and hear" (Acts 2:31–33). Christ dies, according to the text, as a blameless sacrifice (without the blemish of corruption or decay), then is raised in victory over sin and death. He is exalted as Lord in the fullness of the Spirit, to do what only the Lord can do—namely, pour forth the Spirit upon sinful and dying flesh. For Luke, the Spirit is the promise of the Father granted through the work of the Messiah, who conquers and reigns as Lord (vv. 34–35). The Spirit comes bearing witness to the Lord, who mediates the promised life in the Spirit from the heavenly Father. The mediation of the Son's self-offering is necessary for the Spirit to come. *In mediating the Spirit, the Son grants his own life to us in diversely contextual ways.*

In this chapter we explore who this God-man is, the God-man who becomes our Lord and elder brother in the Spirit. From the start, we see two extremes to avoid. One is a kind of "instrumental" Christology, which views Jesus as *merely* the means of imparting life in the Spirit. Against this, the bulwark doctrines of the incarnation and the atonement have revealed Christ's redemptive significance in his own right as necessary for imparting the Spirit and making sinful flesh worthy of receiving the Spirit. As Paul writes, "Christ redeemed us from the curse of the law by becoming a curse for us, for it is written: 'Cursed is everyone who is hung on a pole.' He redeemed us . . . so that by faith we might receive the promise of the Spirit" (Gal. 3:13–14). On the other hand, neither is the outpoured Spirit the mere instrument of Christ; rather, the Spirit is the mediator of Christ's journey in flesh and the culminating point of his messianic mission, turning that mission into a multicontextual, global, and eschatological reality. As James Dunn writes, "The climax and purposed end of Jesus' ministry is not the cross and the resurrection, but the ascension and Pentecost."[1] This is not to deny the pivotal significance of the atonement. But the atonement is a bridge to the Messiah's impartation of new life. The Christ of Pentecost is indeed to be understood in the context of his sojourn from his incarnation to his death, resurrection, and exaltation. The many tongues that now bear witness to Christ seek to be faithful to what Christ revealed of himself and of God on the way to his climactic pouring forth of the Spirit.

Christological Method

John 1:14 declares that the Word of the Father became flesh and dwelt among us. The image is that of the Word descending into flesh, leading theologians to call this a Christology "from above." As we will see below, this approach to Christology dominated the great creeds of the church in the fourth and fifth centuries. There is no question that this Christology from above is biblical. As I will explain below, the divine Son did indeed descend *from above*, so to speak, or from the heavenly Father and into flesh in Mary's womb for our salvation. The Father's Word, who "was God" (v. 1), "became flesh and made his dwelling among us" (v. 14). Dwelling in flesh, the Word of the Father showed forth "the glory of the one and only Son, who came from the Father, full of grace and truth" (v. 14). But this Word or Son of the Father did not just dwell in flesh: he became flesh! He became human to be the Redeemer, the point of reconciliation between humanity and God. We will explore further what that means below, especially when we discuss the atonement. At this juncture I wish only to say that the Christology from above is indeed biblical. Christ says in no uncertain terms, "I came from the Father and entered the world" (John 16:28).

Yet the Christology from above has had its critics. For one thing, it tends to define Christology mainly in terms of the incarnation. What it means to

---

1. James D. G. Dunn, *Baptism in the Holy Spirit: A Re-examination of the New Testament Teaching on the Gift of the Spirit in Relation to Pentecostalism Today* (London: SCM, 1970), 44.

say that the Word became flesh and dwelled among us can take up the lion's share of the christological debate. The atonement was later added as of equal importance. In fact, the Christology of the West reached its fulfillment in the eleventh century, when Anselm showed that the God-man (the divine Son who became flesh) provided us with the only feasible explanation for how Christ could reconcile God and humanity on the cross. As human, Christ could bear our debt of honor to God; as divine, he could break the bonds of sin, death, and the devil so as to pay that debt.

Critics point out that in the Christology from above, Christ is so defined according to the incarnation and atonement that who he was as a *historical figure* in his own time and place can recede into the background as insignificant. Albert Schweitzer (1875–1965) wrote his classic, *The Quest of the Historical Jesus*, in search of the Jesus of first-century Judaism. He masterfully surveyed the modern efforts prior to the twentieth century to reconstruct who Jesus was as a man of history. This effort came to be called the **quest for the historical Jesus.** Schweitzer maintained that creedal Christology (which we call "from above") "cut off the last possibility of a return to the historical Jesus."[2] He even wished to "shatter" christological dogma and become an "ally" in its destruction.[3] Schweitzer conceded that the various efforts at writing biographies of Jesus were not entirely objective. Each biographer ended up shaping Jesus "in accordance with his own character."[4] Schweitzer's own effort focused on Jesus as an apocalyptic (or end-time) Jewish prophet who gave his life over to the coming kingdom of his heavenly Father, dying in an unsuccessful attempt to bring it to earth and to move the wheel of history in his direction. For Schweitzer, Jesus was courageous, but the wheel of history destroyed him. This wheel "rolls onward, and the mangled body of the one immeasurably great Man, who was strong enough to think of Himself as the spiritual ruler of mankind and to bend history to His purpose, is hanging upon it still."[5] *This is Schweitzer's challenge.*

But what if the effort of Christ to inaugurate the kingdom of his heavenly Father on earth did *not* end in failure? This is implicitly the leading question of Wolfhart Pannenberg (1928–2014) in his masterpiece, *Jesus—God and Man*, which implicitly responds to Schweitzer's challenge.[6] Pannenberg does not reject the Christology from above but faults it for not being adequately based

---

2. Albert Schweitzer, *The Quest of the Historical Jesus* (Minneapolis: Fortress, 2001), 5.
3. Schweitzer, *Quest of the Historical Jesus*, 5.
4. Schweitzer, *Quest of the Historical Jesus*, 6.
5. Schweitzer, *Quest of the Historical Jesus*, 371 (see also 365–403).
6. Wolfhart Pannenberg, *Jesus—God and Man*, trans. Lewis L. Wilkins and Duane A. Priebe, 2nd ed. (Philadelphia: Westminster, 1977).

on Christ's journey *from below*—namely, his journey to the cross and the resurrection. The quest for the historical Jesus after Schweitzer's classic—picked up, for example, by Rudolf Bultmann (1884–1976)—went through a phase of significant skepticism about the historical veracity of the New Testament accounts of Jesus. Bultmann wanted to *demythologize* Jesus, or interpret the myths about him allegedly reported in the New Testament, to discover their "existential" meaning—that is, their contribution to our quest for the meaning of our lives as we face an uncertain future.[7] Pannenberg was part of a turn to a greater confidence in the historical veracity of the accounts of Jesus in the New Testament. Jesus as a figure of history, for Pannenberg, is pictured compellingly in the Gospels as wholly given over to the arrival of the kingdom of God. Jesus's model prayer, for example, had as its lead petition that the Father's name be hallowed on the earth through the coming of the kingdom of God (Matt. 6:9–10). Pannenberg notes that the implication throughout Christ's life and teaching is that he is indispensable or essential to the coming of the kingdom. This implication is verified at Christ's resurrection, at which time the kingdom or reign of God ends up being inaugurated in history in the figure of the risen Christ. The risen Christ is shown to be essential to the victory of God's lordship, or reign, in the world. Since the kingdom of God is the victory of God's divine lordship, it is essential to God. If Christ is shown to be essential to the kingdom, *he is also shown to be essential to God* (or one in essence with God). In this light, the dogma of Christ's incarnation is revealed at Christ's resurrection. By revealing that Christ is essential to God, the resurrection shows us that Christ, at his conception in Mary's womb, must have been the incarnation of the divine Son in flesh. The Christology *from above* is thus revealed *from below*, at the conclusion of Jesus's journey to the cross and in the resurrection.[8] The added benefit of this christological method is that when we say, "The divine Son became flesh," we understand much better what we mean by the term "divine," since God's nature and will are fully revealed in Jesus's life, death, and resurrection. We also know better what we mean by "flesh," since Christ also reveals the true humanity he takes up in the incarnation.

I would make two qualifications to Pannenberg's breakthrough method. First, it is important to note that the Christology from below is mediated by the Holy Spirit, a point that is not highlighted by Pannenberg. The Son becomes flesh in the virgin's womb in the presence and power of the Holy

---

7. See Rudolf Bultmann, *Jesus Christ and Mythology* (New York: Charles Scribner's Sons, 1958).

8. Pannenberg, *Jesus—God and Man*, 334–89.

Spirit (Luke 1:35). Christ is installed as the Messiah under the anointing of the Spirit at his baptism (3:22). Christ offers himself on the cross by the eternal Spirit (Heb. 9:14), and Christ was raised from the dead "according to the Spirit of holiness" (Rom. 1:4 ESV). The Spirit's mediation of the divine Son's sojourn in flesh opens the path in flesh for the Son's redemptive mission. As Irenaeus (ca. 130–ca. 200) writes of Christ, "So the Spirit of God descended upon him . . . that we might be saved by receiving from the abundance of his anointing."[9] *The Logos (divine Word) Christology from above needs a Spirit Christology from below.*

Second, tracing Christ's significance as both the divine Son in flesh and the Messiah who bears the Spirit would have taken Pannenberg not only to the resurrection for the completion of Christ's mission, but also to Pentecost, where Christ becomes the Lord and head of his body by imparting the Spirit to all flesh. *Christ as the divine Word or Son in flesh bears the Spirit so as to impart the Spirit to others.* Indeed, Christ as Redeemer in his death and resurrection is also Christ as the mediator of life at Pentecost, for his redemptive work opened a path to the Spirit for us; it made us worthy of bearing the Spirit (Gal. 3:13–14). Irenaeus in the second century wrote that Christ bore the Spirit to fully be the Savior of the human race, because he would not only redeem through atonement but also bring humanity to the fullness of life in the Spirit, whom Christ would impart from his own fullness in the Spirit. M. C. Steenberg summarizes Irenaeus's position well: "Without the unction of the Spirit, Jesus is not Messiah; rather that without the Spirit the incarnate Son is not fully redeemer, since he who redeems recapitulatively does so by uniting humanity to the full life of God."[10]

Paul fittingly climaxes his discourse on the resurrection of Christ with the insight that Christ rises from the dead as a "life-giving Spirit," as the one who comes to us anew in the outpouring of the Spirit that he provides (1 Cor. 15:45). *The divine Son shows his essential unity with God by pouring forth the Spirit on all flesh.* Relocating the decisive moment of Christology from the resurrection to Pentecost allows us to regard Christ's ecclesial (i.e., church-connected) identity as the Lord and head of his body, as well as our elder brother and the firstborn from the dead for the entire creation (Eph. 4:15; Heb. 2:11; Col. 1:15–18). As Eduard Schweizer writes, "Jesus will never be without a church."[11] The Son was elect from all eternity to bear this identity,

---

9. Irenaeus, *Against Heresies* 3.9.3, as quoted in Matthew C. Steenberg, *Of God and Man: Theology as Anthropology from Irenaeus to Athanasius* (London: T&T Clark, 2009), 36.

10. Steenberg, *Of God and Man*, 36–37.

11. Eduard Schweizer, *Church Order in the New Testament*, Studies in Biblical Theology 32 (London: SCM, 1961), 23.

and it is an identity that is expressed and experienced in many unique ways among the peoples of the world.

A full-orbed Spirit Christology that still affirms Christ's deity has recently made an impact on global Christology. For example, New Zealand theologian Myk Habets has highlighted the Spirit's mediation of Christ's incarnation and mission. Habets notes that the disciples came to know Jesus "from below," as the Messiah in the presence and work of the Spirit. It was only at the culmination of his mission in the resurrection that they understood his incarnation as the divine Son "from above."[12] Habets offers a compelling case for integrating both approaches to Christology, from below and from above. He proposes a backward, retroactive reading from Christ's resurrection and presence to us in the power of the Spirit, back to Christ's death, life, and incarnation. This approach to Christology opens our eyes to the pneumatological richness of Christ's entire sojourn to the cross to save us.[13]

Leopoldo Sánchez has, in fact, made an impressive case contending that Spirit Christology is gaining broad support across denominational lines and various areas of theological study.[14] Like Habets, Sánchez notes that a Spirit Christology does not preclude the emphasis of Logos Christology on Christ's deity.[15] Christ bears the Spirit throughout his life, to realize in his flesh his faithfulness as the divine Son. In so doing, Christ can then sanctify us in him "with the same Spirit with whom he previously sanctified himself in his humanity from birth."[16] Spirit Christology invigorates Logos Christology by adding the two elements of dynamism and communal self-giving. Christ's communal self-giving is found in Christ's later sanctification of others in himself by the overflowing ecstasy of the Spirit.[17] The gift of the Spirit at Pentecost becomes "the paschal fruit, the gift of the crucified Christ to the church."[18] In Christ, we can receive forgiveness and sanctification through the Spirit, without whom the victory of the cross could not reach us.[19] In Christ's sharing of his Spirit as the obedient Son, we become adopted sons and daughters of God in him.[20] Sammy Alfaro's *Divino Compañero* also seeks

---

12. Myk Habets, *The Anointed Son: A Trinitarian Spirit Christology*, Princeton Theological Monograph Series 129 (Eugene, OR: Pickwick, 2010), 50–51.

13. Habets, *Anointed Son*, 116–17.

14. Leopoldo A. Sánchez M., *T&T Clark Introduction to Spirit Christology* (New York: Bloomsbury T&T Clark, 2021).

15. Leopoldo A. Sánchez M., *Receiver, Bearer, and Giver of God's Spirit: Jesus' Life in the Spirit as a Lens for Theology and Life* (Eugene, OR: Pickwick, 2015), xx.

16. Sánchez, *Receiver, Bearer, and Giver*, 29.

17. Sánchez, *Receiver, Bearer, and Giver*, 63.

18. Sánchez, *Receiver, Bearer, and Giver*, 69.

19. Sánchez, *Receiver, Bearer, and Giver*, 69.

20. Sánchez, *Receiver, Bearer, and Giver*, 84.

a Spirit Christology that respects the deity of Christ and the Trinity. But he attempts to understand what the Christ of the biblical narrative means for our time, especially among the poor and the oppressed. Jesus is the divine-human companion to people in need, not only because he experienced such need but also because he revealed himself in this way on his way to the cross.[21]

According to African theologian Kwame Bediako, Spirit Christology is important to African theology, noting, "It is hardly surprising that the Christologies that have emerged in African theology so far are predominantly 'pneumatic,' presenting a Christ who is a living power in the realm of Spirit."[22] Bediako confesses Christ as Lord of all, including the deceased ancestors that are venerated in many African cultures. He holds that Jesus ascended to God victorious over the spirits and thus over our lives as well. All ancestors are now to be reevaluated and relativized in his light, and they are no longer to be feared because of Christ's lordship.[23] African (Ghanaian) theologian Esther Acolatse supports the ministry of the church in delivering people from evil spirits in Christ's name, but she also shows that the Bible calls into question the hypersignificance granted to spirits in Africa. She wants to affirm the reality of demonic spirits but finds in Christ the victory over them all.[24] My own effort to write a Spirit Christology that links the incarnation, Christ's reception of the Spirit, the atonement, and Pentecost will be outlined below.[25]

The Incarnation

Why is it important to say, along with John 1:14, that the Word of the Father *became flesh* and dwelled among us? How does it lead to redemption and new life in the Spirit for all flesh? This was the question implicitly posed by the early heresy called **Gnosticism**. This early heresy could not imagine God being involved in material creation; it could not even imagine God creating it. The reason for that is the evil and suffering that plague the material world. For the Gnostics, the God of creation and of the Old Testament was thus not the heavenly Father, but an inferior figure. Salvation was regarded as only of

21. Sammy Alfaro, *Divino Compañero: Toward a Hispanic Pentecostal Christology*, Princeton Theological Monograph Series 147 (Eugene, OR: Pickwick, 2010), 128–48.

22. Kwame Bediako, *Christianity in Africa: The Renewal of a Non-Western Religion* (Maryknoll, NY: Orbis Books, 1995), 176.

23. Bediako, *Christianity in Africa*, 25–27.

24. Esther Acolatse, *Powers, Principalities, and the Spirit: Biblical Realism in Africa and the West* (Grand Rapids: Eerdmans, 2018).

25. For a fuller account, see Frank D. Macchia, *Jesus the Spirit Baptizer: Christology in Light of Pentecost* (Grand Rapids: Eerdmans, 2018).

the soul through enlightened knowledge (*gnōsis*). Some regarded Christ as not having had a material body (a christological heresy called **docetism**). In this scheme of things, the incarnation, the Word or Son of God made flesh, was unthinkable. Contrary to Gnosticism, the incarnation assumes that God, the Father of Jesus Christ, is indeed the Creator and is committed to redeeming and renewing the creation. God determines not to do this from a distance but rather from within creation (within *flesh*) and in a way that invites all flesh to receive and participate in God's redemptive and renewing presence in the world. Thus, the Father sent the divine Son *into flesh* through the mediation of the Spirit.

The incarnation involves not only full humanity but also full deity. "For in Christ all the fullness of the Deity lives in bodily form" (Col. 2:9). First, the Son, the Word incarnate, is fully divine. Since only God can save us (Hosea 13:4), anyone less than truly divine cannot be the Savior. In the fourth century, a presbyter at the church of Alexandria in Egypt named Arius (ca. 260–336) got into a quarrel with his bishop, Alexander (d. 326 or 328), over the nature of Christ. Arius proposed that the Word or Son of the Father was not the "true God" but was of a different nature than this God. He contended that the Word of the Father shared in the divine glory but was deity of a *different and lesser rank*. This idea that the Word or Son of the Father was of a different nature from the true God was also proposed by other church leaders in Arius's day. This position has come to be called **subordinationism**, because it subordinated the Son *in essence* to the "true God" or Father. Subordinationists defended their stance using two arguments. First, for many, it was unthinkable that God, who is perfect in essence, could suffer, for suffering reveals a lack in the one who suffers. But the Word of the Father, who was thought to be of a different and lesser nature, could suffer to mediate the true God to the weakness of flesh. Second, it was thought that if the Son or Word were of the same nature as the true God, a division would occur in the one nature of God. Such a division would reveal a lack of perfection since God's nature would lack unity. So, Arius and other subordinationists reasoned, the Word of the Father must be of a different and lesser nature than the Father so that the Father could be absolutely alone in unity and supremacy as the true God. But Arius went even further to say something that other subordinationists did not say. Arius maintained that the Word of the Father was *created out of nothing* and had an absolute beginning. Therefore, there once was when he was *not*. Arius did maintain that the Word of the Father was created before time itself and was the mediator for the creation of all else. Arius said this because he did not like the idea of a lesser deity of a different nature somehow *emanating* out from the true God. He searched for a more biblical explanation for the coming forth of the Logos or Word of the Father, and he chose "creation."

Arius's bold subordinationism was heretical because it ended up denying Christ's true deity. In the church at that time, being created out of nothing (*ex nihilo*) was widely (and rightly) thought to be one of the major differences between the Creator and the created. To say that the Word of the Father was created out of nothing seemed to completely strip the Word of the Father of deity. Because Arius essentially denied Christ's deity, in his theology Christ ended up "saving" us merely by his godly example, which is no salvation at all. There would be no adequate basis for atonement, for God in Christ reconciling us to Godself. For Arius, Christ was not God in flesh assuming us into the divine life, but rather nothing more than an ideal creature paving a path to the ideal godly life, which none of us can adequately follow.

At the Council of Nicaea in 325 CE, the Arian problem was confronted head-on. The result was a rejection of Arian Christology. The Nicene Creed, formed from that council, contained a bold statement supporting the unity of essence (*homoousios*) and equality of deity between the Father and the Son. The Nicene Creed affirmed of Christ that he is "God from God, Light from Light, true God from true God, begotten, not made; of the same essence as the Father."[26] Notice that the Son is "true God from true God." No lesser rank for Christ! Plus, the Son is also "begotten, not made." The idea that the Son is eternally "begotten" of the Father without beginning was well established in the church—an idea that went back to the third-century church father Origen. The Arian belief that the Son was "made" is fortunately denied. And the unity of essence (*homoousios*) between the Father and the Son is boldly affirmed.

The belief that Christ is fully divine and of the same essence as the Father is necessitated by the scriptural witness. A number of texts affirm this. John 1:1 states that "in the beginning" the Word already "was." The verse then says that the Word was "with God" and the Word "was God." When one moves down to verse 18, one finds that the Son, who was in closest relation to the Father, came to reveal him. So it is clear from the context that verse 1 refers to the heavenly Father when stating that the Word was with "God." But verse 1 declares that the Word *was God*, meaning that the Word was himself divine as well. Verse 18 confirms this interpretation, identifying the Word of verse 1 with the Son of the Father: "No one has ever seen God, but the one and only Son, who is himself God . . . , has made him known." Early manuscript evidence suggests that "one and only Son" should actually be the Greek *monogenēs theos* (μονογενὴς Θεός), which literally means "the only begotten God." The textual evidence for the authenticity of this phrase as

---

26. The wording of the Nicene Creed is available at https://www.crcna.org/welcome/beliefs/creeds/nicene-creed.

belonging to the original text is strong.[27] In either case, this phrase calls the Son "God," just as verse 1 does. In fact, the entirety of the Gospel of John supports the deity of the Son. Christ says that the Son has life in himself as the Father does (5:26). As divine, Christ thus came to give life and life more abundant—something only God can do (10:10). When encountering the disciples on the eve of his resurrection, Christ presents himself as the One who breathes forth the Spirit (20:21)—again, which only God can do. The Holy Spirit in the New Testament even comes to be called the "Spirit of Christ," as if "Spirit of God" and "Spirit of Christ" are interchangeable terms (Rom. 8:9). Upon seeing the risen Christ, Thomas thus worships him with the words "My Lord and my God!" (John 20:28).

In 1 John 5:20 we find this statement, "We know also that the Son of God has come and has given us understanding, so that we may know him who is true. And we are in him who is true by being in his Son Jesus Christ. He is the true God and eternal life." Who is the referent in this latter sentence, "He is the true God and eternal life"? It seems to be Jesus Christ, because "his Son Jesus Christ" is the closest antecedent, grammatically speaking, and the Father is never referred to as the "eternal life" in Johannine literature, whereas Christ is (see John 11:25; 14:12). Moreover, the logic of the passage is that we dwell in the Father by dwelling in the Son, because the Son is true God and eternal life. When Jesus says that the Father is "greater" than he is (14:28), he is noting that the point of reference for discerning his significance transcends what may be apparent to the naked eye. Rather than denying his unity of life with the Father, this statement confirms it.

The book of Revelation also supports Christ's deity. When John sees the exalted Christ, he falls prostrate in an act of worship. Christ says, "Do not be afraid. I am the First and the Last" (1:17); this language is taken from Isaiah 44:6 and 8: "I am the first and I am the last; apart from me there is no God. . . . Do not tremble, do not be afraid." The implication is clear: the exalted Christ identifies himself with God. In the fifth chapter of Revelation, Christ takes the scroll from the hand of the heavenly Father and is worthy to open its seals and reveal its message because he is the Redeemer who will make his people to be "a kingdom and priests" (5:9–10). Then come rounds of praise that reach their crescendo when all of creation grants Christ the same praise that is directed to the heavenly Father: "To him who sits on the throne *and to the Lamb* be praise and honor and glory and power, for ever and ever!" (5:13; emphasis added). If Christ were not fully divine, directing the same praise to him that is given to the Father would be blasphemy. And John would agree.

---

27. For instance, it is found in the Bodmer Papyri of about 200 CE.

On two occasions, he attempts to worship the angel who is showing him the visions, only to be rebuked both times and told to worship God alone (19:10; 22:9). But no one is rebuked for worshiping Christ.

Titus 2:13 notes that we are waiting for the appearance of our "great God and Savior, Jesus Christ." Unless one is waiting for two appearances at Christ's coming, one of God and one of Christ, it seems clear, as the grammar indicates, that Christ in this verse is *both* God and Savior. This dual designation makes good theological sense, since one cannot be the Savior unless one is *also* God (Hosea 13:4). Simply to maintain that God saves *through* Jesus is not adequate, since the Scripture clearly states that Jesus saves too: "You are to give him the name Jesus, because he will save his people from their sins" (Matt. 1:21). God saves through the saving action of Jesus Christ. The same could be said of 2 Peter 1:1.

Notice also Romans 9:5, which says of the Jews, "Theirs are the patriarchs, and from them is traced the human ancestry of the Messiah, who is God over all, forever praised!" The words "who is" are not part of the original Greek text, though their addition brings out the true meaning of the text. The grammar flows more naturally if "God over all" refers to its immediate antecedent, which is "the Messiah." Moreover, in Paul's letters there are numerous places where he uses the terms "God" and "Christ" interchangeably. The Spirit of God is the Spirit of Christ (Rom. 8:9); the grace of God is the grace of Christ (2 Cor. 8:9); the peace of God becomes the peace of Christ (Col. 3:15); the churches of God become the churches of Christ (Rom. 16:16); the kingdom of God is also the kingdom of God's Son (Col. 1:13). Paul has the church glorifying Christ as Lord in and by the Spirit (1 Cor. 12:3). Indeed, throughout the New Testament there are numerous places where Christ is granted the title Lord in the contexts of salvation and worship, used in a way that is true of God alone.[28]

As with Revelation 1:17, discussed above, numerous other verses in the New Testament pick up Old Testament texts that refer to God and use them to refer to Christ. I offer two further examples. The first is the coming of God to fulfill salvation. Isaiah 40:3 announces,

> A voice of one calling:
> "In the wilderness prepare
>   the way for the LORD;
> make straight in the desert
>   a highway for our God.

28. See, e.g., Acts 2:34–36; 7:59–60; 8:16; 10:36; 11:17; 15:11; 16:31; 19:5; 20:21; Rom. 1:4, 7; 10:9–16; 12:19; 14:8–11; 1 Cor. 1:2–3, 8; 4:5; 8:6; 12:3; 2 Cor. 1:2–3, 14; 8:9; Gal. 1:3; 6:18; Eph. 1:2; 4:5; 5:19–20; Phil. 1:2; 2:11; 4:23; 1 Thess. 5:9, 28; 2 Thess. 1:2; 3:18; 1 Tim. 1:2; 2 Tim. 4:8; 2 Pet. 2:20; 3:18; Jude 4, 21, 25; Rev. 17:14; 19:16 ("LORD OF LORDS").

But notice that in Mark 1:3 it is not Jesus Christ who is the messenger preparing the way for the coming of God; it's John the Baptist, and he's preparing the way for the coming of Christ. This puts Christ in the place of the coming God! Notice also Isaiah 6, in which Isaiah has a stunning vision of God, exalted in the holy of holies of the Jewish temple, calling Isaiah to proclaim judgment to Israel. Verse 10 refers to the fact that Israel will be hardened in its rebellion so that its path of suffering might eventually lead to genuine repentance at the right time. But take note of the fact that John 12:40–41 quotes from Isaiah 6:10 with the editorial comment that Isaiah had actually beheld "Jesus' glory and spoke about him." Again, the reader is urged to put Jesus in the place of Israel's God.

If the incarnation affirms Christ's full deity as the Savior and imparter of the Spirit, it also assumes his true and full humanity. Gregory of Nazianzus's famous rule concerning the incarnation is significant here: "What has not been assumed, has not been healed."[29] In other words, only that which is taken up by the divine Son in the incarnation can be healed. So if Christ did not take up *full humanity* with all of its capacities in the incarnation, he could not be the one who redeems and heals every dimension of our human existence. If Jesus did not have a human soul, he could not be the means of redeeming us in our very soul.

Jesus was also sinless, for the one who redeems cannot himself be in need of redemption. The sinlessness of Christ undoubtedly has to do with the fact that Christ is sanctified from the womb for the task of being the spotless Lamb for our redemption (Luke 1:35). This text reads, "The Holy Spirit will come on you, and the power of the Most High will overshadow you. So the holy one to be born will be called the Son of God." It may be said that the eternal Word of the Father spoke his own flesh into existence in the creative and sanctifying power of the Holy Spirit. John the Baptist was *filled* with the Spirit in his mother's womb (1:15), but only Christ was *conceived* by the Spirit in his mother's womb (1:35). Only Christ was to be divine; only he was to be without sin; only he was to have eschatological significance as the one who imparts the Spirit to all flesh, to all contexts globally. This Christ was indeed tempted in every way yet remained sinless (Heb. 4:15). Christ's sinlessness does not mean that his embodied existence was not finite, not bearing human limitations. But at every point, Christ never compromises with sin, never aligns with it. He never denies his calling or acts contrary to it. He was the spotless Lamb throughout his life.

---

29. Gregory of Nazianzus, *Epistulae* 101.32, as quoted in John McGuckin, "The Strategic Adaptation of Deification in the Cappadocians," in *Partakers of the Divine Nature: The History and Development of Deification in the Christian Traditions*, ed. Michael J. Christensen and Jeffery A. Wittung (Grand Rapids: Baker Academic, 2008), 101.

Being human also meant that Christ experienced the full range of human temptation and suffering, with unfathomable fullness and intensity. He was tempted and tried. At Gethsemane, he says to his disciples, "My soul is overwhelmed with sorrow to the point of death" (Mark 14:34). He falls to the ground in despair, gripped in that moment with a lack of clarity, yet he is still unyielding in his willingness to follow the Father's will: "'*Abba*, Father,' he said, 'everything is possible for you. Take this cup from me. Yet not what I will, but what you will'" (v. 36). On the cross, he sinks even deeper into the cloud of darkness: "My God, my God, why have you forsaken me?" (15:34). The goal was to experience the fullness of human suffering and thereby be the means of healing in every way: "During the days of Jesus' life on earth, he offered up prayers and petitions with fervent cries and tears to the one who could save him from death, and he was heard because of his reverent submission. Son though he was, he learned obedience from what he suffered and, once made perfect, he became the source of eternal salvation for all who obey him" (Heb. 5:7–9).

Christ was sinless, but his perfection was ongoing even in the face of ever-new challenges. He could not be perfect in his yielding in death until he died. But he endured it all faultlessly so as to be that perfect offering for our sins, that victory that would redeem and transform our lives in every way.

Certain theologians in the early centuries of the church denied the full humanity of Christ. For example, Apollinaris of Laodicea (ca. 310–ca. 392) maintained that Christ was not fully human: "It is inconceivable that the same person should be both God and an entire man."[30] In his view, Christ did not have a human soul. The divine Son took the place of his soul at the incarnation. Following the rule stated above, if Christ did not have a human soul, he could not have been the Savior of human souls. He redeems that which he assumes in incarnation.

The fifth-century theologian Nestorius (ca. 381–ca. 451) believed that the Son took on complete human flesh, but Nestorius kept the deity from the adverse effects of human suffering by *separating* the two natures (divine and human) from each other. The divine and human natures in Christ were often spoken of in Nestorius's writings as if they were *independently* acting subjects rather than two distinct natures of *one* acting subject or person. The incarnation was viewed as a free act by both the divine Son and the human Jesus throughout Christ's life; both remained in free and mutual *synapheia*,

---

30. Apollinaris of Laodicea, *Fragments* 9, as quoted in Richard A. Norris Jr., ed. and trans., *The Christological Controversy*, Sources of Early Christian Thought (Minneapolis: Fortress, 1980), 108.

or joining, interrelation, and cooperation.[31] The harmony between the two (i.e., the divine Son and the human Jesus), for Nestorius, was so perfect that it was *as if* they were "as one single spirit, one single will, one single intelligence, inseparable and indivisible *as in one single being*, God's will and his will."[32] But it was this "as-if-ness" ("as in one single being") about the unity of Christ's person in Nestorius's language that rankled his opponents, since it implied that Christ was actually a union of two acting subjects or persons, one divine and one human. No matter how hard Nestorius tried to affirm that Christ was only *one person*, he ended up implying that Christ was *two persons* in one body, a divine subject and a human subject.

Nestorius's greatest opponent was the able theologian Cyril of Alexandria (ca. 378–444). For Cyril, there is no need to keep the divine and human natures in Christ separate in order to protect one from distorting the other. God liberates and does not diminish or distort humanity, and humanity was made to attain fulfillment by taking on God. Cyril thus stressed the *unity* of the two natures in the *one person* of Christ (called the **hypostatic union**): "the one Lord Jesus Christ must not be divided into two Sons."[33] Christ was not incarnated in a "human being" as if there were from the beginning a divine person and a human person uniting at the incarnation. Rather, Christ's human personhood was only formed *in union with the divine Son*, having a human mind or soul that served as the visible (human) expression of the Son's mode of consciousness. So Cyril would not say that the Son took on a human being who was formed apart from the Son; rather, a human being was formed in the incarnation of the Son. To avoid confusion, Cyril preferred saying that the Son took on "flesh" rather than a human being, "for Scripture says not that the Logos united to himself the person of a human being but that he became flesh."[34] Cyril saw no need to keep the divine Son from suffering, though he saw the Son as suffering *impassibly*, or in a way that did not show a lack or need in the divine essence: "Since, however, the body that had become his own underwent suffering, he is—once again—said to have suffered these things for our sakes."[35] Though Cyril at times misleadingly referred to Christ as having

31. John A. McGuckin, *Saint Cyril of Alexandria and the Christological Controversy* (Yonkers, NY: St. Vladimir's Seminary Press, 2010), 162.

32. Nestorius, *Book of Heraclitus* 102, as quoted in McGuckin, *Saint Cyril of Alexandria*, 163 (emphasis added).

33. Cyril of Alexandria, *Second Letter to Nestorius*, as quoted in Norris, *Christological Controversy*, 134.

34. Cyril of Alexandria, *Second Letter to Nestorius*, as quoted in Norris, *Christological Controversy*, 134.

35. Cyril of Alexandria, *Second Letter to Nestorius*, as quoted in Norris, *Christological Controversy*, 133.

only *one nature*, he did not mean that Christ's deity and humanity had somehow meshed into one mutated reality that was neither truly human nor truly divine. Cyril did, in fact, distinguish in principle between Christ's divine and human natures; Cyril only meant to convey the point that Christ's humanity was being "deified," or transformed into the divine image through incarnation. "We say that Jesus Christ is one and the same, even though we recognize the difference of natures and keep them unconfused with each other."[36] Cyril strongly emphasized that Christ's humanity was not somehow diminished by the incarnation. The implication is clear: Christ's humanity was fulfilled by being the incarnation of the divine Son in flesh. As we noted above, the divine Word of the Father "spoke" his own flesh into existence in the power of the Spirit. This flesh was full and ideal humanity because humanity was always meant to be the visible revelation of the Word of the Father (John 1:14).

Under the influence of *Pope Leo's Tome*, a letter written by Pope Leo I to the bishop of Constantinople in 449, the Chalcedonian Definition dropped Cyril's reference to Christ as having "one nature." But the rest of the definition was written under the influence of Cyril's theology. It confessed Christ as one person acknowledged in two natures, which are "without confusion, without change, without division, without separation; the distinction of natures being by no means taken away by the union, but rather the property of each nature being preserved, and concurring in one Person."[37] In other words, Christ took on flesh in a way that neither diminished nor changed his deity or his humanity. The two natures remained distinct but also inseparable (united in one person). The natures were neither confused (blended) nor separated. The upshot of this is that the God-man suffered human condemnation and death so as to take humanity up into the glory of the divine life.

Christ's Life

The Nicene Creed and Chalcedonian Definition did not pay much attention to the life of Christ. But the Gospels do indeed grant this life importance, for the crucifixion and resurrection bring his life to fulfillment. It becomes clear that Jesus's death is the offering up of a faithful life, as shown by the character, content, and direction of that life. It becomes clear that Jesus came to be viewed by his disciples as essential to the divine presence and work (and thus

36. Cyril of Alexandria, *Scolia on the Incarnation*, as quoted in McGuckin, *St. Cyril of Alexandria*, 307.
37. The Creed of Chalcedon is available at http://www.prca.org/about/official-standards/creeds/ecumenical/chalcedon.

essential to God) only in the light of his teachings and deeds. It becomes clear that his end cannot only be death; rather, it also includes victory because the signs of that victory dot the landscape of his life. Yet leaping theologically from the incarnation to the cross, without the benefit of Christ's life, would mean the loss of theological depth.

Jesus's life mission is launched with his baptism at the Jordan River. The setting is significant since the Jordan played an important role in Israel's history. Following Joshua and the priests as they carried the ark of the covenant, the Israelites passed through the Jordan on dry ground, on their way into their promised land (Josh. 3:17). Under John the Baptist, various Israelites (i.e., Jews) reenter the Jordan with repentant hearts, leaving their sins behind. They reemerge from the river a renewed people, burning with hope for the coming Messiah and the era of the Spirit that he will bring. Jesus enters these same waters to be baptized too, except he is the one who will *realize* the promised era of the Spirit for which they hope. He does not need to repent, for he is the sinless Messiah. John seems to know as much: "I need to be baptized by you, and do you come to me?" (Matt. 3:14). But Jesus joins the sinners in the water to symbolize his taking their place, his overcoming sin on their behalf: on the cross and in the resurrection he opens a path for them to the Spirit. In this way will divine justice or righteousness be fulfilled: "It is proper for us to do this to fulfill all righteousness" (v. 15). Christ's emerging from the water under the power of the Spirit symbolizes his emerging later from the grave in the fullness of the Spirit at his resurrection. The fourth-century Eastern church father Ephrem the Syrian (ca. 306–373) thus notes that Jesus's water baptism "hurried" and served as a precursor to his death and resurrection as the redemptive events that release the Spirit to all flesh at Pentecost.[38] John's water baptism seems to have no clear precedent within the religion of Israel.[39] In baptizing the Messiah in water, John the Baptist "does not belong within the kingdom; he stands before it."[40] Christ's reception of the Spirit after his water baptism is "the decisive change in the ages."[41] A contrast exists, then, between Jesus and John the Baptist—namely, "the antithesis of preparation

---

38. Referenced in Killian McDonnell, *The Baptism of Jesus in the Jordan: The Trinitarian and Cosmic Order of Salvation* (Collegeville, MN: Liturgical Press, 1996), 168–69.

39. Morna D. Hooker, *The Gospel according to Saint Mark*, Black's New Testament Commentary (Peabody, MA: Hendrickson, 1991), 39. All that we can connect it with are the cleansing rituals needed for entry to the temple, with which John's father as a priest would have been familiar.

40. W. Marxen, *Der Evangelist Markus* (Göttingen: Vandenhoeck & Ruprecht, 1956), 31, quoted in Knox Chamblin, "John the Baptist and the Kingdom of God," *Tyndale House Bulletin* 15 (October 1964): 13.

41. Chamblin, "John the Baptist and the Kingdom of God," 26.

and fulfillment, of shadow and substance."[42] Yet Jesus's water baptism under John does indeed reach for his death and resurrection as the victory that will make way for the Spirit, which Jesus will pour forth onto all peoples.

The key moment that launches Jesus's ministry is thus the descent of the Spirit upon him. The incident is given for us in all four Gospels, but I'll use Luke's version of it: "When all the people were being baptized, Jesus was baptized too. And as he was praying, heaven was opened and the Holy Spirit descended on him in bodily form like a dove. And a voice came from heaven: 'You are my Son, whom I love; with you I am well pleased'" (3:21–22). The descent of the Spirit on Jesus at his baptism was not Jesus's first encounter with the Spirit. As noted above, Christ was conceived by the Spirit in the virgin's womb (Luke 1:35). That event occasioned the incarnation, the divine Son's union with flesh. Christ's flesh is already sanctified from the beginning to be the tabernacle set aside for life in inseparable union with the Son. At Christ's baptism in the Spirit at the Jordan, Christ's sonship is actualized further in flesh: "You are my Son," declares the Father from heaven, and Jesus is publicly installed as the anointed Messiah for his mission.

Three points of emphasis need to be made here. First, the Old Testament foretells that the Lord will usher in the time of salvation by pouring forth the Spirit "on all people" (Joel 2:28). This event is also tied to the ministry of the anointed Messiah, for he will come bearing the Spirit—"The Spirit of the Sovereign Lord is on me" (Isa. 61:1). When John the Baptist sees the Spirit descending on Jesus, he knows that Jesus is the Messiah and that the time of salvation is at hand (see John 1:33).

Second, Jesus will later pour forth the Spirit, and he will bear the Spirit for this purpose. In this context, Jesus's reception of the Spirit becomes paradigmatic, the standard for all other receptions of the Spirit—analogous to that of the church's later reception of the Spirit through him. Luke crafts his Luke-Acts narrative to highlight the link between Jesus's baptism in the Spirit and ours. Jesus receives the Spirit while praying (Luke 3:21), and so do the early believers (Acts 1:14; 2:1–4). The Spirit descends on Jesus with a theophany, a visible manifestation of God (as a dove), which points to a new era dawning (Luke 3:22); so also the Spirit descends on the disciples, but the theophany is tongues of fire and a sound of a rushing wind (Acts 2:2–4). Jesus proclaims the meaning of the event (Luke 4:18–19); so also does Peter concerning the outpouring of the Spirit on the disciples (Acts 2:14–36). Jesus moves forth in power for his mission, being persecuted while having his ministry vindicated by signs and wonders of the Spirit; so also the disciples. Being ideal, Christ

42. Chamblin, "John the Baptist and the Kingdom of God," 19.

receives the Spirit with immeasurable fullness (John 3:34), and the Spirit rests on him, remaining with him (1:33). Both qualities of his reception of the Spirit are due to his deity and his sinless flesh, which is perfectly yielded to the Spirit. His yielding to the Spirit expands as it faces new challenges, both in Jesus's human development and in changing contexts. So also, with less perfection, do we live by the Spirit drawn continuously from him, growing in the sanctified life and in our empowered witness to Christ.

Third, the event of the Spirit's descent upon Jesus is described, especially in Luke, with eschatological significance, pointing to the ultimate renewal of all things. The Spirit arrives accompanied by a theophany of a dove, which is a symbol of new creation. One recalls that after the flood the dove that Noah sent out came back with an olive branch in its beak, revealing that the newly purged earth can now be inhabited. Moreover, heaven opening at Jesus's Spirit baptism also implies an announcement that refers to the latter days (Luke 3:21–22).[43] In McDonnell's words, "Eschatology begins at the Jordan."[44]

The euphoria of Christ's reception of the Spirit and his vindication of his sonship from the Father led, by contrast, to the start of Christ's trial; the sign of his future exaltation led to the start of his suffering. Christ is led by the Spirit from the Jordan and into the desert, to be tempted by the devil. At the descent of the Spirit upon Jesus, the Father declares that Christ is indeed the beloved Son, with whom the Father is pleased. The devil immediately seeks to call that declaration into question. He sets up a series of challenges that put Jesus's sonship to the test. Ironically, if Jesus seeks to pass these tests, they will only lead him astray from that very sonship. Rather than accepting these deceptive tests, Jesus reminds the devil of what true sonship in the moment requires of him. Jesus has just come from a forty-day fast. So the devil starts by posing a direct challenge aimed at his moment of weakness, his intense hunger: "If you are the Son of God, tell these stones to become bread" (Matt. 4:3). Jesus responds with penetrating insight into the meaning of life: "Man shall not live on bread alone, but on every word that comes from the mouth of God" (v. 4). We should recall that Israel grumbled in the desert for more food (Exod. 16:3). Jesus did the opposite; he yearned above all else to nourish his soul with the "bread" of the Father's word. He purposely fasted, not eating material bread so he could reveal the all-surpassing value and sufficiency of God's word to meet the depth of human need. Since Christ was himself the Word of the Father (John 1:1, 14), his dedication to the Father's word was

---

43. John Nolland, *Luke 1:1–9:20*, Word Biblical Commentary 35A (Dallas: Word, 1989), 162; Donald A. Hagner, *Matthew 1–13*, Word Biblical Commentary 33A (Dallas: Word, 1993), 58.
44. McDonnell, *Baptism of Jesus in the Jordan*, 148.

self-affirming, bringing his flesh into deeper conformity to his divine sonship. He knew that a life focused on bread alone is a living death. Death by bread alone! In chapter 6 of Matthew, Jesus does include in his model prayer a petition for daily bread, but it comes after the prayer for God's will to be done above all else (vv. 9–11). Christ then instructs his followers to seek the kingdom of God *first*, and their needed food, clothing, and shelter will be added (v. 33).

The second temptation challenges Jesus to throw himself down from the pinnacle of the temple, trusting the Father to save him. His answer is that one is not to put the Lord to the test (Matt. 4:7). Jesus knows that his own testing will eventually lead to a cross, on which he will offer up his life to save others in obedience to the Father's will. He will indeed entrust his life into the hands of his Father. But to take matters into his own hands in the desert in the way that the devil suggests subjects the Father to a foolish test in a manner that is flagrantly senseless and disobedient. Again, Jesus has already shown in his fast that he lives above all else by the Father's word.

The final test has Satan offering the kingdoms of the world to Jesus if only he will bow down to Satan. But the kingdoms of this world are, like bread, not alone sufficient for life. To live for material things alone is a living death. What good is it if one gains the whole world and loses their soul (Matt. 16:26)? It's God's kingdom, or liberating reign, that will transform the kingdoms of this world into the kingdom of Christ (Rev. 11:15). At that time Satan will be locked into the abyss (20:1–3). How foolish it would be for Christ to submit to the devil in exchange for passing material power that will crumble into dust! Of course, Christ maintains his loyalty to the Father; he grants the devil a final and decisive rebuke: "Away from me, Satan! For it is written: 'Worship the Lord your God, and serve him only'" (Matt. 4:10, citing Deut. 6:13).

Christ's spiritual devotion to the Father involves addressing the Father as *Abba* (an intimate word for "father") with unprecedented frequency.[45] In submission to the Father, Christ in his prayer life accents his role as the divine Son in flesh and anointed as Messiah to bring the kingdom of God to earth. His model prayer starts this way,

> Our Father in heaven,
> hallowed be your name,
> your kingdom come,
> your will be done,
>   on earth as it is in heaven. (Matt. 6:9–10)

---

45. Though I would not say that "Daddy" quite captures this term either, since it lacks the reverence also implied in *Abba*.

The relationship of the Son to the Father is here opened up to others. Christ's "my Father" is, in the presence of the disciples, adjusted to "our Father," for Christ came to reveal the Father and to open the blessings of sonship to others (John 1:14–18). The entire gospel is implied in that "our Father." In Ezekiel 36:23, Israel is rebuked for profaning God's name before the nations. So God will show the glory of the divine name: "I will show the holiness of my great name, which has been profaned among the nations." God will bless Israel with the Spirit so that they can obey God and bear a different witness (v. 27). Christ, as the divine Son and the bearer of the Spirit, is the one in whom this goal will be fully accomplished; he will invite his "body" on earth to be his instruments, in the power of the Spirit, to participate in its fulfillment. So Christ leads his disciples in this missional prayer—asking that God's name may be hallowed throughout the earth—as the prelude to the kingdom's coming. They will move out in the power of the Spirit to the ends of the earth in witness to Christ (Acts 1:8).

Christ, during his life on earth, understands himself to be the new temple of the divine presence in the world. At the temple courtyard, when he drives out the money changers who are driven by profit, Jewish leaders question his authority to do this. His response is a challenge: "Destroy this temple, and I will raise it again in three days" (John 2:19). They thought he was referring to the Jewish temple, but he was obviously referring to his body. Elsewhere, Christ proclaims judgment on the temple. The day is coming "when one stone will not be left on another" (Luke 21:6). The temple was subsequently destroyed by the Romans in 70 CE, and it was never rebuilt. In Jesus's day, the temple was viewed as the locus of God's presence in the world; as the place of atonement in the sacrificial system, it was thought to be the link between God and humanity. Here in John 2:19–21, *Christ* is shown to be the true locus of God's presence in the world, and *he* will be the true place of atonement. The Jewish temple and sacrificial system were but a shadow of the reality to come in Christ (Heb. 10:1; see 10:1–10). The Jews who challenge Jesus are clinging to the shadow and will seek to destroy the reality to which it points. What they treasure will be destroyed, and the one they seek to destroy will be raised up.

Christ fulfills the law with mercy and a justice that is shown to be re-demptive. He criticizes those Jewish leaders who hold rigidly to external rules without the true devotion of the heart (Matt. 5:21–30). He rebukes those who accent lesser matters of purity rituals while flouting the weighty matters of mercy and justice (23:23). "You strain out a gnat but swallow a camel" (v. 24). Loving God and neighbor are inseparable (Mark 12:29–31), and the neighbor includes all those in need. Jesus tells the parable of the good Samaritan to show that those in respected positions in Judaism fail to attend to a stranger in need of help, while a despised Samaritan shows mercy to him. The Samaritan shows the kind of mercy and justice that the law requires (Luke 10:25–37). Moreover, Christ invites "outcasts and sinners" of Israel to his table fellowship. Some Jewish leaders misuse the law to exclude them, but Christ identifies the law as a witness to the gospel, the gospel of the coming kingdom of God, a gospel rooted in mercy and aimed at redemption. When Jewish leaders complain that Jesus eats with sinners and outcasts (Luke 15:1–2), Jesus tells them parables involving a woman who seeks a lost coin and a shepherd who seeks a lost sheep to illustrate that God loves sinners and seeks them out with mercy and love, in order to bring them into the mercy and righteousness of the kingdom of God. A younger son squanders his inheritance, but he is received as a royal guest when he returns to the household of his father in repentance. The elder son refuses to join the celebration of the younger brother's return, much like select Jewish leaders refuse to join Jesus at the table of hospitality with the outcasts and sinners. The father reminds the elder son that all benefits of sonship are a gift of grace, which must be shared compassionately with those who repent. The justice of the kingdom is offered in mercy; it promises redemption by grace to those who receive it and will seek it above all.

The kingdom of God, for Christ, is not human made; it is not erected by human-made systems. It is not a place or an institution. The kingdom is God's presence in Christ and the Spirit to overthrow the dark powers and liberate human communities to participate in the divine communion and mission. As Jesus says, "If it is by the Spirit of God that I drive out demons, then the kingdom of God has come upon you" (Matt. 12:28). The kingdom is thus celebrated as one celebrates a wedding feast in which the host saves the best wine for last (John 2:1–12). It is "righteousness, peace and joy in the Holy Spirit" (Rom. 14:17). It is also lived out in the discipleship of costly love. The kingdom of God is both now and not yet for Christ. It is likened to a tiny mustard seed that is planted in a field and that bears visible fruit throughout the world; it's also likened to yeast hidden in bread, causing it to rise for all to see and enjoy (Matt. 13:31–33). The liberating reign of God is hidden, and its full impact is yet to be felt. Still, those who discover it realize that it is incomparably valuable. It is like a treasure hidden in a field or a rare pearl hidden among less-valuable objects in an outdoor market. Others may walk by and not notice. But when someone catches a glimpse of its inestimable value, they will give all to have it (vv. 44–46). Even though it is free, granted entirely by grace, those who receive it will give all to do so.

Christ proclaims the good news of the coming kingdom to all, but especially to the downtrodden of this world, to those who suffer most from the
personal and systemic evil in the world.

> The Spirit of the Lord is on me,
>   because he has anointed me
>   to proclaim good news to the poor.
> He has sent me to proclaim freedom for the prisoners
>   and recovery of sight for the blind,
> to set the oppressed free,
>   to proclaim the year of the Lord's favor. (Luke 4:18–19)

These words definitely have a spiritual dimension. Jesus's ministry is filled
with incidents of him casting out demons and healing the sick: "And He healed
many who were ill with various diseases, and cast out many demons" (Mark
1:34 NASB). But there is also a social dimension to the term "oppressed" since
it includes the poor. In Jesus's time and place, the Jews were accustomed to
viewing the woes of sin and the blessings of salvation in a holistic way that
involves both body and soul. To restrict the power of the Spirit to the soul
would have sounded strange to their ears.

Thus, in the kingdom of God, simple acts of generosity to the socially
marginalized and oppressed are valued highly. Granting someone something
to eat, drink, and wear is praised, as is giving a stranger a place to sleep or
visiting one of them in prison. Christ receives such things as done unto him
(Matt. 25:37–40). The society shaped by the kingdom of God is indeed the
body of Christ. Yet the church's witness to the world extends grace to people
in the world in a way that specially attends to those who are marginalized
and oppressed, as Jesus did with his open table fellowship. Surely, showing
grace to people for whom Christ died, extending brotherhood and sisterhood
to them, is also to be valued, as shown in the parable of the good Samaritan
(Luke 10:25–37).

Juan Luis Segundo notes that the righteousness or justice of the kingdom
of God that Christ announces and inaugurates is more than an individual
experience; it is also a new creation, a new social order, a new humanity
that follows the way of the cross, the way of self-giving love.[46] The resistance
of Jewish leaders to Christ is thus not only religious but political. Segundo
points to Mark 3:6: "The Pharisees went out and immediately held counsel
with the Herodians against him, how to destroy him" (ESV). This alliance

---

46. Juan Luis Segundo, *The Historical Jesus of the Synoptics* (Maryknoll, NY: Orbis Books,
1985), 3–5.

with the Herodians is political.[47] We can add that in John, the ruling Jewish authorities are fearful that Jesus's movement, enthused by his raising Lazarus from the dead, will provoke an attack from the Romans that will strip Israel of its temple and its land. They thus conspire to kill Jesus in order to hold on to political power and influence (John 11:45–57). Rumors of a resurrection are indeed revolutionary in their implications. Those who rule by using the fear of death as their weapon have reason to fear a movement that no longer fears death. Jesus gives rise to a new humanity, which will live the way of the cross, of self-giving love—a new community shaped by that love and living in the burning hope of its ultimate victory over sin and death. This community turns to proclaim the Lord's favor especially to those who suffer the most from social systems callously marginalizing them. Those who are yearning for God welcome it. Those who are only concerned with their hold on political power fear it.

Death, Resurrection, Pentecost

There is no question that the death and resurrection of Jesus Christ are pivotal for linking the Jesus Christ of the Gospels to the Jesus Christ present in the Holy Spirit today. Christ's death on the cross is on the horizon even at Christ's conception and birth. According to Hebrews 2:14, the Son of God took on flesh for this reason: "Since the children have flesh and blood, he too shared in their humanity so that by his death he might break the power of him who holds the power of death—that is, the devil." The Son of God took on human flesh to die and defeat death and the devil! At Jesus's dedication at the temple as an infant, the prophet Simeon pronounced an extraordinary prophecy of Christ's future significance. He will be "a light for revelation to the Gentiles, and the glory of your people Israel" (Luke 2:32). But the path to that glorious fulfillment is one of trials culminating in an abrupt and horrific ending to his time among us. Turning to Jesus's mother, Mary, the prophet adds that a sword will pierce her soul (v. 35). The horizon of Jesus's coming into flesh is not only glory but a cross. In fact, the glory will come through the victory of divine love at the cross.

After the midpoint of his mission, Christ turns toward Jerusalem with a premonition that he will be rejected by the majority of the Jewish leadership and will be killed. He says as much in Mark 8:31, prophesying that the "Son of Man" will be rejected and killed but that he will be raised. Peter has just confessed him as the Messiah when Christ makes this stunning prediction

47. Segundo, *Historical Jesus of the Synoptics*, 76–77.

(v. 29). The title **Son of Man** is Jesus's favored self-designation. This title is mentioned eighty-one times in the Gospels. It harkens back to Daniel 7:13, where God's chosen Messiah will be granted sovereign power to reign; he will be worshiped by all nations, and his kingdom will last forever. This title serves Jesus well since it exceeds Israel's nationalistic hopes (indicated by titles like **Son of David**) and points ahead to the Christ of Pentecost, who will reach all nations. But notice that Christ says the Son of Man must suffer and be rejected and killed. How does that fit Daniel 7:13, which has the Son of Man worshiped and reigning forever? Being rejected and killed fits better with the suffering servant of Isaiah 53, who appears to have no majesty. He will be despised and rejected, even crushed for our iniquity (vv. 3–5). In an unprecedented move, Christ applies this destiny of the suffering servant to the Son of Man depicted in Daniel 7:13, leaving open the question as to how the Son of Man, who reigns forever, ends up being rejected and killed. How can the Messiah be rejected and killed? Moreover, if Jesus will be rejected and killed, what will happen to his disciples? Peter has reason to be deeply concerned about Christ's prediction of his coming death. Not only does it seem to contradict Christ's messianic identity; it places the disciples in danger as well. I doubt that Jesus's added assurance that he will rise again offers much consolation. The part about rejection and execution will most likely be ringing in the disciples' ears, blocking out everything else.

Peter thus pulls Jesus aside to rebuke him. But Christ rebukes *him*: "Get behind me, Satan!" he says. "You do not have in mind the concerns of God, but merely human concerns'" (Mark 8:33). Peter's confession of Christ's messianic identity is an important insight. But with his rebuke of Christ, Peter shows a profound lack of awareness; he oversteps himself. Just prior to Peter's confession of Christ, a blind man eventually healed by Christ sees people as "trees walking around" before gaining full sight (v. 24). Peter is like that man, except the sight involved is spiritual rather than physical. His sight is coming into focus at the time of his confession, but it is not yet entirely clear. In rebuking Peter, Christ once more rejects Satan. Christ must be detecting behind Peter's rebuke a temptation from Satan to pursue a path other than the one the Father wills for him. Christ has as his focal point only the fulfillment of the Father's will. In Christ's view, Satan has no place there. "Get *behind* me, Satan!" (emphasis added).

There is no turning back from the destiny Christ has before him. He feels the pressure to prepare the disciples for his coming rejection and death. "For even the Son of Man did not come to be served, but to serve, and to give his life as a ransom for many" (Mark 10:45). If even the Son of Man will serve by giving his life, then the disciples must be prepared to give all in this way as well. Discipleship involves carrying a cross; Jesus needs to make this point clear. We need to make this point clear today as well.

But only *his* death is the ransom needed for the atonement of all others. The term "**atonement**" refers most basically to redemption and reconciliation with God through Christ's death and resurrection. Even the word implies as much: "at-one-ment" refers to a state of reconciliation. How does Christ's death atone for us? To start with, notice Christ's description of his death as a **ransom**. A ransom is a payment made to deliver someone from bondage, a slave or a prisoner of war. A ransom *redeems* someone from bondage; it purchases freedom for them. Jesus's death, which represents this offering, fulfills his entire life of faithful service and honor to God. Hebrews 10:10 states it succinctly: "We have been made holy through the sacrifice of the body of Jesus Christ once for all" (10:10). The passage surrounding this text, however, depicts this offering as also involving a lifetime of self-sacrificial giving: "He said, 'Here I am, I have come to do your will'" (v. 9). Philippians 2:8 makes this point by saying that Christ becomes "obedient to death—even death on a cross!" Christ decisively brings to fulfillment a self-offering that spans his entire life. Christ offers himself by the eternal Spirit once and for all on the cross (Heb. 9:14).

We should also consider the notion of **sacrifice**. The sacrificial offerings of the Old Testament, which were part of the law, could not atone. Humanity cannot atone for itself by means of the law. "It is impossible for the blood of bulls and goats to take away sins" (Heb. 10:4). Old Testament sacrifices were only a shadow of a future fulfillment that would come through Christ, providing a way for the Israelites to be saved "on credit" or through hope (vv. 1–7). The fact that Christ's entire self-sacrificial life is implied in the offering of his death makes it clear that the payment involved in the ransom of Christ's death was not made to Satan. Christ did not direct his obedient life to Satan. Rather, Christ's obedient or faithful life was offered up to his heavenly Father on our behalf.

The self-offering of Christ's perfect life for our redemption and reconciliation requires unpacking. How are we to understand this? Why would God choose this means of atonement? Swedish Lutheran theologian Gustaf Aulén (1879–1977) wrote a well-known book titled *Christus Victor*, in which he placed front and center the idea that God sent the divine Son into flesh to conquer sin, death, and the devil and thus to open a path to God for us all. The text quoted above is key: "Since the children have flesh and blood, he too shared in their humanity so that by his death he might break the power of him who holds the power of death—that is, the devil" (Heb. 2:14). Christ "disarmed the powers and authorities" and "made a public spectacle of them, triumphing over them by the cross" (Col. 2:15). Aulén's accent on divine victory holds that God crashes through whatever imprisons us, taking up our God-given cause on our behalf and doing so in a way that serves divine love. The justice of the cross is not defined by human merit. The justice of the cross is redemptive, coming through the divine victory over humanity's enemies. Justice is served on the cross as God sovereignly defines it, and that includes the overthrowing of dark powers on our behalf: "The New Testament idea of redemption constitutes in fact a veritable revolution; for it declares that sovereign divine love had taken the initiative, broken through the order of justice and merit, triumphed over the powers of evil and created a new relation between the world and God."[48]

The question left open by Aulén's atonement theory is what, if anything, Christ's perfect obedience to the Father's will and consistent submission to the leading of the Spirit have to do with the victory of the cross. Anselm of Canterbury's satisfaction theory of atonement helps us to explain the atonement with this issue in view. Anselm defended the so-called **satisfaction theory of atonement**. His classic, *Cur Deus Homo* (*Why the God Man*), vindicates Chalcedonian Christology by showing why Christ's being both fully divine and fully human in one person is needed to accomplish atonement for us. During the Middle Ages, "satisfaction" consisted of a payment to make amends for a wrong committed and an honor offended. Anselm argued that humanity denied the honor due to God by granting allegiance to the devil. It would not befit divine justice if God were to simply ignore the offense and provide a way out of humanity's bondage to the devil. What is required is satisfaction, the restoration of honor to God through perfect human obedience. "So then, everyone who sins ought to pay back the honor of which he has robbed God; and this is the satisfaction which every sinner owes to God."[49] Anselm noted that only God could overcome sin, death, and the devil and heal the breach between creation and God caused by human disobedience. But only humanity is obliged to pay the debt of honor that it owes to God and make satisfaction. Thus, for Anselm, the one who brings about atonement must be in the very same person both divine and human.

Here we must bear in mind four additional points. First, God the Father is not to be viewed as a passive observer, waiting for the Son in flesh to satisfy the Father's honor on behalf of humanity before atonement can be made. Instead, the Father, out of love for humanity, sent the Son into flesh through

---

48. Gustaf Aulén, *Christus Victor: An Historical Study of the Three Main Types of the Idea of Atonement*, trans. A. G. Hebert (London: SPCK, 1931), 155.

49. Anselm, *Cur Deus Homo* 1.11, in *St. Anselm: Basic Writings*, trans. S. N. Deane (La Salle, IL: Open Court, 1968), 217.

the Spirit so that honor may be restored for the sake of human redemption. God's restoration of divine honor on humanity's behalf was accomplished primarily by God as an act of altruistic love. In satisfying divine honor, love is ultimately satisfied. Second, it is not only the Father who was honored and glorified in the redemption of humanity, but the Son and the Spirit as well—the triune God. As Anselm notes of Christ, "Since he is very God, the Son of God, he offered himself for his own honor as well as for that of the Father and the Holy Spirit."[50] This means that the atonement reconciles us not only to the Father but also to the way of the Son and to the leading of the Spirit. Atonement opens up the entire path of discipleship for us! The means of atonement provides the path of redeeming love for us to mimic. Third, Aulén is wrong to contrast his *Christus victor* atonement theory with Anselm's satisfaction theory, as if the latter focuses merely on Christ's human righteousness without a divine-victory motif. Anselm's satisfaction theory involves God's defeat of sin, death, and the devil as well.

Fourth, atonement is indeed an objective accomplishment. It provides an open door to victory in the Spirit for all of creation. Both the medieval theologian Peter Abelard (1079–1142) and modern liberal theologians are wrong to reduce atonement to our conversion to God's cause of love in the world. The justice fulfilled for creation is an important component of atonement. Christ offered himself up for our sins "to demonstrate his righteousness at the present time, so as to be just and the one who justifies those who have faith in Jesus" (Rom. 3:26). Yet the victory of divine love over sin and death is still a movement, from incarnation through atonement to Pentecost, which can be obscured if we separate atonement from Pentecost too sharply. Christ's victorious self-offering is also an invitation for us to offer ourselves in repentance and faith as sacred offerings to God by the Spirit and through Christ. "Therefore, I urge you, brothers and sisters, in view of God's mercy, to offer your bodies as a living sacrifice, holy and pleasing to God" (Rom. 12:1). Our self-offering is perfected and made acceptable to God through Christ's self-offering on the cross. In this way, Christ continues to intercede for the saints from his once-and-for-all-time atonement for us (8:34). He is the great high priest who empathizes with our struggles and will offer grace in time of need (Heb. 4:14–15).

In atonement, God turns to humanity in grace, but it is not a turning from something contrary; rather, it is consistent with the eternal heart of God. The **penal-substitutionary theory** of atonement should accent the point that divine judgment is overcome for the sake of mercy and grace. In this theory,

---

50. Anselm, *Cur Deus Homo* 2.18, in Deane, *St. Anselm*, 297.

Christ, sent by the Father and led by the Spirit, takes our place and suffers our condemnation and death in order to free us from this fate. The text most often used in support of this is Isaiah 53:4–6:

> Surely he took up our pain
> and bore our suffering,
> yet we considered him punished by God,
> stricken by him, and afflicted.
> But he was pierced for our transgressions,
> he was crushed for our iniquities;
> the punishment that brought us peace was on him,
> and by his wounds we are healed.
> We all, like sheep, have gone astray,
> each of us has turned to our own way;
> and the LORD has laid on him
> the iniquity of us all.

The suffering here is vicarious, such that Christ bears our wounds, the wounds of our flight from God, the wounds of our alienation and estrangement. "We all, like sheep, have gone astray." Earlier we noted that wrath is not reducible to divine anger, an internal disposition in God. Though God is passionate in loving us and resistant to the evil that destroys us, wrath, objectively speaking, is God's handing us over to the wayward path of sin and death that we have willed for ourselves (Rom. 1:24–28). But God hands the *divine Son* over to the same destiny so as to provide a path through that terror and back to God. "He was delivered over to death for our sins and was raised to life for our justification" (Rom. 4:25). Human condemnation, alienation, and death are overcome by God in Christ so as to reconcile us to God. "God was reconciling the world to himself in Christ, not counting people's sins against them" (2 Cor. 5:19). However, God has no need to "convert" to us! God loved us and sent the Son to die for us *while we were yet sinners* (John 3:16–17; Rom. 5:8). We need to convert to God. The idea that Christ converts the Father from wrath to love for us is manifestly unbiblical. Wolfhart Pannenberg notes rightly, "The world must be reconciled to God, not God to the world."[51]

One could view the atoning death of Christ as a kind of exodus by which Christ passes through the fire of judgment unharmed and thus opens passage to communion in the triune God—the "promised land," so to speak, of life

---

51. Wolfhart Pannenberg, *Systematic Theology*, trans. Geoffrey W. Bromiley (Grand Rapids: Eerdmans, 1991–98), 1:437.

in the Spirit. In Luke's Gospel, John the Baptist foretells that the Messiah will baptize all flesh "with the Holy Spirit and fire" (3:16). The next verse makes it clear that the baptism in fire is judgment: "His winnowing fork is in his hand to clear his threshing floor and to gather the wheat into his barn, but he will burn up the chaff with unquenchable fire." Christ is baptized in the Spirit directly after his baptism in water under John. Little does John know that Christ will also bear the baptism in fire for humanity so that it can be freed and be baptized in the Holy Spirit. Luke 12:49–50 implies as much: "I have come to bring fire on the earth, and how I wish it were already kindled! But I have a baptism to undergo, and what constraint I am under until it is completed!" Christ wishes that the fire of judgment were already kindled on the earth because that would mean that the end-time kingdom of God would be near at hand. But he knew that he had a "baptism" to endure first—namely, the baptism of his death, which is the baptism in fire. And what constraint he was under until it was completed! Joseph Fitzmyer notes of this text that Christ's fire baptism "is not one that he merely administers to others but that he must undergo; he who baptizes with fire must himself face the testing and *krisis* that the figure connotes."[52] James Dunn draws the same conclusion from Luke 12:49–50, noting that Christ "drains the cup of wrath which is the portion of others." He adds that, in Acts 1:5, Christ only mentions to his disciples the coming baptism in the Spirit, because the baptism in fire was already overcome.[53]

Christ died to redeem "persons from every tribe and language and people and nation" (Rev. 5:9). He did not die to redeem "humanity" as a generic mass. He passes through judgment in order to save all peoples in all of their diversity. He invites them all to pass with him through the fire of judgment so that, purged by passing with him safely through it, they might come forth in all their beauty as persons created in God's image and re-created after the glorious likeness of Jesus Christ as people of the Spirit. They will bear this likeness in various contexts and ways, each reflecting Christ in diverse ways. The atonement thus leads to Pentecost. Redemption leads to the life of the Spirit: the overcoming of sin and death opens the path to the Spirit. The Spirit rested on Christ so that, after the cross and the resurrection, a path would be opened to the promised Holy Spirit, which includes communion with the Father in Christ and conformity to the way of Christ in the world. Christ's redemption makes us worthy of the Spirit, worthy of

52. Joseph Fitzmyer, *The Gospel according to Luke X–XXIV: Introduction, Translation, and Notes*, Anchor Bible 28A (New York: Doubleday, 1970), 995.

53. Dunn, *Baptism in the Holy Spirit*, 43.

the communion the Spirit brings, worthy of the image of Christ into which the Spirit shapes us. "Christ redeemed us from the curse of the law by becoming a curse for us, for it is written: 'Cursed is everyone who is hung on a pole.' He redeemed us . . . so that by faith we might receive the promise of the Spirit" (Gal. 3:13–14).

But redemption through the atonement involves not only the cross; it involves also the resurrection. The cross reveals the depth of victory won at the resurrection. Indeed, the cross of Jesus means that we cannot appreciate hope until we first stare down into the pit of hopelessness and despair and realize that we are not alone because Christ is with us, even and especially there. The resurrection does reveal the victory of the cross. But the resurrection also fulfills it. The resurrection is a redemptive event in its own right. Without it, we are still in our sin. "And if Christ has not been raised, your faith is futile; you are still in your sins" (1 Cor. 15:17). At Christ's resurrection, Christ is vindicated and appointed the Son of God in power, "according to the Spirit of holiness" (Rom. 1:4 ESV). He is condemned as a blasphemer in crucifixion, but the Father overturns that verdict by raising him in the fullness of the Spirit, in the power, sanctity, and freedom of immortal flesh. "He appeared in the flesh, was vindicated by the Spirit, was seen by angels, was preached among the nations, was believed on in the world" (1 Tim. 3:16). He was vindicated in resurrection as the favored Son, blessed with the Spirit for our sakes: "He was delivered over to death for our sins and was raised to life for our justification" (Rom. 4:25). It is from his fullness in the Spirit as the favored Son that Christ pours forth the Spirit onto all flesh at Pentecost, thus to grant us, in all our diversity, the blessings of sonship and daughtership in him.

Theologians commonly *imply* that Christ poured forth the Spirit at Pentecost. They write of Christ's objective victory at the cross and the resurrection over sin and death to save us and then also of the Spirit's witness to that victory and his incorporation of us into it. But the passage from the former to the latter through Christ's pouring forth of the Spirit often goes unexplored. One must recall here that Christ arose in the fullness of the Spirit when he was raised from the dead. From that abundance, Christ poured forth the Spirit upon us. Christ overflows at Pentecost. He gives himself over to the overflowing ecstasy, global diversity, and eschatological reach of the Spirit of Pentecost. What does this say about Christ? What does it say about his mission and identity? The Christ of Pentecost is the penultimate climax of the christological mission and identity of the Messiah. He is the one who not only wins our victory over sin and death but also gives himself over to it, so as to mediate this victory to all flesh. He remains our Lord and mediator of life, the one who is to come and make all things new.

FINAL REFLECTIONS

Christological method starts with a Christology *from above*, which points to the descent of the Son into flesh at the incarnation. There is also a Christology *from below*, which accents Christ's life journey in the Spirit toward the fulfillment of his mission and the full actualization and revelation of his identity as the divine Son in flesh. The former (from above) focuses on John 1:14, which claims that the Word of the Father became flesh. The latter (from below) centers on Luke 1:35, which declares that Christ is conceived by the Spirit in Mary's womb as the one who will fulfill the divine mission in history. The former is sometimes called Logos Christology, and the latter, Spirit Christology. Logos Christology is favored by the ancient creeds, and Spirit Christology has recently gained global interest. When Christ rises from the dead and pours forth the Spirit, he shows that he is essential to God's reign and salvific work—which means that he is essential to God. If Christ is essential to God, he must be the divine Son from above at the incarnation. The Christology from below reveals the Christology from above. Christ's reception of the Spirit at the Jordan actualizes Christ's sonship in flesh more profoundly; it also installs Christ as the Messiah and Spirit Baptizer, who will baptize the flesh of all believers in the Spirit. He remains true to the cause of God's love in the world, the mercy and justice of the kingdom of God, giving himself entirely over to redemptive mission. He passes through the baptism in fire (the judgment of sin and death) on the cross and rises in the fullness of the Spirit so as to pour forth the Spirit on all flesh. Christ remains our Lord and head, the one who redeems us so that we can become worthy to receive the Spirit and to follow in his footsteps, in his likeness. He remains the mediator of new life. Christ in the Spirit is contextualized in many cultures and other contexts in ways that are faithful to the gospel and relevant to our deepest quests for meaning and purpose.

TOPICS FOR REVIEW

1. What did Arius believe, and exactly how did the Council of Nicaea refute him?
2. How do John 1:1, Romans 9:5, Titus 2:13, 1 John 5:20, and Revelation 1:17 support Christ's deity? In your own words, summarize (in one or two sentences) what each verse says.

3. Explain Gregory of Nazianzus's dictum "What has not been assumed, has not been healed."

4. What did the Chalcedonian Definition teach?

5. What does "atonement" mean? Briefly, use concepts like ransom (Mark 10:45), sacrifice (Heb. 10:1–7), and *Christus victor* (Heb. 2:14) to explain it.

6. Explain Anselm's satisfaction theory of atonement.

7. Summarize the explanation of the penal-substitutionary theory of atonement.

4

HOLY SPIRIT, CREATION, AND SALVATION

The doctrines of the atonement and justification by grace through faith have often been called the doctrines by which the church stands or falls. So important are these doctrines that the church can only "stand" by affirming them. But the nineteenth-century Scottish Reformed theologian George Smeaton tells us rightly that more can be added to this list: "Whenever Christianity has become a living power, the doctrine of the Holy Spirit has uniformly been regarded, equally with the atonement and justification by faith, as the article of a standing or falling church."[1] The juxtaposition of the atonement and the outpouring of the Holy Spirit at Pentecost as the two towering doctrinal themes upon which the church stands or falls is telling. There is no question that the church, especially in the West, anchored the significance of Christology in the atonement—or, more fully, in the incarnation and the atonement. As I noted in the preceding chapter, Anselm in the eleventh century vindicated the doctrine of the incarnation espoused by the Chalcedonian Definition in 451 CE—that Christ is one person acknowledged in two distinct but inseparable natures, fully divine and fully human—by showing how this understanding of Christ explains his atoning death and the redemption that it brings to all of creation. Christ, as human, can take

---

1. George Smeaton, *The Doctrine of the Holy Spirit* (1889; repr., Edinburgh: Banner of Truth, 2022), 1.

on our debt of honor to God and confront the barriers of sin and death that stand in the way of our paying our debt; but as divine, Christ has the ability to remove the barriers and pay that unimaginably enormous debt on our behalf. This incarnation-atonement link resisted any tendency to reduce Christ to a mere instrument of the Spirit. He is indeed constituted and empowered by the Spirit, but he is also the incarnation of the divine Son in flesh, who redeems humanity on the cross, thus opening a path to the Spirit for us all. There is no experience of the Spirit without this. On the other hand, we dare not reduce the Spirit to a mere instrument of Christ, bearing witness to a christological work that may be described quite apart from the Spirit's presence and work. Such a thought is manifestly absurd theologically, since the very title "Christ" literally means "anointed one." If Christ is by his very identity the one anointed by the Spirit, how can the person and work of Christ be conceptualized without granting the Spirit a vital role to play? Does not the anointed Messiah redeem us under the Spirit's anointing so as to open a path to the Spirit (and to Christ's own crucified and risen life) for us? The answer is an unequivocal *yes*. He bears the Spirit as human and imparts the Spirit to us as divine. Only God can impart God! Only by granting the Spirit a vital role to play in both Christ's redemptive work and our participation in his crucified and risen life can we arrive at a deep understanding of Christ's person and work.

Though pneumatology was part of the story of Christ, the Spirit was first a powerful and transformative *presence* before the church came to understand pneumatology as a bulwark theme in the church's dogmatics. Finnish theologian Veli-Matti Kärkkäinen is quite right that before the Spirit was a vital theological doctrine, the Spirit was behind a transformative and empowering *experience*. The experience, of course, was provoked and contextualized fundamentally by the Scripture and by the proclamation, liturgies, and mission of the church. But the experience of the Spirit also provoked further theological inquiry and moved the understanding of the church into deeper waters when it came to conceptualizing the Spirit's person and work.[2] Both the history of theology and the global voices of theology today can offer the churches much wisdom in their task of responsible and faithful God talk. It is fitting to start with a reminder of the deity and personhood of the Spirit. The Spirit's presence and work give valuable clues for such fundamental insights into **pneumatology**, which is the doctrine of the Holy Spirit.

2. Veli-Matti Kärkkäinen, ed., introduction to *Holy Spirit and Salvation: The Sources of Christian Theology* (Louisville: Westminster John Knox, 2010), 3.

The Deity and Person of the Spirit

As I pointed out in chapter 2, the Holy Spirit may be termed the third person of the Trinity—fully divine, as is the Father and the Son. One arrives at this conclusion, for example, by following the logic of Jesus's sayings in the Gospel of John. Jesus states in 5:26, "As the Father has life in himself, so he has granted the Son also to have life in himself." In other words, the Father has life in himself as *divine*, which means that he has life in a way that is not dependent on any other source for life but is rather the source of life to all else (note 1:1–5). In 5:26, Jesus states something remarkable: "The Father . . . granted the Son" to share deity and "also to have life in himself," in the same way. Of course, this sharing of deity between the Father and the Son is eternal, without beginning, for the Son shares the glory of deity with the Father from before all things (as the Word of the Father, reflecting this glory back to the Father, 1:1; 17:5). By extension, Christ later informs the disciples that he will send the Holy Spirit from the Father, the Spirit who "proceeds" from the Father (15:26). One could reasonably extend the truth of the Son's sharing deity with the Father to involve the Spirit as well, except that the Spirit is not the Son, especially with respect to not being begotten. The Spirit eternally *proceeds* from the Father or is breathed forth, figuratively speaking, which is unique to the Spirit. The Spirit in one in deity with the Father and the Son, as they are one with the Spirit.

We speak of one God because one divine life, one divine essence, is shared equally from the Father, through the Son, and in the Spirit: the Father being the one who loves, the Son being the beloved, and the Spirit being the bond, witness, and ecstatic delight of this love. To part from John for a moment, one sees this truth in Luke 3:22, where the Father pours forth the Spirit with immeasurable fullness upon the Son, saying, "You are my beloved Son, whom I love; with you I am well pleased" (cf. John 1:33; 3:34). The Son moves forth in the Spirit, in return showing love and devotion to the Father. The communion shared in the life of the triune God allows the persons of the Godhead to interpenetrate one another in an unimaginably intimate communion. Thus, Jesus says to the Father concerning his disciples, "I pray . . . that all of them may be one, Father, just as you are in me and I am in you. May they also be in us so that the world may believe that you have sent me" (17:20–21). The Spirit is the overflowing ecstasy of the love shared in intimate communion between the Father and the Son, opening the triune God to participation by others, indwelling others so as to incorporate them into this communion. First John 4:13 states, "This is how we know that we live in him and he in us: He has given us of his Spirit." Jesus thus shows that he breathes forth the

Spirit from the heavenly Father upon his disciples to open his life with the Father (and his mission on behalf of the Father) to them (John 20:21). As he is in the Father and the Father is in him, in the bond of the Spirit's love, now by way of the Spirit and the mediation of the Son, the disciples can commune in the embrace of the triune God. Jesus's redemptive work in the power of the Spirit breaks through the barriers of sin and death, opening the path to this communion for all flesh.

Five lines of argument may be used to confirm the full deity of the Spirit. First, the Spirit functions as the presence and power of God in creation (Gen. 1:1–2). Only God can be said to have created all things (Isa. 45:12). Second, the Spirit is essential to providing salvation for creation, not merely bearing witness to salvation but also providing salvation, making it happen. Only God can do this. As Hosea 13:4 states, we are to acknowledge no Savior except God. In other words, only God can save. John's Gospel points out that the Spirit, mediated by Christ, is the very life that enlivens the soul and wells up in us unto life eternal (4:14). The Spirit is essential to salvation: "God our Savior . . . saved us, not because of works done by us in righteousness, but according to his own mercy, by the washing of regeneration and renewal of the Holy Spirit, whom he poured out on us richly through Jesus Christ our Savior" (Titus 3:4–6 ESV). The blood of Christ that washes away our sin is followed by the purification of our souls and our heart's affections by the regenerating and renewing work of the Spirit. In this ongoing work, the Spirit also sanctifies us, sets us apart from sin, and consecrates us unto God (1 Cor. 6:11; 2 Thess. 2:13; 1 Pet. 1:2). The presence of God to reign and overthrow the dark powers arrives in the Spirit: "If it is by the Spirit of God that I drive out demons, then the kingdom of God has come upon you" (Matt. 12:28). The risen Christ imparts the Spirit as a "life-giving Spirit" (1 Cor. 15:45), and the glory of God comes to us in our reading of Scripture, "from the Lord, who is the Spirit" (2 Cor. 3:18). So intimately unified are Christ and the Spirit in their saving action toward us! Christ is thus present in us by the indwelling of the Spirit—Christ in us, the hope of glory (Col. 1:27)—just as the Spirit in us is the down payment, indicating the fullness of redemption to come (Eph. 1:13–14). The Father will also raise us up from the dead by the Spirit, as Christ was raised (Rom. 1:4; 8:11). If the Spirit is essential to the provision of salvation, to God's saving presence, the Spirit is also essential to God, because only God can save.

Third, the Spirit's name is "Holy," implying that the Spirit, in an unqualified sense, represents the perfect holiness of God. Being divine, there is no corruption or evil in the Holy Spirit. The Spirit is rather God's purgative fire, for "God is a consuming fire" (Heb. 12:29). As the Holy Spirit, the Spirit sanctifies;

the Spirit is in no need of sanctification. The Spirit is the Spirit of truth and discernment, which comes to us in the gift of God's presence; there is thus no deception or duplicity involved in the Spirit (John 15:26; 16:13; 1 John 5:6).

Fourth, the Holy Spirit is listed with the Father and the Son in the church's communion and worship as essential to the divine presence and work. We baptize people in water "in the name of the Father and of the Son and of the Holy Spirit" (Matt. 28:19). This implies that we are lifting up the sovereign authority of the Spirit by baptizing under his name alongside the names of the Father and the Son. We are also recognizing that we are symbolizing our incorporation into the communion of these three in water baptism. Such reverence and adoration belong to God alone. Spiritual gifts in the church are of the "same Spirit," the "same Lord," and the "same God," as if God's involvement in this mutual sharing of life and ministry may be distinguished in these three ways (1 Cor. 12:4–6). In fact, the Spirit decides how the gifts are diversified, which is a divine prerogative. "One Spirit," "one Lord," and "one God" unite the church, granting all three, including the Spirit, a divine function. In this one Spirit we all have access to the Father (Eph. 2:18), granting the Spirit, again, an essentially divine function.

Fifth, the Spirit is sometimes referred to implicitly as God. Isaiah 63:10 says of Israel's rebellion against God,

> But they rebelled
>   and grieved his Holy Spirit;
> therefore he turned to be their enemy,
>   and himself fought against them. (ESV)

Notice how grieving the Holy Spirit grieves God, causing God to turn against them. So also, Ananias and Sapphira in Acts 5 are said to have lied to God because they lied to the Spirit (vv. 3–4). In the psalmist's effort to flee God's saving presence, he writes of an effort to flee the Holy Spirit, as though the two are the same. The Spirit is omnipresent, as is God (Ps. 139:7–10). Having the Spirit dwell within makes people God's temple, since the Spirit's indwelling is God's indwelling: "Do you not know that you are God's temple and that God's Spirit dwells in you?" (1 Cor. 3:16 ESV).

Though the Spirit is obviously divine, as declared in the Bible, it took the church centuries to bring this important insight to creedal expression. The christological confession in the Nicene Creed of 325 CE, which confessed Christ as divine, merely concluded with the phrase "and in the Holy Spirit." I suppose one might take this to mean that the Spirit is to be confessed as divine as well. But this implication is not simply to be assumed, especially with the amount of uncertainty about the Spirit in the fourth century. The great Eastern theologian Gregory of Nazianzus wrote as late as 380 CE: "Of the wise men among ourselves, some have conceived of him [the Holy Spirit] as an activity, some as a creature, some as God; and some have been uncertain which to call him."[3] The **Constantinopolitan Creed**'s additional words concerning the Spirit in 381 CE are thus timely: "the Lord, the giver of life. He proceeds from the Father and the Son, and with the Father and the Son is worshiped and glorified. He spoke by the prophets."[4] No text of Scripture explicitly directs praise to the Spirit, but the reason is surely not a denial of the Spirit's *deity*. Rather, it is much more likely an indication of the Spirit's *function* as the presence and power *in and from whom* we worship (we worship "in the Spirit and in truth," John 4:23). The Spirit is not the Lord *to whom* the worship is directed. Yet, as noted above, in multiple instances the Spirit is revered as divine by the ways in which Scripture and the church identify the Spirit or the Spirit's actions as divine. And as the Constantinopolitan addition to the Nicene Creed illustrates, there is nothing unorthodox about glorifying the Spirit along with the Father and the Son. We should bear in mind that Paul instructs us to live "to please the Spirit" (Gal. 6:8). Does that not implicitly depict a life that glorifies the Spirit?

Perhaps more relevant to pneumatology today is the personhood of the Spirit. In light of the fact that impersonal symbols are used of the Spirit in the Bible, such as wind or breath (Ezek. 37:9–14; John 20:22) or water (7:38–39), it is tempting for some to view the Spirit as an impersonal power or energy. But ample evidence shows that the Holy Spirit is personal. The Spirit is grieved (Isa. 63:10; Eph. 4:30), blasphemed (Matt. 12:31), and lied to (Acts 5:3). The Spirit witnesses to our spirits that we are children of God (Rom. 8:16), testifies of Jesus (John 15:26), speaks on Christ's behalf (Rev. 2:11), proves the world wrong about the things of Christ (John 16:7–11), helps us and intercedes for us in our weakness (Rom. 8:26), distributes spiritual gifts among the congregants diversely as "he wills" (1 Cor. 12:11 ESV), and "searches all things, even the deep things of God," in deciding what to reveal to us (2:10). Christ receives the Spirit from the heavenly Father to pour forth the Spirit onto others, revealing the personal distinctions among Father, Son, and Spirit (Acts 2:33). The same distinctions are shown in John 15:26: "When the Advocate comes, whom I will send to you from the Father—the Spirit of truth who goes out from the Father—he will testify about me."

3. Gregory of Nazianzus, *Oration* 21.33, as quoted in Jaroslav Pelikan, *The Emergence of the Catholic Tradition*, vol. 1 of *The Christian Tradition: A History of the Development of Doctrine* (Chicago: University of Chicago Press, 1971), 213.

4. The Nicene Creed can be found at https://www.crcna.org/welcome/beliefs/creeds/nicene-creed.

The Spirit's unique personhood is the bond, freedom, glory, and ecstatic delight of the love shared between the Father and the beloved Son. While reading the New Testament about the Holy Spirit, one is struck by the connection between the Spirit and love. The Father declares love for the Son while pouring forth the Spirit upon him (e.g., Luke 3:22). As John's Gospel adds, John the Baptist knew that Christ was the favored or chosen one when he saw the Spirit descending upon him from the Father (1:33–34). The Spirit overflows the love shared between the Father and the Son (which the Spirit fully shares as well) to incorporate us into this communion. Jesus prays to the Father that just as he is in the Father and the Father is in him in intimate communion, so may Christ's followers "be in us" (John 17:20–21). John tells us elsewhere that the Spirit overflows this communion between the Father and the Son to incorporate us into it: "This is how we know that we live in him and he in us: He has given us of his Spirit" (1 John 4:13). John adds that the Son of the Father will thereby be with us "in truth and love" (2 John 3). Paul confirms also that "God's love has been poured out into our hearts through the Holy Spirit, who has been given to us" (Rom. 5:5). We are incorporated into Christ and into his communion with the Father through the Spirit (1 Cor. 12:13). Augustine boldly made the claim that "the Holy Spirit's gift is nothing other than the Holy Spirit." He elaborated by saying that the Spirit is "the mutual . . . love by which the Father and the Son love one another"—being also the mutual love imparted to us.[5] Robert Jenson rightly states that this was an "audacious doctrine," one that the subsequent tradition wanted to qualify by maintaining that the Spirit imparts gifts of love to us without actually imparting the Spirit's very person to us. But Jenson dissents. When it comes to the Spirit, "the gifts are nothing but the giver."[6] Indeed, our bodies are temples of the Spirit (1 Cor. 6:19), as is our corporate life together as a local body of Christ (3:16). Singaporean theologian Simon Chan notes that the Spirit, as the "third person" of the Godhead, is the divine person of the "many." Christ as the "only Son" is alone the mediator and Redeemer, but the Spirit of Pentecost opens the one mediator to many anointed instruments. It is in the formation of the church as Christ's body (the *totus Christus*, or total Christ) "that the Spirit as Third Person comes to his own."[7] The people of God will all contextualize Christ globally in many different ways, causing the love of the Father and the very person of the Son to be diversely contextualized

5. Augustine, *De trinitate* 15.36, 15.27, as quoted in Robert W. Jenson, *The Triune God*, vol. 1 of *Systematic Theology* (New York: Oxford University Press, 1997), 148.
6. Jenson, *Triune God*, 149.
7. Simon Chan, *Liturgical Theology: The Church as Worshipping Community* (Downers Grove, IL: IVP Academic, 2006), 33.

as well. The Spirit is not just personal but superpersonal. In us and in all of creation, the Spirit perfects the love of the Father and the redemptive work of the Son. The fourth-century Cappadocian church father Gregory of Nyssa summed up the work of the Spirit in the context of the triune God in history with this standard expression: The divine work in us "has its origin from the Father, and proceeds through the Son, and is perfected in the Holy Spirit."[8]

The Spirit of Creation

In the early church, the Gnostic heresy struck a blow against pneumatology (not only Christology, as we mentioned in the preceding chapter) by calling into question God's role as Creator and as the one who indwells and renews creation. The material creation was thought to be too evil and corrupt to have been created or redeemed by God. Within such a heretical framework, the Holy Spirit's work was confined to inward illumination concerning the spiritual significance of Christ. In that restrictive framework, salvation was viewed as freedom from the material world through enlightened *gnōsis*, the Greek term for "knowledge" (from which we derive the terms "Gnosticism" and "Gnostic"). But Genesis 1:1–2 is clear: the Holy Spirit of God hovered over the deep to bring the material creation into being. The work of the Spirit is not to be confined to inward illumination of the message of spiritual renewal. The Spirit brought the material creation into being, sustains it, and wills to renew it through bodily resurrection and the new heaven and new earth. Indeed, as Wolfhart Pannenberg explains, "The same Holy Spirit of God who is given to believers in a wholly specific way, namely, so as to dwell in them (Rom. 5:9; 1 Cor. 3:16), is none other than the Creator of all life in the whole range of natural occurrence and also in the new creation of the resurrection of the dead."[9] The Spirit's work is vast and involved in the entire creation to bring it into being and to renew it in Christ's immortal image.

The Spirit encompasses all of creation. One only needs to turn to the first two verses of the Bible to discover the vastness of the Spirit's work. Let us look more deeply at Genesis 1:1–2: "In the beginning God created the heavens and the earth. Now the earth was formless and empty, darkness was over the surface of the deep, and the Spirit of God was hovering over the waters." The

8. Gregory of Nyssa, On "Not Three Gods," in *A Select Library of the Nicene and Post-Nicene Fathers of the Christian Church*, 2nd series, trans. Henry Austin Wilson, ed. Philip Schaff and Henry Wace (Edinburgh: T&T Clark, 1893), 5:334.

9. Wolfhart Pannenberg, *Systematic Theology*, trans. Geoffrey W. Bromiley (Grand Rapids: Eerdmans, 1991–98), 3:1–2.

Spirit in the second verse is the great *ruach*, or wind of God, that proceeds from God as though it were a mighty breath. I agree with Pannenberg that in the context of the following verses, which shift the focus to the divine *fiat*, or speaking, the wind should be viewed as the "breath" involved in the divine speaking and its fulfillment.[10] This wind swirls over the deep as a mighty creative storm. Korean Pentecostal preacher David Yong-Gi Cho (1936–2021) likens the Spirit here to an "incubator" of life, in which the creation spoken into being by the Word of the Father incubates and comes to life.[11] One cannot help but also notice an overcoming of darkness by light, of emptiness or voidness by form and beauty, as life reaches to attain its God-intended form by the grace of God. "And God said, 'Let there be light,' and there was light" (v. 3). The divine "Let there be" reveals an enabling and freeing of life to come forth and flourish by grace. The brooding Spirit is not oppressive or tyrannical but rather freeing and enabling.[12] Elsewhere in the Bible, God creates from "nothing," from "things that were *not*" (Rom. 4:17; emphasis added). But here in Genesis 1:1–2, the scene starts with creation already in process, so the enabling and freeing work of the Spirit is accented. Such is typical of the Spirit's work. In the Spirit, there is "freedom" from the destructive force of unbelief (2 Cor. 3:17). Grace does not diminish or oppress human life but frees it to be what God intended. But in the case of Genesis 1, the context is creation rather than new creation.

Genesis 1 depicts the vastness of the Spirit's work in bringing the cosmos into being. The Spirit mightily fulfills the Word's command by bringing the beautiful heavens and earth into being "in all their vast array" (Gen. 2:1). It seems that all of it is intended to be God's dwelling place; that is the meaning of God's "rest" when the work is completed. God does not require rejuvenation from labor. The "rest" is God's taking up residence in the temple of the creation so as to enjoy it. "He stretches out the heavens like a canopy, and spreads them out like a tent to live in" (Isa. 40:22). Of course, the heavens cannot contain God (1 Kings 8:27). Yet God does indwell them. Humans are created as the priests of this temple of creation: they occupy a special role on the earth to "image" God by stewarding life under God's lordship (Gen. 1:27–28). The creation of the cosmos in Genesis 1 turns to highlight the creation of humanity in Genesis 2. Here we find that the scene changes. God gets more intimately involved. Instead of breathing forth a great wind, God stoops low; forms the first *adam*, or human being, from dust; and breathes

---

10. Pannenberg, *Systematic Theology*, 2:78.

11. David Yong-Gi Cho, *The Fourth Dimension* (Alachua, FL: Bridge-Logos, 1983), 2:17–19.

12. Walter Brueggemann, *Genesis,* Interpretation: A Bible Commentary for Teaching and Preaching (Atlanta: John Knox, 1982), 30.

the Spirit into the nostrils so as to impart life (v. 7). The woman is formed from Adam's rib, presumably with the aid of the same dust and breath—the rib taken from Adam functioning as a symbol of their one flesh or shared humanity (v. 23). All of humanity could rightly declare, "The Spirit of God has made me; the breath of the Almighty gives me life" (Job 33:4).

With this intimate divine involvement in the creation of humanity, the inquiry of Psalm 8 is answered.

> When I consider your heavens,
>   the work of your fingers,
> the moon and the stars,
>   which you have set in place,
> what is mankind that you are mindful of them,
>   human beings that you care for them? (vv. 3–4)

Why does God attend to us, care for us so well, given the vastness of the cosmos? In fact, we today know even more about how large the cosmos is than people did in biblical times. We are aware of the billions of stars that make up our galaxy and the billions of galaxies that make up the cosmos. Genesis 2 tells us the story as to why we warrant such attention amid such a vast creation. The Spirit of God's work is both vast and intimately personal. God breathes life personally and intimately into humans: they are elect or set apart from the animal kingdom for a special purpose, to be the priests of creation; to be brothers and sisters of God's Son, the High Priest of creation; and to be minitemples of the Spirit dwelling within, eventually shaped in the immortal image of the risen Christ.

Humanity is created in God's image equally as male and female (Gen. 1:27). The Genesis 2 account that has God creating the woman from Adam's rib does not make the woman inferior. The narrative depicts her in equality to Adam. Though Adam is among animals, he is still *alone* (v. 18). The reason is that there is no animal present who is his *equal*. There is no animal with whom he can share humanity. So God creates the woman, using Adam's rib only to symbolize their shared humanity: "This is now bone of my bones and flesh of my flesh" (v. 23). The term "helper" does not imply inferiority, for the term is also used of God (Ps. 54:4). The man is to be so grateful for a covenant partner with whom he shares God's image that he should be willing to leave his father and mother and unite loyally to her, which in the patriarchal cultures of biblical times was uncharacteristic. The woman left her household to join the man's. He now prioritizes her in the same way, exercising the same freedom from parents and shift in loyalty to the spouse that she has shown in uniting to him, even if they remain in proximity to his parents' household (Gen. 2:24). The subordination of the woman is not mentioned until the curse of sin is described (v. 16)—hardly a source of guidance for holy wedlock.

Women and men practice their shared image of God in the natural realm by filling the earth with diverse progeny and caring for life in a way that reveres it and respects difference (Gen. 1:26–27). Indeed, according to Bulgarian theologian Daniela Augustine, "the Spirit gardens difference," and "authentic flourishing depends on mutuality" across difference.[13] Since our diverse presence as a human race is meant to be a living icon of God's own presence, dehumanizing or effacing others because they are different is an "iconoclastic act."[14] "Homogeneity grieves the Spirit."[15] For this reason, the new creation through Christ and by the Spirit is announced in many tongues at Pentecost, a symphony of diverse sounds that are harmonized by the Spirit. God is not praised or witnessed to in one dominant or all-determinative language or culture. In Christ, sons and daughters, servants and their masters, and old and young participate as equals in the Spirit's prophetic witness in the world (Acts 2:17–18).

Humanity is created by the Spirit as a living soul, as an embodied soul (Gen. 2:7). We are a unity with distinct but inseparable dimensions: physical and spiritual. Death separates the two—which is the very meaning of death, the separation of soul from body necessitated by the failure of the body to live. The dust reclaims it (3:19). Paul thus defines death as a *departure* to be with Christ (Phil. 1:23). Seventeenth-century philosopher René Descartes (1596–1650) sought to explain the capacity of the soul to depart from the body at death by defining the soul even now as a separate entity functioning independently of the body. This extreme dualism was typically Greek but arguably not Hebrew; instead, Hebrew thought sought a more unified anthropology in which soul and body function currently as a unified whole (as two distinct but inseparable dimensions of existence), only made separable by God at death. At death, God miraculously sustains the soul when the body fails in its unique function.

But how do we know that we *are* a soul? Why can we not explain human experience solely on physical terms? One could answer that *human consciousness* is indeed a mystery. No scientific theory has as yet adequately explained it. And it may very well be that science may never explain it since it is inextricably involved in a spiritual awareness. But one must use caution when explaining

13. Daniela C. Augustine, *The Spirit and the Common Good: Shared Flourishing in the Image of God* (Grand Rapids: Eerdmans, 2019), 9, 14.
14. D. Augustine, *The Spirit and the Common Good*, 3.
15. D. Augustine, *The Spirit and the Common Good*, 46.

a phenomenon spiritually just because science cannot definitively explain it as a physical phenomenon. This can be a case of the "God in the gap" approach to science, which fits God into those areas of human experience or natural processes currently inadequately understood by science. As scientific knowledge increases, the gaps grow narrower or disappear altogether, causing theology to lose some of its credibility. It is thus better to reason theologically about the soul in ways supported by Scripture.

In line with Scripture, what seems the more pertinent point of interest is not so much that we are conscious beings but rather *where our consciousness seems inherently directed*. Human experience across the globe and down through the centuries gives abundant evidence of the fact that humanity inherently reaches for transcendence. Consciousness reaches beyond itself to the ultimate mystery that lies beyond material existence. I do not deny that science may be able to explain this too. But is it not curious that we *are* this way? This is the point raised by Scripture when it comes to the soul: "As the deer pants for streams of water, so my soul pants for you, my God" (Ps. 42:1). Religions may be diverse, but the quest for something transcendent to give meaning to it all is remarkably present throughout. Jesus's delivery of his soul to his heavenly Father on the cross, as his final act of obedience in offering his life for our salvation, is the ultimate answer to the soul's meaning and destiny (Luke 23:46). The destiny of Jesus's soul to unite with an immortal body fills out the picture. The soul and the physical life that embodies it belong to God, and Christ gave all to open a path to reconciliation and healing for them *both*. The existence of a soul in humanity means that our existence belongs to God, down to the deepest depth of human life and consciousness. Indeed, "even in his innermost being, man cannot escape God," writes Heinrich Ott. He then concludes, "*We do not possess our souls, they are not at our disposal.*"[16] Our souls belong to God, along with the entire life that embodies them. We do not just ask questions that reach beyond; we *are* such questions!

I speak here as a so-called **dichotomist**, someone who views human beings as made up of body and soul rather than of body, soul, and spirit—the **trichotomist** position. I take the dichotomist position because terms like "soul," "spirit," and "heart" seem interchangeable in Scripture, different terms to describe the same spiritual dimension to life. For example, Mary the mother of Jesus proclaims, "My soul glorifies the Lord and my spirit rejoices in God my Savior" (Luke 1:46–47). It seems that "soul" and "spirit" are used interchangeably here, distinguished for poetic purposes but referring to the same reality. I don't think Mary meant to say that two different parts of her were

16. Heinrich Ott, *God* (Atlanta: John Knox, 1974), 61 (emphasis original).

separately reacting to God. It is much more likely that she, as an embodied soul, was glorifying and rejoicing from deep within. Genesis 35:18 states that Rachel's "soul" departed at death (ESV); Luke 23:46 reports that Jesus's "spirit" departs at his death. But where in Scripture does it say that *both* the soul *and* the spirit depart at death together? Clearly, soul and spirit are referred to interchangeably in the above verses.

Hebrews 4:12 does list soul and spirit together: "For the word of God is alive and active. Sharper than any double-edged sword, it penetrates even to dividing soul and spirit, joints and marrow; it judges the thoughts and attitudes of the heart." But this verse only illustrates my point. Dividing soul and spirit is like dividing joints and marrow. But joints, which by definition involves bones, are partially made up of marrow! These two are not separate realities; by way of extension, neither are soul and spirit. The point is poetic; God's word can do the impossible, like separating things that are basically the same. Moreover, 1 Thessalonians 5:23 states, "May your whole spirit, soul and body be kept blameless." Here we have the stacking of synonymous terms for poetic effect. One's spirit and soul being kept pure stresses every ounce of our being, like saying we should love God with all our heart, soul, and strength (Deut. 6:5). The author does not intend to say that one's total strength is necessarily a different part of us than our hearts. It is just two different ways of saying essentially the same thing. We stack up synonymous terms to say, in different ways, that we love (or are to be pure) with all that we are. The different terms are not meant to be analyzed and separated out; rather, they are stacked together for poetic or emotional emphasis.

The love of God that pours forth from the divine life to create and care for humanity also cares for all of creation. Psalm 104 tells us that God cares for the animal kingdom amid their suffering and need. "When you send your Spirit, they are created, and you renew the face of the ground" (v. 30). God continues to bless the natural life of humans, for example, by filling artisans with the Spirit so that they will be at their best in designing and crafting the tabernacle (Exod. 35:30–35). God provides us with the breath we breathe and our natural sustenance. God is involved in the migrations of diverse peoples and the lands that they occupy. In God, "we live and move and have our *being*" (Acts 17:28; emphasis added). All this is due to the love of the Creator, but it also sets the stage for our destiny to find, in the Son, deliverance from sin and death and supernatural regeneration unto life eternal in Christ's image.

In the Bible, it is assumed that something has gone wrong with humanity (Gen. 3). We fell from God; we became alienated from the supernatural grace meant to sustain us in communion with God and bring us to our eternal destiny. Communion was broken with God from deep within our souls, and the body became subject to the curse of death. In the fifth century, Augustine notes that humanity was created as entirely dependent on God for its destiny. Created from nothing, humanity is made to reach for the fulfillment of being from God. This means that, from the beginning, humanity was able to fall by turning from God under the illusion of self-sufficiency. Fulfillment from God remains the call; nothingness remains the threat. Referring to the Son and the Spirit as the "two hands" of the Father, Colin Gunton explains Augustine's point eloquently: "Through his Son and Spirit, his two hands, the Father both prevents the creation from slipping back into the nothingness from which it came and restores its teleology, its movement towards perfection."[17]

Irenaeus in the second century notes that, though humanity was created innocent, it needed from the beginning to progress toward the absolute perfection intended by God. Being immature at the beginning, humanity "was unable to lay hold of it."[18] Rather than journeying toward this goal, humanity took a wayward turn into the captivity of sin and death. Irenaeus explains that Christ as the last Adam came to "sum up" (i.e., recapitulate) in himself the new humanity that would, through him, attain what Adam and Eve failed to attain—namely, immortality and perfect glory. "He summed up in himself the long history of the human race and so furnished us with salvation in a short and summary way, to the end that what we had lost in Adam . . . we might recover in Christ Jesus."[19] Christ came in the form of humble flesh in order to relate to us on our level, to meet us where we are, so as to redeem us and impart the Spirit to us from Christ's own fullness. Christ thus came in mortal flesh "so that we would be able to hold in ourselves the one who is the bread of immortality, the Spirit of the Father."[20]

Having fallen into sin and death, humanity is helpless, without the grace of Christ and the Spirit, to take steps toward its salvation. In the fifth century, **Pelagius** took issue with this assumption. He argued that human nature is inherently good and able, by obeying its inner propensity for good, to please God. Speaking of human conscience, he writes, "We should learn its goodness from the mind itself rather than from somewhere else."[21] He gives a long

17. Colin Gunton, "The Spirit Moved over the Face of the Waters: The Holy Spirit and the Created Order," *International Journal of Systematic Theology* 4, no. 2 (July 2002): 197–98.

18. Irenaeus, *Against Heresies* 4.38.1, in J. Patout Burns, trans. and ed., *Theological Anthropology*, Sources of Early Christian Thought (Philadelphia: Fortress, 1981), 23.

19. Irenaeus, *Against Heresies* 3.18.1, in Alexander Roberts and James Donaldson, eds., *Apostolic Fathers with Justin Martyr and Irenaeus*, vol. 1 of *The Ante-Nicene Fathers* (Peabody, MA: Hendrickson, 1994), 446.

20. Irenaeus, *Against Heresies* 4.38.1, in Burns, *Theological Anthropology*, 24.

21. Pelagius, *Letter to Demetrias* 4, in Burns, *Theological Anthropology*, 43.

list of examples in the Bible of righteous people who do so, concluding, "We have spoken much about nature, and through the examples of the saints have illustrated and proven its goodness." Further, Pelagius recognizes that we can do wrong, but he wishes to "refute the charge that nature's inadequacy forces us to do evil." Only the exercise of our will "causes different merits in the same nature," either punishment or favor from God.[22] Pelagius does recognize that there is a sense in which nature can be corrupted and obedience harder to accomplish. After humanity sinned, nature "had been covered over by vices and corroded by the rust of ignorance." So "the Lord applied the law like a file to polish nature by repeated correction and restore its original luster." Doing good "has become difficult for us only because of the long custom of sinning, which begins to infect us even in our childhood." Sinning becomes "an addiction," "holding us bound with what seems like the force of nature itself."[23] But it isn't; nature is entirely good. Doing evil is simply a bad habit that needs to be broken. We just need help. Pelagius notes that it was thus more possible during the era of the law to please God from the power of our human nature because of the liberating influences of the law. But he adds that Christ's coming grants us an even greater advantage, for "Christ's grace taught us and regenerated us as better persons. His blood has purged and cleansed us; his example spurred us to righteousness." Christians should "be better than people who lived before the law, therefore, and better than people who lived under the law."[24]

What is glaringly absent from Pelagius's account is what may be termed **original sin**—namely, the inborn corruption of our nature due to the mortal and sinful nature that we inherited from Adam and Eve. Human nature is thoroughly good, for Pelagius. Our challenges are therefore due to external conditioning, which lures us to sin and turns sinning into an addiction. Pelagius thus sees human history as humanity's gradual climb toward realizing its God-created potential. The era of the law is one level of aid, and the coming of Christ grants us the maximal advantage. Christ not only provides forgiveness, he "regenerates us," which, in the larger context of Pelagius's theology, appears to be a kind of rejuvenation of a goodness that is already there. Pelagius's theology appears as a kind of self-help philosophy that draws from resources (i.e., the law and then further help from Christ and the Holy Spirit) that allow us to become our best selves in fulfillment of God's purposes.

22. Pelagius, *Letter to Demetrias* 7–8, in Burns, *Theological Anthropology*, 48, 49.
23. Pelagius, *Letter to Demetrias* 8, in Burns, *Theological Anthropology*, 50.
24. Pelagius, *Letter to Demetrias* 8, in Burns, *Theological Anthropology*, 50.

In opposing Pelagius, Augustine attacks the notion that our nature is entirely good, as though we can please God "by the energies of our own will."[25] He accuses Pelagius of "extravagantly" praising our natural capacity for God.[26] Augustine digs deeper into the human problem to place a spotlight on the inherited corruption of the human will itself, arguing that we need divine grace even to produce goodwill in us. Augustine concedes that, for Pelagius, God "works in us to will what is good, to will what is holy."[27] But Augustine adds that Pelagius refers here to "the law and the instruction."[28] For Augustine, more is needed, for not even the law is adequate without the Spirit to produce the fruit of righteousness in our lives. The word of God and the Spirit fundamentally change us and direct the heart toward God.[29] Thus, grace is not merely removing barriers in the way of our achieving our destiny by inherent human capacity. If that were the case, we would be meriting our favor with God. "How is it grace if it is paid as our due?"[30] Rather, we stand corrupted and condemned to death. Only Christ's death and resurrection can reverse this destiny; only the gift of his Spirit can apply this solution to our lives. "God shows that when he redeems by Christ's blood, he himself converts people from evil and makes them eternally good."[31] We must yield to this grace *by* this grace, for Augustine. But nature being polished or rejuvenated is not enough. Nature must be transformed and elevated from its created state to new creation by the death and resurrection of Christ and the work of the Spirit.

Perhaps it is going too far to suggest that Pelagius simply believes that we merit our salvation. When reading Pelagius, I don't get the impression that he thought we deserve the help that God gives us, especially forgiveness through the cross. Yet Augustine has a point. Salvation is a great deal more than help in achieving our natural potential. Pelagius had a blind spot when it came to the depth of our inherited corruption and the depths to which grace must go to heal us. He also needed to face more penetratingly the extent to which grace must transform us to take us from mortality to immortality—how dependent we are on the justice of the cross and the resurrection to make us worthy of such a transition and to make it happen, including its onset in regeneration. In that light, he needed to understand the silliness of using a metaphor like "polishing" our nature to describe the path of salvation.

25. Augustine, *On the Grace of Christ* 2.2, in Burns, *Theological Anthropology*, 62.
26. Augustine, *On the Grace of Christ* 50.55, in Burns, *Theological Anthropology*, 96.
27. Augustine, *On the Grace of Christ* 10.11, in Burns, *Theological Anthropology*, 68.
28. Augustine, *On the Grace of Christ* 10.11, in Burns, *Theological Anthropology*, 69.
29. Augustine, *On the Grace of Christ* 14.15, in Burns, *Theological Anthropology*, 72.
30. Augustine, *On the Grace of Christ* 23, in Burns, *Theological Anthropology*, 77.
31. Augustine, *On Rebuke and Grace* 11.30, in Burns, *Theological Anthropology*, 101.

The Spirit and New Creation

The Spirit is thus the Spirit not only of creation but also of new creation. The supernatural work of the kingdom of God is inaugurated by Christ in the presence of the Holy Spirit: "If it is by the Spirit of God that I drive out demons, then the kingdom of God has come upon you" (Matt. 12:28). The point was made in the previous chapter that Christ bears the Spirit all the way to the cross, offering himself "through the eternal Spirit" (Heb. 9:14) and then being raised in power "according to the Spirit of holiness" (Rom. 1:4 ESV) to save us. The world condemned him at the cross, but God was at that same cross, providing the means for their salvation, "reconciling the world to himself in Christ, not counting people's sins against them" (2 Cor. 5:19). He ascended to the Father's right hand to reign, justified as the faithful Son and bearer of the Spirit so as to justify us. From there, as Messiah and Lord, he pours forth the Spirit by which he will unite us to himself in communion and empower us for participation in his mission (Acts 2:33). He opens up the liberating reign of God to us in the presence of the Spirit. The life of the church is not primarily about ceremonies or practices but rather about the life of the Spirit, of which they are at best mere instruments. Speaking in the context of Jewish food laws, Paul wants to make it clear that "the kingdom of God is not a matter of eating and drinking, but of righteousness, peace and joy in the Holy Spirit" (Rom. 14:17).

Salvation occurs from the Father, through the Son, and in the presence of the Holy Spirit. The Holy Spirit offers sinners what theologians call "**prevenient grace**," or the enablement to repent and believe. In the Spirit, the gospel is the power of God unto salvation, enabling us to repent and believe. This grace (all grace, for that matter) can be resisted; as Paul warns the Corinthians, they are not to receive the grace of God "in vain" or without its attaining its goal in the person's heart (2 Cor. 6:1). The person must yield to this grace (by this grace) in repentance and belief to be saved. **Repentance** and **faith** are two elements of one movement. Repentance is turning away from sin, and faith is turning to God in trust and loyalty. This turning or **conversion** is accompanied by what theologians call **regeneration**, or the full awakening of the soul to God, having been "born again" (1 Pet. 1:23). In receiving the gift of the Spirit at the point of faith, we are united to Christ, for "if anyone does not have the Spirit of Christ, they do not belong to Christ" (Rom. 8:9). This **union with Christ** makes us sons and daughters of God, sharing in all the benefits of Christ's sonship. Using the exodus as a metaphor, Paul tells us that God makes us sons and daughters by delivering us from condemnation and death at the cross and the resurrection so as to bring us to the "promised land" of life in the Spirit. We should have no fear of returning to bondage or slavery, for we have the Spirit within assuring us that we belong to Christ. Notice the wording of Romans 8:15–16: "The Spirit you received does not make you slaves, so that you live in fear again; rather, the Spirit you received brought about your adoption to sonship. And by him we cry, 'Abba, Father.' The Spirit himself testifies with our spirit that we are God's children." The Old Testament exodus was only a type or a shadow of the true exodus to come, an exodus from the bondage of sin and death through Christ and in the Spirit. The promised land given to Israel was only a type or a shadow of the new heaven and new earth, sanctified for the heavenly city, the kingdom of God.

All of the blessings of salvation occur in this union with Christ by the Spirit. In the Spirit, Christ is present to us and in us: "Christ in you, the hope of glory" (Col. 1:27). This redemption is received by the Spirit and makes us worthy of the Spirit. Notice Paul's reasoning in Galatians 3. The Galatians were most likely under the impression that one must earn the life of the Spirit. Paul strikes at the heart of this misconception by pointing to the cross (and implicitly its victory in the resurrection) as that which wins the gift of the Spirit for us. Paul thus starts his argument in Galatians 3:1 by asking how they can be so misled, when, before their very eyes, Jesus Christ was presented as crucified. He then asks them how they received the Spirit—Was it by the law or by believing the proclamation of Christ crucified and risen (v. 2)? The answer is clearly that they received the Spirit as a gift, by faith alone. He gets clearly to the overall point in verse 14: "[Christ] redeemed us . . . so that by faith we might receive the promise of the Spirit." In his death and resurrection, Christ redeemed us by overcoming the barriers of our sin, condemnation, and death, breaking open a path of reconciliation with God and life in the Holy Spirit.

In saying this, Paul describes **justification by grace** as a declaration of favor with God that is founded on the atonement and is heard and received by the Spirit through faith. Justification refers to *being set in right relation with God*; sinners are declared to be right with God in the gospel, enabled to live freely for God by faith. Justification is founded on the grace of God at work in the atonement, for "all are justified freely by his grace through the redemption that came by Christ Jesus" (Rom. 3:24). God fulfilled justice for creation on the cross and in the resurrection "so as to be just and the one who justifies those who have faith in Jesus" (v. 26). Christ was handed over to death for our sins but "raised for our justification" (4:25 ESV). The world condemned Christ on the cross, but in Christ's resurrection, God overturned that verdict and declared Christ the faithful Son, doing so in power "according to the Spirit of holiness" (Rom. 1:4 ESV). We are now justified in Christ by faith. We, too, are declared right with God as sons and daughters, accomplished in power by the Spirit in the gospel, which we receive by the Spirit through faith. Justification received by the Spirit makes us worthy of the Spirit. We will also be declared just or right with God in power at our resurrection one day.

James reminds us that justification is received by grace through faith, but he adds that justifying faith shows itself (or is vindicated as authentic) in works. Abraham was credited as righteous when he believed the promises of God (Gen. 15:6), but when he acted to sacrifice his son Isaac on the altar in total trust in God's promise (Gen. 22), his faith was shown to be authentic (James 2:21–24). "Show me your faith without deeds, and I will show you my faith by my deeds" (v. 18). James is not saying that we are saved by works. Salvation by "grace alone" (*sola gratia*) is not denied. This is clear from James 1:17–18: "Every good and perfect gift is from above, coming down from the Father of the heavenly lights, who does not change like shifting shadows. He chose to give us birth through the word of truth, that we might be a kind of firstfruits of all he created." No way of earning one's salvation here! James's complaint is in the realm of faith. He protests a faith that has been reduced to a mere confession of right belief, a confession without any trace of works in which such faith is incarnated so as to be living, so as to be *real*. "Faith by itself, if it is not accompanied by action, is dead" (2:17). The Jews confessed that God is one, but that is hardly adequate: "You believe that there is one God. Good! Even the demons believe that—and shudder" (v. 19).

Paul uses the term "justification" differently than James does. For Paul, justification is not the vindication of faith but rather our right standing before God. Still, Paul would agree with the substance of James's protest; he writes to the Galatians, "The only thing that counts is faith expressing itself through love" (Gal. 5:6). Indeed, Paul tells us that we are not saved by good works (Eph. 2:8–9), for we ourselves are *God's* good work: "For we are God's handiwork, created in Christ Jesus to do good works, which God prepared in advance for us to do" (Eph. 2:10). God prepared us in advance, by grace, for the marvelous work to be accomplished through us. A life rich with divine purpose and good works brings glory to God and, in turn, enriches life with further meaning and fulfillment. Our life becomes a rich garden of good fruit rather than a barren desert. There is good news about good works. We should not ask whether we *have* to do good works; we should feel *grateful* that we are freed by grace to do them!

Sanctification is our being set aside from sin and consecrated unto God. When speaking of this *positionally*, we are cleansed because of the atonement ("sprinkled with his blood," 1 Pet. 1:2) and by "the washing of rebirth" (Titus 3:5). All of this means that the atonement is the basis of forgiveness, and the born-again experience is the moment when it is applied to us by faith. But our *position* before God of being cleansed from sin still requires an *actualization* of purity in life, or a *progression* of conformity to Christ in ever-increasing holiness of life. In his *Plain Account of Christian Perfection*, John Wesley (1703–91) speaks of the need to strive for "simplification of intention" and purification of desire. He writes, "I saw that 'simplicity of intention and purity of affection,' one design in all we speak or do and one desire ruling all our tempers, are indeed 'the wings of the soul,' without which [the soul] can never ascend to the mount of God."[32] What he means here is that our intentions or goals should find their unity in the love of Christ. All of our goals need to be governed by this overarching intention. The purification of desire should transform all desires so as to subordinate them to a longing for the love of Christ in all things. Wesley believed that it was possible to attain these goals in life, which he termed "Christian perfection." He never intended this goal to be confused with absolute perfection, only with the alignment of our intentions and longings with the love of Christ. But even that qualification would sound too optimistic for some Protestant theologians. Can we, in this life, attain simplicity of intention and purity of desire in all things? The Calvinist and Lutheran traditions would disagree. They hold to the doctrine of **total depravity**, which maintains that sin has disabled and tainted all dimensions of human capacity, including the intentions and desires, making it impossible in this life to attain perfection in any sense. Still, the Wesleyan simplicity of intention and purification of desire is a goal worth fighting for—with every ounce of our being.

Interestingly, Paul focuses on the *desires* when talking about our progress in conforming to Christ in the Spirit: "So I say, walk by the Spirit, and you will not gratify the desires of the flesh. For the flesh desires what is contrary to the Spirit, and the Spirit what is contrary to the flesh" (Gal. 5:16–17). Acting on distorted desires "of the flesh" (i.e., of our fallen existence) gratifies these desires. Desires that are consistently gratified grow stronger. But refusing to act on these distorted desires and yielding rather to the longings implanted by the Word of God and the Holy Spirit will cause the right desires to be gratified and to grow stronger. It seems that the question related to the affections, what we long for, is the fundamental question we need to ask ourselves. According to whose affections are we living—those of the flesh or those of the Spirit? Indeed, Paul urges, "Clothe yourselves with the Lord Jesus Christ, and do not think about how to gratify the desires of the flesh" (Rom. 13:14).

Though we are cleansed from all sin before God in Christ (our positional sanctification), we must still strive to actualize our purity in life and strive

---

32. John Wesley, *A Plain Account of Christian Perfection,* ed. George Lyons, Christian Classics Ethereal Library, https://www.ccel.org/w/wesley/perfection/perfection.html.

toward perfect love in all things (progressive sanctification). Life in the Spirit is to be a constant self-crucifixion and ever-deeper discovery of resurrection power as we grow stronger in our conformity to Christ: "I have been crucified with Christ and I no longer live, but Christ lives in me. The life I now live in the body, I live by faith in the Son of God, who loved me and gave himself for me" (Gal. 2:20). As Cornel West is fond of saying, love is a form of death.[33] There are people in your life who need you to be winning this battle of the sanctified life. We should fight this battle not only for ourselves but even more importantly for them. Do it for them; do it for love. But in the power of the resurrection, holy love is also a great force for good in the world. Holy love translates into social justice out of mercy for the oppressed and neglected. Holy love is indeed the force that will win in the end. The resurrection teaches us this point, and we should never forget it. Even now, we overcome evil with good; good is a force of resistance against evil and is the only path to justice and healing. Good breaks the cycle of violence and replaces it with an entirely different way of life in the world, one that is graced.

Glorification is the ultimate attainment of the fullness of the Spirit in the Christian life. The reference here is to the resurrection of the dead. Christ was glorified at his resurrection and exaltation. Before his death, he prays to his Father, "Now, Father, glorify me in your presence with the glory I had with you before the world began" (John 17:5). He prays for the glory of his deity to be actualized and manifested in his embodied life as the Christ. He will only pour forth the Spirit upon his glorification (7:38–39), because it is only then that his atoning work is completed and his embodied life is perfected as the Word and mediation of the Spirit to all flesh. Imparting the Spirit through his glorified life, he shows us that the crucified life of self-giving love is the only path to glory, the only path to the victory of love. He also imparts to us the victory of the Spirit in sanctification and healing, as well as the ultimate attainment of glory in resurrection.

Glorified in resurrection, Jesus's risen life is permeated by the perfect sanctity, liberty, beauty, and majesty of the Spirit. Glorified, Jesus comes to us in the presence and power of the Spirit. Without confusing the persons of the Son and the Spirit, Christ comes to us as the life-giving Spirit (1 Cor. 15:45). The first Adam became a living soul as a natural man, who was both taken from the dust and destined to return to the dust (Gen. 2:7; 3:19). We are his seed, bearing his natural image. But the glorified Christ, the last Adam, is life-giving. We are meant to receive the Spirit from him and bear his

---

33. Cornel West, "Love Is a Form of Death," YouTube video, 5:56, September 18, 2015, https://www.youtube.com/watch?v=irs62hK_nm0&ab_channel=TheTable%7CBiolaCCT.

immortal image by being born again into a living hope (1 Pet. 1:3; cf. 1 Cor. 15:46–49).

"For you died, and your life is now hidden with Christ in God. When Christ, who is your life, appears, then you also will appear with him in glory" (Col. 3:3–4). We will be raised again and glorified in him. The Holy Spirit is the down payment of this glorification. The communion, sanctity, and freedom of the risen life should already be affecting the life we now live, since the Spirit lives within. At the resurrection, we will be "swallowed up by life" (2 Cor. 5:4).

Paul ties our sonship and daughtership to the gift of the Spirit. When Christ imparts the Spirit, he opens our lives to the benefits of his sonship, his election from all eternity as the beloved and favored Son. As bearers of the Spirit, we cry "Abba" to the heavenly Father alongside Jesus Christ, our Lord and elder brother. In times of trial, the Spirit bears witness with our spirits that we are indeed children of God. We will never be abandoned, nor will we be cast back into slavery to sin and death (Rom. 8:15–16). Paul also speaks of our waiting for adoption as sons and daughters of God, which Paul defines as "the redemption of our bodies," or the resurrection (v. 23). How can we be children of God *already* as bearers of the Spirit and still be, in the Spirit, *waiting for* our adoption as children of God? The answer is in the "now" and "not yet" of eschatological salvation. In ancient adoption law (as is often the case today), adoptions were carried out in two stages. The parents took their adopted children into their homes and gave them the privileges of sonship or daughtership. But at the end of a probation period, the adoption was finalized. I think Paul had something like this in mind. Now, we are the children of God as bearers of the Spirit in Christ; but then, at our resurrection of the dead, our adoption will be finalized. Our ultimate day of adoption is our resurrection! At that time, we will be perfectly conformed to Christ's image. Our life is currently "hidden with Christ in God." But "when Christ, who is your life, appears, then you also will appear with him in glory" (Col. 3:3–4).

Salvation in the Spirit is not only deeply personal; it is also *communal* or social. Christ opens his risen life to all peoples by pouring out the Spirit on all flesh. The life of the church is the school of the soul in the ways of the Spirit. We seek to be as Christ to one another, and we minister to one another in multiple gifts of the Spirit. Evil inhabits corporate and institutional realities. Evil endures and grows more devastating once it is institutionalized, encoded in patterns of behavior, laws, and corporate powers. The church, in the sanctifying and empowering presence of the Spirit, is to be the mercifully just community that becomes a counterforce, subverting the evil powers at work in the world by the example it sets, the gospel it preaches, the compassion it shows, and the prophetic voice of protest it speaks forth. People of the Spirit dare not turn a deaf ear to the cries of suffering or treat evil as if it is just the way things are meant to be. The segregation and denigration of people because of their race or the subjugation of women is to be resisted in every way. Poverty and sickness are to be eradicated as much as possible. If we are not on the side of compassion and justice, we are not a righteous people.

The life of the Spirit is indeed central to the Christian life. The Christian is submerged into the realm of the Spirit's work. According to James Dunn, the **baptism in the Holy Spirit** is in fact the key to soteriology, or the doctrine of salvation, in the New Testament.[34] John the Baptist announced that the coming Messiah will baptize in the Holy Spirit. John baptized in water, but the Messiah will occasion a "river" of the Spirit into which he will "baptize" those who repent unto new life (Matt. 3:11; Mark 1:8; Luke 3:16; John 1:33; Acts 1:5). Dunn views Spirit baptism as occurring at the moment one repents and believes in Christ. It is the gift of the Spirit that unites us to Christ and incorporates us into his body (1 Cor. 12:13) at the moment we believe in the gospel. This is the **evangelical view of Spirit baptism.** Dunn views water baptism as a symbolic response to Christ's baptism in the Spirit, a way for us to bring to ritual and public expression our repentance and faith and to show gratitude for the gift of the Spirit that was granted to us, which is the gift of the Father's love and of Christ himself, his crucified and risen life.

Some sacramental traditions, like Catholic and certain mainstream Protestant traditions, take a different view of Spirit baptism, tying it instead to the sacraments of initiation, such as water baptism and confirmation. Spirit baptism is the spiritual side of the sacraments of initiation. This is the **sacramental view of Spirit baptism.** Catholic theologians George Montague and Kilian McDonnell maintain that though it is a sovereign act of God, Spirit baptism (or at least the granting of the gift of the Spirit) is occasioned by water baptism. Not coincidentally, they point out that Jesus received the Spirit at his baptism and that both 1 Corinthians 12:13 and Acts 2:38 imply that the Spirit is granted at our baptism too. In response to this position, Dunn notes that the gift of the Spirit in the New Testament is sometimes given apart from any mention of water baptism, both in Jesus's case (John 1:33) and among the cases of the early churches (Acts 2:1–4). In Acts 10:44–48, Cornelius's household is baptized in the Spirit *before* they are baptized in water, and the later report of the incident does not even mention their water

34. James D. G. Dunn, *Baptism in the Holy Spirit: A Re-examination of the New Testament Teaching on the Gift of the Spirit in Relation to Pentecostalism Today* (London: SCM, 1970), esp. 4–7.

baptism (11:15–18). The Samaritans in Acts 8:9–25 are baptized in the Spirit significantly *after* their baptism in water.

Pentecostals hold that Spirit baptism is *postconversion*, having to do with empowerment for witness rather than initiation into Christ by faith or water baptism (Luke 24:49; Acts 1:8). The case involving the Samaritans is often cited by Pentecostals as a case in point. They typically ask, "If Spirit baptism were the gift of the Spirit granted at one's initial union with Christ by faith or water baptism, why don't the Samaritans receive it when they are saved?" (Acts 8:14–17). Pentecostals also note that the original disciples had already believed in the risen Christ before they are filled with the Spirit on the day of Pentecost in Acts 2.

Dunn argues, by way of response, that the outpouring of the Spirit at Pentecost introduces a new era of the Spirit that brings the disciples from a pre-Pentecost experience of salvation to a post-Pentecost experience of salvation, which is richer and more intimate spiritually. Non-Pentecostal scholars usually respond to the Samaritan incident by noting that it is an exception to the rule. The fact that Philip is alarmed enough to notify Jerusalem when the Spirit does not descend on the Samaritans when they are converted is telling. This implies to some that the early church considered it unusual that the Spirit was not felt as present at the event of conversion. Some Pentecostals reason that the Spirit coming upon a person may have been evidenced by some sort of inspired speech that was assumed to be a characteristic consequence, such as testifying, prophecying, or speaking in tongues (Acts 2:4; 4:31; 10:44–46; 19:6). The common expectation among the early churches seems to have been that new converts believe with their hearts, confess with their lips that they have accepted Christ, and welcome the Spirit into their lives (Rom. 10:9). But most Pentecostals find a postconversion empowerment evidenced in Acts.

Pentecostals generally agree that the Spirit enters the Christian life and unites us to Christ from the moment we first believe and that water baptism is certainly an important confirmation and public witness to this event. Their only point is that there is more of God, more love and power, yet to be experienced in the Spirit—a filling to overflowing that drives one outward into service to others. Spirit baptism is meant to be experienced powerfully as overflowing love! This is a point that theologians from all traditions can affirm regardless of how they interpret the term "baptism in the Holy Spirit." Christians should pray for the Spirit to empower them for their service to others. From the moment of their initial faith in Christ, the Spirit within them will overflow in power as they bear witness to Christ (John 7:38). The Spirit comes upon us so as to facilitate our yielding to the overflow of the Spirit from within. Regardless of how one views Spirit baptism as a technical matter, the need to affirm one's possession of the Spirit from the start of the Christian life (Rom. 8:9) and the need for empowerment for service—a filling to overflowing (Eph. 5:18)—are both important for our response to the teaching of Scripture about the Christian life.

FINAL REFLECTIONS

The Holy Spirit, a fully divine person of the triune God, is utterly unique, like a mysterious wind that rests upon the darkness and the chaos, creating light and beautiful form. Such was and continues to be the case in creation and also in new creation, or immortality. The Spirit is not without its source in the depths of the Father's love, nor is it without its Word that mediates the form and structure of the Spirit's powerfully free, creative, and renewing activity, holding all things together in its developing design (Col. 1:17). Creation lives in the Spirit; yet, natural life is still subject to atrophy and death. Humanity lives in the Spirit too. Even in its fallen state, humanity lives and moves and has its being in the Spirit (Acts 17:28). Natural human capacities and talents flourish in the Spirit as well. But such natural flourishing is not enough when it comes to the grace necessary for salvation or for new creation as a supernatural reality. The incarnation, death, and resurrection of Jesus Christ, which are themselves mediated by the Spirit, are necessary both for our worthiness to receive the Spirit's supernatural work and for our reception of the transformative power necessary to take us from creation to new creation. Contrary to anything Pelagius says, there is no natural bridge from the mortal to the immortal. Justification, or being made right with God, is by grace alone through faith alone. Yet the faith that justifies is never actually alone. It expresses itself in acts of love; it authenticates itself and attains its telos, or end goal, in this way. Such acts are, by grace, a freeing and joyous enrichment of the life that we have in God.

Sanctification, our separation from sin and consecration unto God, is a positional reality that overlaps with justification. We are cleansed by Christ of all sin at the moment we accept him as Savior and Lord by faith. But sanctification is also to be a progressive reality by which our intentions are simplified under the sole direction of Christ's love, and our desires are purified of corruption and directed to the same goal. The path of the Spirit is the crucified path of self-giving love in the power of the risen life. Glorification fulfills salvation at the point of resurrection, at which point we are "swallowed up by life" (2 Cor. 5:4). Our baptism in the Holy Spirit has this swallowing up by life as its horizon. Seek more of God; seek to be filled with the Spirit. We have a mission to fulfill! The Spirit in us now, allowing us to partake of the benefits of Christ's sonship, is the down payment of the fullness of liberty to come in the resurrection. Conformed to Christ's image, we will be able to see him as he is and discover our destiny as human beings in communion.

TOPICS FOR REVIEW

1. Briefly put, what are the five lines of argument for the Spirit's deity?
2. Briefly summarize five scriptural texts that support the Spirit's personhood.
3. Describe the dichotomist and trichotomist positions on human nature, as well as the position advocated in the chapter. Do you agree with this position? Why or why not?
4. What did Pelagius believe about the human condition, and how did Augustine respond?
5. What is justification by grace through faith? What is James's position on the matter? Does it basically align with Paul's?
6. What is sanctification? What does Wesley teach, and how do I respond to him in this chapter? Consider what Paul says about the desires in your response.
7. What is baptism in the Holy Spirit, according to James Dunn and Kilian McDonnell? What is your view?

5

CHURCH

The church is unique. Nothing else quite like it exists in the world. We are on sacred ground when we discuss it. First Peter 1:2–3 refers to the churches as consisting of those "who have been chosen according to the foreknowledge of God the Father, through the sanctifying work of the Spirit, to be obedient to Jesus Christ and sprinkled with his blood." Election from the Father, redemption through Christ, and sanctification through the Spirit are involved in the *gift* called the church. But, as we will see, the church is also a *challenge*, for we are called to participate by God's grace in this wonderful communion of the people of God (and in its mission). The Greek word for "church" is ἐκκλησία (*ekklēsia*), from which we derive the term "ecclesiology" (the study of the church). The term literally refers to those who are "called out" and gathered together. It was a term used of public gatherings in the ancient Greek-speaking world. But the church is gathered by the prior act of the triune God to call them, incorporating them into the life of communion and sending them forth to open this communion to the world, inviting an ever-more diverse inclusion of people from all contexts and walks of life.

A Trinitarian Gift

The church is born in God's self-giving to the world. From the depths of the Father came forth the love to save the world. Note James 1:17–18: "Every good and perfect gift is from above, coming down from the Father of the

123

heavenly lights, who does not change like shifting shadows. He chose to give us birth through the word of truth, that we might be a kind of firstfruits of all he created." On the basis of the redemptive work of the Son, who is faithful to the Father, sin and death are overcome as barriers between us and God, and the blessings of sonship and daughtership are extended to us all. In the abundant Spirit, who overflows the love shared between the Father and the Son, we receive the victory of Christ, along with all of its blessings, as we are incorporated into the communion of the triune life. The church is incorporated into the communion of the triune God and is sent forth to be the chief sign and instrument of God's mission in the world. The church is indeed to be the "icon" of the Trinity. But we must use caution when saying this, for the communion shared among the trinitarian persons is infinitely and unimaginably interpenetrating. Our communion is at best an incredibly vague and woefully inadequate image of that. But a woefully inadequate icon is still an icon! Even the unfathomable difference between our communion and God's communion can inspire us to give of ourselves to each other in richer ways.

The church is born in the communion and missions of the triune God. The fact that God is a communion of persons implies that salvation brings us from alienation to communion with God and with one another in God. Divine communion is thus essential to the church's understanding of its own life. Christ prays "that all of them may be one, Father, just as you are in me and I am in you. May they also be in us so that the world may believe that you have sent me" (John 17:21). Notice that Jesus starts with the intimate communion (interpenetration) that he has enjoyed throughout eternity with the Father: "as you are in me and I am in you." He then follows with a request that others may be in them: "May they also be in us." The point here is the intimate communion of the triune God: the Father in the Son, the Son in the Father, the Spirit in them both, and both in the Spirit as the bond and celebration of their shared love. It is then through the overflowing Spirit that we are brought into the communion of divine love. The church is born in the outpouring of the Spirit! The Spirit gives birth to the church. But that great moment of the Spirit's outpouring is birthed eternally in the heart of the Father, in the Father's elect will, since the Spirit proceeds from the Father with this consequence in mind (1 Pet. 1:1–2). The Spirit's outpouring was made possible by the redemptive atonement of the Son, who overcame the barriers of sin and death so that we may be worthy of the Spirit: "He redeemed us . . . so that by faith we might receive the promise of the Spirit" (Gal. 3:14). The end result is that the Spirit is poured out upon us so that we may be brought into the communion of the triune God. This is the gift of the church; this is the essence of our mystery as the church, as a communion of saints. This truth is adduced in 1 John 4:13: "This is how we know that we live in him and he in us: He has given us of his Spirit."

The church is thus characterized as a **koinonia** (κοινωνία, *koinōnia*), or a communion of saints. "They devoted themselves to the apostles' teaching and to fellowship, to the breaking of bread and to prayer" (Acts 2:42). The word for "fellowship" here is *koinōnia*. The term refers most essentially to a sharing of life in the Holy Spirit. It's derivatively a sharing of like-minded faith (represented in the above text as the teaching of the apostles) and other practices such as prayer, breaking of bread (especially the Lord's Supper), ministry, and mission. Communion has become very important to ecclesiology across denominational and cultural lines. Under the umbrella of this term, various streams of the global church have been able to find a degree of common ground when it comes to their practices. As Lorelei Fuchs has shown in her massive study on koinonia, the fact that communion can be experienced by degrees has helped divided churches to form degrees of unity and common life together even though they remain loyal to their different denominations. The goal is to show the world that they regard each other as one even though they are denominationally diverse (more on this later).[1]

The church is also a **mission**. Given that the triune life is missional, that the Father has sent the Son and the Spirit into the world to save it, the church that is incorporated into the triune communion will see itself as a mission as well. If the triune communion is open to the world and extended to the world through the triune missions, so is the church by God's grace to be an open and hospitable communion extended to the world. Mission is not simply what the church *does*; it's what the church *is*. Jesus said that as *he* was sent, he is sending *us* (John 20:21). As he was sent by the Father under the anointing of the Spirit to fulfill the divine mission in the world, so is he sending his church to the nations under the Spirit's anointing.

Missional ecclesiologies are helping to renew the church by reminding it that as Christ came out of love for the world to save it (John 3:16), so are we to be directed to the world in his name. As Christ is the divine "man for others," so are we to be "his people for others." Our theology and church life cannot be closed in upon ourselves if we are to be like the Christ who gave of his life for the world. Gary Tyra's *Missional Orthodoxy* is a fascinating example of how Christian theology can be done with the church's missional life at the horizon.[2] Missional ecclesiologies are indeed helping to renew the

---

1. Lorelei F. Fuchs, *Koinonia and the Quest for an Ecumenical Ecclesiology: From Foundations through Dialogue to Symbolic Competence for Communionality* (Grand Rapids: Eerdmans, 2008).

2. Gary Tyra, *A Missional Orthodoxy: Theology and Ministry in a Post-Christian Context* (Downers Grove, IL: IVP Academic, 2013).

church and its theology. If we view the Spirit figuratively as the breath of God, by analogy we can say that as God inhales, the people of God gather in communion with and enjoyment of the divine self-giving. But as God exhales, the people of God are sent out into the world in power to bear witness. The church is not merely a mission. After all, the church, as the bride of Christ, is not wedded to her groom merely to serve in his mission. This bride also enjoys communion with and in the groom. But neither is the church only a communion with Christ. To commune with Christ is to share in his life, and that surely involves his mission. If we share in his life, we share in his love for the world, which he died to save. Surely, we are a mission as well. The love of Christ compels us (2 Cor. 5:14–15).

I desperately need this gift called the church. My tendency is to surround myself with people I enjoy being with, who I feel complement me. It's fine to enjoy the company of such people. Friendship is often uplifting. But to be like Christ, I need to have my soul expanded beyond this, becoming close to others who are different from me and, especially, who I may not particularly enjoy being with. God places me in fellowship with many such people in the church and asks me to love them, to help bear their burdens, and to rejoice with them when they are blessed. "If one part suffers, every part suffers with it; if one part is honored, every part rejoices with it" (1 Cor. 12:26). I can only bear their burdens if I care about them, and I can only rejoice with them when they're blessed if I don't envy them or covet their success. In this way, my soul expands; I gain a greater capacity to love as Christ loves. The church is to be the school of the soul, the infirmary of the sick. I am to become an "ecclesial personality" who is open and willing to embrace. The church needs me to be all that I can be in Christ. When I was born again, I was born into a family. If Christ is not ashamed to call us his brothers and sisters (Heb. 2:11), neither should we be too proud to enter the church with the same attitude toward those who have gathered.

Election

The church is the elect people. First Peter 1:1 addresses churches with the terse greeting "To God's elect." Election refers to *choosing*; the elect are God's chosen. The people of God may be called "chosen" of God. Election is trinitarian in nature. The churches are said to be "chosen according to the foreknowledge of God the Father" (v. 2). Election is also tied to sonship, ultimately to God's Son, who is favored and chosen by the Father from all eternity. Peter continues by saying that Christ "was chosen before the creation of the world, but was revealed in these last times for your sake" (v. 20). The implication is that the elect churches in 1 Peter 1:2 are members of Christ's body, the body of the one and only elect of the Father. The Chosen One was revealed in time for our sakes, for the sake of our inclusion in him and his election. Election in time is thus linked to *favored sonship*. Referring to the exodus, God says of Israel in Hosea 11:1, "Out of Egypt I called my *son*" (cf. Exod. 4:22–23, emphasis added). He follows this with a complaint concerning Israel's unfaithfulness: "But the more they were called, the more they went away from me" (v. 2). By denying their sonship, the Israelites were denying their election.

Sonship, though, does not belong primarily to Israel but to God's eternal Son, who took on flesh in the person of Jesus Christ, Israel's Messiah. When telling the story of the baby Jesus being taken to Egypt by his parents to escape Herod's effort to kill him and then, after Herod's death, being brought back home, Matthew quotes the above-mentioned Hosea text, "Out of Egypt I called my son," but this time in reference to Christ (Matt. 2:14–15). Significantly, the following verse, Hosea 11:2, about Israel's waywardness, is left out in Christ's fulfillment. This is because Jesus is the *faithful* Son of God. He was such from all eternity (John 1:18). Israel was elect and called by God as God's "son" to foreshadow *him*. Their election was derived from his election, and it serves his election too. Lastly, election is actualized in time by the Holy Spirit. First Peter 1:2 states that the Father has elected us "through the sanctifying work of the Spirit," who sets us apart from sin and consecrates us unto God through inclusion in Christ, including our adoption into the full benefits of his favored sonship. Note also Ephesians 1:13–14: "And you also were included in Christ when you heard the message of truth, the gospel of your salvation. When you believed, you were marked in him with a seal, the promised Holy Spirit, who is a deposit guaranteeing our inheritance until the redemption of those who are God's possession—to the praise of his glory." Notice the election language describing the people of the Spirit as God's "possession": "You will be my treasured possession" (Exod. 19:5).

With this larger background in mind, let us explore election in greater depth, especially in light of the church's relationship to both Israel and the expanding mission of the church to the nations. First, election in the Old Testament occurs *in time* as God interacts with people to fulfill the divine plan for history. As we will note, election is also eternal, but we should first recognize that it occurs *in time*. As Kurt Koch states, the election of Israel is portrayed as "a concrete historical act on God's part that forms the starting point and basis of the salvation history of God and his people."[3] Sigurd Grindheim also

---

3. Kurt Koch, "*Zur Geschichte der Erwählungsvorstellung* in Israel," quoted in Wolfhart Pannenberg, *Systematic Theology*, trans. Geoffrey W. Bromiley (Grand Rapids: Eerdmans, 1991–98), 3:442.

points out that, in the Old Testament, "election is never explicitly associated with a time before or at creation."[4] Election occurs *in* time as a commitment to the patriarchs of Israel (Neh. 9:7; Pss. 105:6; 135:4; Isa. 41:8; 51:1–3) or as a promise to Israel in relation to the exodus or the wilderness wanderings (Deut. 4:37; 7:6–7; 10:15; Ezek. 20:5; Hosea 11:1; 13:4–5). God chooses Israel in part because they are oppressed and the fewest in number among the peoples of the earth (Exod. 3:7; Deut. 7:7–9). God purposed to use them to show the mighty power and glory of divine love and justice to the much larger and mighty nations. God's election fulfills divine and not human purposes. It is a sovereign act of God. It is not earned. Yet human faithfulness to God does play a role in one's reception of it. When Abraham was willing to sacrifice his son Isaac on the altar, he received a response from the angel of the Lord: "The angel of the LORD called to Abraham from heaven a second time and said, 'I swear by myself, declares the LORD, that because you have done this and have not withheld your son, your only son, I will surely bless you and make your descendants as numerous as the stars in the sky and as the sand on the seashore" (Gen. 22:15–17). Abraham had a faith that expressed itself through a willingness to sacrifice his son Isaac—which foreshadowed the Father's love that sent the one and only Son to the cross to save us!

This Old Testament presentation of election, as played out in time, may surprise some readers who are accustomed to viewing election exclusively as a timeless decree. Some hold that God chose who would be saved and who would be passed over or destined to damnation. Those who are predestined to be saved are then thought to be awakened to salvation through irresistible grace, and those predestined to damnation will without question continue on their path of rejection to the end. This predestinarian view is traceable to Augustine in the fifth century, but today it is most often associated with John Calvin (1509–64), the great sixteenth-century Reformer, and referred to today under the label of **Calvinism**. Later in the sixteenth century, Jacob Arminius (1560–1609) regarded the Calvinist understanding of eternal predestination as removing any determinative significance to human free will; he tried to rectify this neglect by basing divine election on God's foreknowledge of what *humans* freely choose—a view called **Arminianism**. For Arminius, grace is not irresistible, though it enables our response to God, so human choice ends up having a role to play in whether people are included in God's predestined plan. The debate that raged as a result was between the Calvinist emphasis

4. Sigurd Grindheim, *The Crux of Election: Paul's Critique of the Jewish Confidence in the Election of Israel*, Wissenschaftliche Untersuchungen zum Neuen Testament, 2nd series, vol. 202 (Tübingen: Mohr Siebeck, 2005), 8.

on the all-determinative significance of God's predestination and sovereignty (in which the human choice for God is predetermined and brought forth by irresistible grace) and the Arminian emphasis on free will (that is foreknown by God and predestined on that basis but not predetermined nor guaranteed by irresistible grace). Some don't feel at ease in either camp. They might attempt to argue that election is a mystery. It is played out in heaven, as if all depended on God's choice, but it is also played out on earth, as if human responses to God, by enabling grace, were of real and determinative significance. These folks have felt the pressure to take sides. There is, however, another alternative.

Twentieth-century Swiss Reformed theologian Karl Barth opened up a fresh perspective on election by describing it as a triune act, centering on Christ and extending to others through the Spirit. For Barth, election is thus not primarily about *us* but about *God*, being God's *self-determination* for creation. The Father elects the Son from all eternity to be the chosen Son, in whom others are chosen and included by way of *adoption*. Christ's election is indeed unique, for he is the one and only Son who will redeem us and bestow the Spirit upon us, granting us access to the benefits of his sonship, including election. In all its uniqueness, his election is thus *also* opened to us; its benefits and mission are shared with us by grace. For Barth, *all favor* with the Father is mediated in and through the one and only Son: "Before Him and without Him, and beside Him, God does not then elect or will anything."[5] The Spirit, for Barth, is the seal and the expanding boundary of election in Christ. Election in the Spirit is thus, for Barth, "a divine activity in the form of the history, encounter and decision between God and man."[6] As Suzanne McDonald has argued as well, election in the Spirit overflows Israel to bless the nations through the expanding mission of the church, which is the mission of the triune God.[7] Election is thus both *eternal* and *in time* because the triune God has determined from all eternity to give of Godself to history in a way that opens *all* people to the divine call.

Let us linger on the theme of Christ-centered election a bit longer. Christ is the elect Son and the bearer of the Spirit, so that by imparting the Spirit he can open up his elect sonship to us. *Christ thus reveals not only elect humanity but also the God who elects.* John's Gospel reports that John the Baptist said this of Christ: "And I myself did not know him, but the one who sent me to baptize with water told me, 'The man on whom you see the Spirit come

5. Karl Barth, *Church Dogmatics*, vol. II/2, *The Doctrine of God*, trans. G. W. Bromiley, ed. T. F. Torrance (Edinburgh: T&T Clark, 1957), 94.

6. Barth, *Church Dogmatics*, II/2, 175.

7. Suzanne McDonald, *Re-Imaging Election: Divine Election as Representing God to Others and Others to God* (Grand Rapids: Eerdmans, 2010).

down and remain is the one who will baptize with the Holy Spirit.' I have seen and I testify that this is God's Chosen One" (1:33–34). Christ bears the Spirit as the favored Son so as to impart the Spirit of sonship to others. Recall that election is inextricably tied to favored sonship in Hosea 11:1: "Out of Egypt I called my son." This is said of Israel. But, as noted above, Matthew records that *Christ* is actually the chosen Son called out of Egypt (2:14–15), implying that Israel's election foreshadows his; in a sense, it is derived from him. We then find the Father declaring Christ's favored and beloved sonship from heaven as the Spirit descends on Jesus at his baptism: "This is my Son, whom I love; with him I am well pleased" (3:17). Christ passes through the waters of the Jordan River at his baptism under the anointing of the Spirit, in a way similar to Israel's passing through the waters of the sea accompanied by the Spirit as the chosen people in the exodus:

> Then his people recalled the days of old,
>   the days of Moses and his people—
> where is he who brought them through the sea,
>   with the shepherd of his flock?
> Where is he who set
>   his Holy Spirit among them,
> who sent his glorious arm of power
>   to be at Moses' right hand,
> who divided the waters before them,
>   to gain for himself everlasting renown? (Isa. 63:11–12)

Israel's election under the anointing of the Spirit foreshadowed the election of Christ, who fulfilled election for all time and, for more than Israel, indeed for all nations. Matthew 12:18 says as much concerning Christ:

> Here is my servant whom I have chosen,
>   the one I love, in whom I delight;
> I will put my Spirit on him,
>   and he will proclaim justice to the nations.

When God tells Abraham that he will give the promised land "to your off-spring" in Genesis 12:7, Paul takes this to refer to Jesus Christ. "The promises were spoken to Abraham and to his seed. Scripture does not say 'and to seeds,' meaning many people, but 'and to your seed,' meaning one person, who is Christ" (Gal. 3:16). It is not Israel that fulfills the promise given to Abraham that all nations will be blessed; it is Israel's Messiah, born from Israel as Abraham's seed. Israel's election foreshadows and serves Christ's election.

Within this christological election, the promised land for which Israel is chosen ends up foreshadowing the new heaven and new earth over which Christ will reign. He will declare justice to the nations as God's righteous ruler. "He was given authority, glory and sovereign power; all nations and peoples of every language worshiped him. His dominion is an everlasting dominion that will not pass away, and his kingdom is one that will never be destroyed" (Dan. 7:14). Election is thus connected to the Father's will but also to the Son's favored sonship and to the Spirit as the blessing of that favor shared with us. *To be elect is to be adopted to sonship and daughtership in Christ under the anointing, seal, and blessing of the Spirit.*

Election in time is thus also *eternal*. God is not bound by time. The Lord who reigns over history does indeed inhabit and experience time, but God is not limited by time *as we are*, discovering new things and deciding things along the way. "I make known the end from the beginning, from ancient times, what is still to come. I say, 'My purpose will stand, and I will do all that I please'" (Isa. 46:10). But the eternality of election is also due to the fact that it has its meaning primarily in the eternal self-determination of the triune God. Herein is the link to time as well. God's self-election in eternity involves the election of others. God freely self-determines to be the God *for others*. As we will see, there is a sense in which we are chosen in Christ in all of eternity *and* we actualize this election by being included in Christ by faith in time, adopted into the benefits of Christ's elect sonship by the Spirit. Such has always been the Father's predestined plan. Notice the flow of Paul's logic in Ephesians 1:3–5: "Praise be to the God and Father of our Lord Jesus Christ, who has blessed us in the heavenly realms with every spiritual blessing in Christ. For he chose us in him before the creation of the world to be holy and blameless in his sight. In love he predestined us for adoption to sonship through Jesus Christ, in accordance with his pleasure and will."

Consider how people are blessed from all eternity by being chosen "in him" or "in Christ" to favored sonship by way of the Spirit of adoption. We are called to *his* elect sonship. We are only chosen in him! Notice also verses 13–14, where people actualize their election in time by being included in Christ, sealed unto the day of redemption to be God's "treasured possession," which is election language (Ps. 135:4). Are only a select few chosen in eternity in Christ? Ephesians 1:10 indicates that Christ's elect sonship is an eternal gift to all, for the goal is to unite all of humanity—indeed, all of creation ("all things")—under *Christ*.

The issue therefore arises as to whether election is *corporate* in nature and, if so, how individual choice factors into it. Ancient peoples typically thought primarily in corporate terms. A person thought of himself or herself primarily as a member of a clan, tribe, or people group. In the modern era, the issue of persons as individuals has become prominent. The question thus arises as to what extent we may be reading our individualism into texts on election. It's not that God does not see or regard us as individuals or that individuals don't matter in the Scriptures. It's rather the question of whether election in Scripture is primarily a corporate issue. When Paul writes in Romans 8:30 that "those he called, he also justified; those he justified, he also glorified," is he referring to an indiscriminate body open to *all* or to individuals predetermined in eternity? New Testament theologian Alan Richardson (1905–75) argued for the former.[8] When Luke writes, "All who were appointed for eternal life believed" (Acts 13:48), is he referring to those who had arrived at an "appointed" moment in God's guidance and their spiritual preparation to receive eternal life, like the Ethiopian eunuch, who had a divinely arranged meeting with Philip in the desert (8:26–40)? Or Cornelius, who had a similarly arranged and appointed meeting with Peter (10:1–48)? Or even the nations that were led by God to their "appointed times in history" (17:26)? In the book of Acts, people are constantly arriving at key moments appointed by God for eternal life. Must we read more into it than this? Aren't such moments ordained by God for all? Don't such opportunities require faith for fulfillment, a faith decision that is foreknown by God but not thereby predetermined? Is there no place in the history of election as actualized in time for willfully missed opportunities?

We need to explore what the term "predestine" means. In ancient Greek literature outside of the New Testament, the term simply refers to something ordained. Any other assumptions, such as the belief that what is ordained is guaranteed to occur, must be justified by the context of the term's usage.[9] Election in Romans does in fact seem ordained (predestined) by God for all, but it also seems to be dependent on faith to be actualized by all, a faith that is not guaranteed in advance. Paul writes in 9:2–5 that elements of election, like adoption to sonship and its future glory, "belong" in fact to *all* of Israel, including many whom Paul does not expect will believe, causing great sorrow and anguish for him:

> I have great sorrow and unceasing anguish in my heart. For I could wish that I myself were cursed and cut off from Christ for the sake of my people, those of my own race, the people of Israel. Theirs is the adoption to sonship; theirs the

8. Alan Richardson, *An Introduction to the Theology of the New Testament* (New York: Harper & Row, 1958), 279.

9. This is from New Testament scholar Bo Reicke, as summarized by Robert Sloan in "'To Predestine' (προορίζω): The Use of a Pauline Term in Extrabiblical Tradition," in *Good News in History: Essays in Honor of Bo Reicke*, ed. Ed. L. Miller (Atlanta: Scholars Press, 1993), 128.

divine glory, the covenants, the receiving of the law, the temple worship and the promises. Theirs are the patriarchs, and from them is traced the human ancestry of the Messiah, who is God over all, forever praised! Amen.

In the above passage, all of the glories of election to sonship belong to *all* of Israel, presumably according to God's ordained plan. Yet faith is required for them to actualize this election in time. Thus, in chapter 11, Paul can also refer to believing Jews as "the elect among them" (the people of Israel), the elect among the elect, who are distinguished from the unbelieving Jews who are "hardened" (v. 7) and have not actually taken part in an election that, as Paul makes clear in 9:2–5, *belongs to them*. They possess an unfulfilled calling, a rejected sonship, like the wayward prodigal son who, in Luke 15, abandons his sonship and squanders his inheritance.

But their hardening was not meant to be permanent. When Isaiah asks God how long Israel will be hardened, God answers, "until the cities lie ruined" (6:11). There is a desired end to it that leads to repentance:

> "Come now, let us settle the matter,"
>   says the LORD.
> "Though your sins are like scarlet,
>   they shall be as white as snow;
> though they are red as crimson,
>   they shall be like wool." (1:18)

Here's the point for Paul in Romans: The Jews who are hardened need not remain that way. They, too, may reclaim the election ordained for them and become part of the body of Christ, even though they had previously been cut off from it due to unbelief. Paul writes of the Jews who were cut off from the tree of God's people due to a lack of faith in Christ: "And if they do not persist in unbelief, they will be grafted in, for God is able to graft them in again" (11:23). Speaking of hardened Israel, Paul writes in verses 11–12 that they may yet be included if they come to believe: "Again I ask: Did they stumble so as to fall beyond recovery? Not at all! Rather, because of their transgression, salvation has come to the Gentiles to make Israel envious. But if their transgression means riches for the world, and their loss means riches for the Gentiles, how much greater riches will their full inclusion bring!"

The hardened ones of verses 7–10 may yet be included in the elect people, according to verses 11–12. The "transgression" of Jewish unbelief that caused riches for gentiles was expressed in their handing Christ over to the Romans to be crucified. That transgression brought riches to the gentiles, much like pharaoh's earlier effort to destroy Israel at the sea brought mercy to the

Israelites. At key points in salvation history, God uses the transgressions of hardened sinners to show grace to others, but this is not the whole story. God intends this same mercy for those who are hardened, which will bring further blessing.

Paul also refers to this use of transgressions to show grace in Romans 9:22–23, where he writes about God's bearing patiently with "pottery" being prepared for destruction: he uses their transgression to show mercy to vessels being prepared for glory. One must look to the cases of pharaoh and of the Jewish leadership that handed Jesus over to be crucified to understand the meaning of this text. The vessels being prepared for glory because of their faith benefit from the triumph of divine mercy over human transgression. But the hardening of the others is not meant thereby to be permanent; pottery being prepared for destruction is meant to receive mercy too. Such people are not a mere foil for the divine triumph, to be tossed into the ash heap of history once they've served their purpose. Hardening in Romans is a form of judgment that is not meant to be permanent but rather to lead the hardened ones to grace as well. The divine hardening is not primarily imposed by God but chosen by *us*. Paul describes the hardening of sinners in Romans 1:24 as a divine handing over of sinners to their chosen destructive paths: "Therefore God gave them over in the sinful desires of their hearts." Here one is reminded of Psalm 81:12: "So I gave them over to their stubborn hearts to follow their own devices." But in Romans, God bears patiently with sinners on their destructive path, not only to manifest grace in triumph over their transgressions but also to lead them through their hardship to repentance: "Do you show contempt for the riches of his kindness, forbearance and patience, not realizing that God's kindness is intended to lead you to repentance?" (2:4). God hands God's own Son over to damnation on the cross to save those who are handed over to destruction (4:25).

As Karl Barth noted, Christ is the only individual in history predestined to damnation. He bears it on the cross for all of humanity, so that all may share in his eternally ordained election to glory.[10] In fact, we are *all*, apart from grace, vessels being prepared for destruction, called to become vessels prepared for glory by grace: "All have sinned and fall short of the glory of God" (Rom. 3:23). Paul concludes his lengthy discourse on election in Romans 9–11 with an elaboration of this very point: "For God has bound *everyone* over to disobedience so that he may have mercy on them *all*" (11:32; emphasis added). In Romans, election in Christ is open to all; the adoption to sonship and the glory belong to all because of what Christ has done. Israel's

10. Barth, *Church Dogmatics* II/2, 172–73.

election serves Christ's and is meant to be open to the nations. This fact weighed heavy on Paul's heart and drove his missionary ventures to many uncharted territories.

Does the fact that God foreknows who will end up in Christ's body mean that they are indeed predestined in the sense that their justification and glorification are guaranteed (Rom. 8:30)? God does indeed know in eternity what occurs in time. But if God's knowledge in eternity *guarantees* what will happen among individuals in time, it seems that salvation history is nothing more than a play acted out according to a divinely prescribed script. Many, including myself, cannot see how the Calvinist can avoid this conclusion. It seems to me that this exclusive focus on divine determination of all things does not account for the fact that election in Romans is genuinely ordained and purposed by God for *all* of Israel, as Romans 9:2–4 makes clear. In fact, God purposes it for all of humanity: "For God has bound everyone over to disobedience so that he may have mercy on them all" (11:32). Neither does Calvinism, in my view, grant human choice the determinative significance granted in Scripture. The angel of the Lord says to Abraham, "I swear by my-self, declares the LORD, that *because you have done this* and have not withheld your son, your only son, I will surely bless you and make your descendants as numerous as the stars in the sky and as the sand on the seashore" (Gen. 22:16–17; emphasis added). So also, in Romans, though election in Christ is a sovereign act of God that is a gift, it is indeed actualized by an act of faith that is not guaranteed to occur or to fail to occur by divine determination. Rather, Paul warns gentile believers to take with utmost seriousness the grav-ity of their choice when it comes to the privilege of claiming election in Christ: "Consider therefore the kindness and sternness of God: sternness to those who fell, but kindness to you, *provided that you continue in his kindness*. Otherwise, you also will be cut off. And if they do not persist in unbelief, they will be grafted in, for God is able to graft them in again" (11:22–23; emphasis added). Note also Peter's admonition to "make every effort to confirm your calling and election. For if you do these things, you will never stumble" (2 Pet. 1:10). Does not the gravity of human choice dissipate if election is a one-way street, from God to us, determined solely by God, rather than a relational dynamic?

Granted, God is the one who acts to establish our covenant relation and to enable it from beginning to end. God is the dominant partner in this relation. Election is a gift opened up to humanity in the self-determination of the God who freely chooses to be the God for us. But do the sovereignty and all-significant divine action not also allow for genuine creaturely self-determination, choices enabled by God but not irresistible nor guaranteed by divine determination? What if we were to say that what God knows in eternity is indeed conditioned by creaturely actions? This would not represent a loss of divine sovereignty, nor would it necessarily imply salvation by works, since it is not the case that autonomous human agents are acting toward God from their own resources. It is rather the case that human actions, freed and enabled by divine grace, are playing a role in what God knows in eternity. The Calvinist cannot imagine how a person's will, freed and enabled by grace, can do anything but respond favorably. But I can imagine a will that still resists that which lures it to freedom. Grace received must find fulfillment in the completion of that human yielding, or it is received "in vain" (2 Cor. 6:1). Neither am I saying that God is being reduced to a human potential that we can use or not use. Instead, *humanity* is the potential that God has created and has willed to use for divine glory and human fulfillment, a potential that is created by grace for grace but that can resist that grace and willfully choose to recede into bondage. Without divine enablement, humanity remains helpless. If we resist God, we remain unfulfilled. God remains perfectly fulfilled with or without us, though God prefers to be with us.

One last point that needs to be made here concerns divine compassion. If God determines all things, does this not make God the author of evil? One could say in response that God wills primarily the good and authors the evil to serve the good. But what about those consumed by the evil, with no realistic chance to escape and to know the good? The Calvinist may strain to make the case that such a fate is still just, since these poor souls who are passed over and used to show mercy toward others deserve their fate. Leaving aside the questionable assumption that this kind of divine selectivity is truly just, what about compassion? Is it compassionate to pass over an unimaginable number of souls without doing everything to save them? Paul was willing to be an outcast for the sake of saving all those who belong to the Jewish race (Rom. 9:2–5). Can we say anything less of divine compassion? Is not this compassion infinite? Does it not therefore extend to all? "The Lord is not slow in keeping his promise, as some understand slowness. Instead he is patient with you, not wanting *anyone* to perish, but *everyone* to come to repentance" (2 Pet. 3:9; emphasis added). Can anything less than a universally offered compassion be infinite or drive the global mission of the church? Indeed, the love of Christ compels us (2 Cor. 5:14)![11]

---

11. For a more expansive treatment of election, see Frank D. Macchia, *The Spirit-Baptized Church: A Dogmatic Inquiry*, T&T Clark Systematic Pentecostal and Charismatic Theology (New York: Bloomsbury T&T Clark, 2020), chap. 2.

Models of the Church

The church is nowhere defined in the New Testament in so many words. What we have instead are various models drawn from everyday life that are rich with implications. These models invite exploration. The church is, for example, the family of God. The Father sends the only Son so that in the Spirit we could be adopted into sonship. Christ is the firstborn Son of all creation, the firstborn from the dead, willing to share his inheritance with us all (Col. 1:15–18). Indeed, he was appointed the Son for many sons and daughters in power at his resurrection, "according to the Spirit of holiness" (Rom. 1:4 ESV). We are now no longer slaves but sons and daughters through the Spirit of adoption (8:15–16). Though humanity lived in the condemnation and shame of sin, Christ was not ashamed to call us his brothers and sisters. Indeed, he bore our shame so that we could take on his glory. Note Hebrews 2:10–11: "In bringing many sons and daughters to glory, it was fitting that God, for whom and through whom everything exists, should make the pioneer of their salvation perfect through what he suffered. Both the one who makes people holy and those who are made holy are of the same family. So Jesus is not ashamed to call them brothers and sisters." When we are "born again," we are born into a family, the family of God.

Another model is the church as the field of God. "You are God's field" (1 Cor. 3:9). Not only are we the plants; we are also the farmers. The farmers are only instruments of God. They are only servants; it is God "who makes things grow" (v. 7). We must not receive the glory for ministry success! The seed is the word of God, and the Spirit is the nourishment: "For you have been born again, not of perishable seed, but of imperishable, through the living and enduring word of God" (1 Pet. 1:23). And "we were all given the one Spirit to drink" (1 Cor. 12:13). Christ encourages his disciples not to grow weary when laboring in the field of God's people. As with any farming, results will be mixed and sometimes discouraging (Mark 4:13–20). Some seed will be stolen by the birds (as people allow themselves to be deceived), while some seed will only take shallow root and won't endure due to the hardness of the soil (the hardness of people's hearts). Still others will be choked by material cares and worries (like those who are lured away by greed). Even among those who bear fruit, the flourishing will be mixed, "some thirty, some sixty, some a hundred times what was sown" (v. 20). Yet the implication is clear that those who endure in the work and trust in God will have reason for rejoicing. We can also ask what kind of soil *we* are in this parable. Jesus says that he is the vine and we are his branches. Those branches that don't bear fruit will suffer judgment. We are called upon to bear fruit. But we must remain in him and draw from his Spirit to do so (John 15:1–6). And why would we not want to do this? Who wants a life that is barren and purposeless? Who does not want a life that resembles a flourishing garden that blesses others?

The church is also likened to the body of Christ, which is a prominent image in theological literature. "Now you are the body of Christ, and each one of you is a part of it" (1 Cor. 12:27). The body-of-Christ model stresses the unity of the church: "There are different kinds of gifts, but the same Spirit distributes them. There are different kinds of service, but the same Lord. There are different kinds of working, but in all of them and in everyone it is the same God at work" (vv. 4–6). The Corinthians were divided and therefore required this model to renew their appreciation for the unity of their corporate life. The church is not a community of competing factions that descend into fighting and chaos. But Paul also wants to stay clear of any thoughts of uniformity. Not everyone is to try to do the same thing, to engage in the most popular forms of service while leaving other needful ministries neglected. "If the whole body were an eye, where would the sense of hearing be? If the whole body were an ear, where would the sense of smell be? But in fact God has placed the parts in the body, every one of them, just as he wanted them to be" (vv. 17–18). The church is not meant to lack any spiritual gifts while waiting for the Lord to return (1:7). Until we see Christ face-to-face, all of the gifts are needed (13:8–12). It is the Spirit who decides who shall be blessed with which gifts for the edification of others (12:11). Such matters are out of our hands. It is best to allow the Spirit to exercise freedom in this matter. No one should want to quench the Spirit (1 Thess. 5:19). Churches outside of the West tend to emphasize gifts like healing, deliverance, words of knowledge, and speaking in tongues, of which churches in the West are more mixed in their reception. African theologian Esther Acolatse from Ghana, for example, defends the gift of deliverance from demonic oppression as a legitimate gift in the church, though she cautions against placing too much emphasis on it.[12] Korean pastor David Yong-Gi Cho encourages churches to live more intentionally in the "fourth dimension"—that is, the realm of supernatural gifts, such as healing, dreams and visions, and spiritual discernment.[13] Spiritual gifts will be shown to be valid if they exalt Christ alone as Lord (1 Cor. 12:1–3), are exercised in conformity to divine love (13:1–13), and edify, or build up, the church (14:26).

The church is also the temple of the Holy Spirit. "Don't you know that you yourselves are God's temple and that God's Spirit dwells in your midst?"

12. Esther Acolatse, *Powers, Principalities, and the Spirit: Biblical Realism in Africa and the West* (Grand Rapids: Eerdmans, 2018).
13. David Yong-Gi Cho, *The Fourth Dimension* (Alachua, FL: Bridge-Logos, 1983).

(1 Cor. 3:16). The Jewish temple and its sacrificial system were but a shadow of things to come (cf. Heb. 10:1). It was thought to be the central link between God and humanity, but the actual link would be Christ. Christ says to the Jewish leadership that if they seek to destroy "this temple"—meaning his body—he will raise it up (John 2:19). They thought he meant the Jewish temple, but he was referring to his body. Christ is now the chief cornerstone or foundation of the church as the temple of the Spirit that is built on him. "For no one can lay any foundation other than the one already laid, which is Jesus Christ" (1 Cor. 3:11). It is no longer a building but a people that most defines the church today. We are spiritual stones built on Christ and on one another: "You also, like living stones, are being built into a spiritual house" (1 Pet. 2:5). We are to be a holy people who offer ourselves as spiritual sacrifices in worship and life to God (Rom. 12:1–3).

We are also to be the army of God: "Put on the full armor of God, so that you can take your stand against the devil's schemes" (Eph. 6:11). The Roman army of the day was a highly trained and disciplined force. Paul points to that as an example of the people of God in the spiritual realm. There is an enemy that opposes the justice and compassion of the kingdom of God, an enemy that wills our destruction. But God casts out the dark powers through the witness of the church and liberates people to fulfill their divine calling (Matt. 12:28). Being the church is a serious matter. There is a lot at stake. In this context spiritual discipline takes on a sense of urgency, especially on the edge of the church's mission to the world. Similar to the military is the athletic model of the church. "I strike a blow to my body and make it my slave so that after I have preached to others, I myself will not be disqualified for the prize" (1 Cor. 9:27). Spiritual discipline is meant to make us spiritual athletes. The chief prize is Christ himself. Referring to his accomplishments as a leader in the Jewish religion, Paul writes, "I consider everything a loss because of the surpassing worth of knowing Christ Jesus my Lord, for whose sake I have lost all things. I consider them garbage, that I may gain Christ" (Phil. 3:8). There is no higher prize. Of course, we do not win Christ through our own merits. He is a gift above all else, but one that we will gladly give all to possess. We must "throw off everything that hinders and the sin that so easily entangles. And let us run with perseverance the race marked out for us, fixing our eyes on Jesus, the pioneer and perfecter of faith" (Heb. 12:1–2).

In all these models, there is an important coming together of indicative and imperative, gift and work. Paul writes, "You are God's field" (1 Cor. 3:9). But Jesus says that his followers must bear fruit, as if saying, "Now *be* that field of plants!" Likewise, Paul insists that we are Christ's body (1 Cor. 12:27), but then he tells us how to live like it—glorifying Christ, edifying one another, conforming to divine love. Peter says that we are the temple of the Spirit but then tells us to be a holy priesthood, offering ourselves as spiritual sacrifices to God (1 Pet. 2:5). It is as if the Bible is saying, "You are this by grace; now live like it—grow toward it! You are the church; now be the church!"

Practices

The church is born at Pentecost in the outpouring of the Spirit, with practices such as proclamation; the sacraments (i.e., baptism and the Lord's Supper); spiritual gifts, including the ministry of oversight; and mission. These practices were not simply chosen by the church. It was not as if the churches gathered after Pentecost and voted on which practices would be best for them. Christ founded the church with these practices, and the Spirit gives birth to the church with these practices in place. This is how believers will be the church and do church.

With these practices established, the church becomes the instrument of Christ and his Spirit in the world. The church does not have the power to mediate God. *God self-mediates*. Indeed, "there is one God and one mediator between God and mankind, the man Christ Jesus" (1 Tim. 2:5). Christ mediates in and through the Spirit. The church serves God's self-mediation in the world by acting as God's instruments. Even Scripture is instrumental, though it is the chief and most authoritative instrument of the Lord's self-giving through the Spirit. This means that the church's chief role is that of a witness. Writing of the glory of Christ's self-giving through the Spirit, Paul asserts of the church, "We have this treasure in jars of clay to show that this all-surpassing power is from God and not from us" (2 Cor. 4:7).

The kingdom of God in the world is God's sovereign reign brought to bear on creation through the mediation of Christ and in the presence of the Spirit. Jesus says, "If it is by the Spirit of God that I drive out demons, then the kingdom of God has come upon you" (Matt. 12:28). The kingdom is not a place or an institution; it is *God* present and active to set people free and make all things new. The kingdom of God is both now and not yet. It is like a mustard seed that is planted in the soil and will grow into a tree (13:31–32). Above all else, the church seeks the liberation, mercy, and righteousness of the kingdom in the world (6:33). When Paul deals with the controversy over food laws between Jewish and gentile believers, he reminds both sides of what is truly essential to the life of the church: "For the kingdom of God is not a matter of eating and drinking, but of righteousness, peace and joy in the Holy Spirit" (Rom. 14:17). The kingdom of God takes priority in the church.

The church must prioritize the kingdom in all that it does. The church is the chief sign and instrument of the kingdom. The practices of the church aid in the church's signification and instrumentality.

Proclamation is one such practice. It is necessary to the life of the church. Christ is himself the Word of the Father in flesh in the power of the Spirit (Luke 1:35; John 1:14). Christ in his resurrection is the proclamation in flesh of the Father's love. As his body in the power of the Spirit, the church bears witness to him. The Scripture is Christ's chief witness. So the church seeks to bear witness to Christ in obedience to Scripture. As the lead witness to Christ in the church, the Scriptures are the canon, the living measure of the church's life and witness. Christ speaks through the proclamation of the church; his Spirit is the voice through which he speaks: "Whoever has ears, let them hear what the Spirit says to the churches" (Rev. 2:17). The whole church participates in proclamation: "Instead, speaking the truth in love, we will grow to become in every respect the mature body of him who is the head, that is, Christ" (Eph. 4:15). But there are also pastors who are ordained to preach before the congregation or to lead in the church's proclamation. Timothy, a young pastor, needed experience. He required Paul to give him courage to continue practicing: "Until I come, devote yourself to the public reading of Scripture, to preaching and to teaching. Do not neglect your gift, which was given you through prophecy when the body of elders laid their hands on you. Be diligent in these matters; give yourself wholly to them, so that everyone may see your progress" (1 Tim. 4:13–15). When Paul wrote later, Timothy still needed reminding not to neglect his gift to preach and to teach (2 Tim. 1:6). He needed to lean on the Spirit-inspired text as the strong arm of his ministry (3:14–17).

Christ is not only the Word of the Father in flesh, crucified and risen, the living Word among all forms of proclamation in the church; Christ, in his Spirit-sanctified and glorified flesh, is also the sacrament of the church. It is he who is present and celebrated in the Spirit in both baptism and the Lord's Supper. The **sacraments** (or ordinances) of the church are observed in unison. They are not private but public and open to all who believe in the Lord. They celebrate and witness to the church's *union* (baptism) and then *communion* (the Lord's Supper) with Christ in the Spirit and by faith. Christ commissioned his disciples to disciple all nations, "baptizing them in the name of the Father and of the Son and of the Holy Spirit" (Matt. 28:19). Baptism is mentioned here as important to the beginnings of discipleship, which also includes teaching them all that Christ had commanded (v. 20). Catechism and baptism are thus part of the church's evangelistic commission. Christ promised to be with his church in this mission "to the very end of the age"

(v. 20) and, one could add, to the ends of the earth (Acts 1:8)! The early church also baptized in Jesus's name (Acts 2:38), which may have also included the trinitarian reference as well. I myself was baptized "in the name of Jesus Christ for the remission of sins, in the name of the Father, the Son, and the Holy Spirit." The two formulae are not to be viewed as inconsistent with each other, since the name of Jesus Christ cannot be viewed apart from the names of the trinitarian persons. Jesus Christ is the Son of the Father and is anointed by the Spirit. How can one utter the name of Christ while leaving out the Father and the Spirit? Theologically, the name of Christ is shorthand for the name of the triune God. The name of Christ was most likely accented in Acts (e.g., 4:12) due to the fact that baptism done under his authority was being contrasted with the older baptism under the authority or commission of John the Baptist.

Baptism is the rite of union with Christ in the Spirit and by faith. It is not ordinarily the place where regeneration occurs or the Holy Spirit is received, since that takes place at the moment of one's initial expression of faith in Christ (Gal. 3:2). The household of Cornelius is cleansed and accepted by God before being baptized in water (Acts 10:44–47; 15:8–9). Indeed, one cannot even belong to Christ without the Holy Spirit (Rom. 8:9). Water baptism is still important, though, since it is a public witness of one's union with Christ that confirms and deepens one's faith commitment. In Romans 6, believers in baptism dramatize in public their prior act of putting to death the old self, which is ruled by sin and death and condemned (v. 6). They symbolize a baptism into *Christ's* death, which conquers sin and death and leads to glory (v. 4). We rise from the water in newness of life, looking forward to resurrection. "For if we have been united with him in a death like his, we will certainly also be united with him in a resurrection like his" (v. 5). Paul reminds the Romans that they are not to take sin lightly (vv. 1–2). He tells them that they have been baptized in water to symbolize repentance, in celebration of the new life granted us by Christ and in the Spirit. Let us live that way! In Matthew 28:19, one even gets the feeling that baptism is like a commissioning ceremony of Christians for their service to the kingdom of God. Jesus starts by declaring that all sovereign authority belongs to him and then commissions the disciples to make disciples of all nations, baptizing them under the name or sovereign authority of the triune God and teaching them to obey all that Christ commanded. There is a ring to this passage of a military commission. I like to call baptism the ordination and commissioning service of all Christians. Yes, baptism is indeed a celebration of our union with Christ as a gift of God. But it also a commissioning for our service to Christ and his mission in the world.

In light of the above discussion, pedobaptism, or infant baptism, appears incomplete because it does not involve the repentance and faith that are symbolized by the baptismal rite as it is described in the New Testament. Infant baptism has the value of celebrating and welcoming a very young and precious life into Christ and the family of God. And that certainly has value. But baptism as presented here needs more. In the New Testament, baptism brings to expression one's repentance and faith. The biblical argument for infant baptism has therefore not been strong. The World Council of Churches Faith and Order Commission admits as much: "While the possibility that infant baptism was also practiced in the apostolic age cannot be excluded, baptism upon personal profession of faith is the most clearly attested pattern in the New Testament documents."[14] The argument is often made in favor of infant baptism by identifying it as the New Testament fulfillment of Old Testament circumcision, which was applied to infant males. This passage is used for support: "In him you were also circumcised with a circumcision not performed by human hands. Your whole self ruled by the flesh was put off when you were circumcised by Christ, having been buried with him in baptism, in which you were also raised with him through your faith in the working of God, who raised him from the dead" (Col. 2:11–12).

There is indeed a connection between baptism and circumcision here. But circumcision is used figuratively as a symbol of heartfelt repentance and faith, as with the admonition in Deuteronomy 10:16: "Circumcise therefore the foreskin of your heart, and be no longer stubborn" (ESV). The term "circumcision" used in this way is applied to the exercise of repentance and faith: "You were also raised with him through your faith." The fact that the above passage can be fully understood without a reference to infants seems obvious to me.

The theological support for infant baptism is more interesting to me. The great reformer Martin Luther stressed the fact that faith is required for the gospel to be received and for the rituals of the church to be effective. One would think that he would therefore have sided with the Anabaptists (who rejected infant baptism) in affirming believer's baptism. But he didn't. Instead, he offered two major theological arguments in support of it. First, he argued that infants do exercise a faith of sorts. In their simplistic and very primitive dependence on God, they give evidence of faith, in all of its weakness and fragility. Second, and tied to this, is the emphasis of infant baptism on the objectivity and overwhelming strength of God's grace. The faith of the infant is weak, but the strength of God's grace that accepts the infant is *strong* and

14. Faith and Order Commission, *Baptism, Eucharist and Ministry*, Faith and Order Paper 111 (Geneva: World Council of Churches, 1982), 3.

more than sufficient. Luther claims to be able to say in times of trial, "Bapti-
zatus sum!" ("I have been baptized!").[15] Reformed theologian G. C. Berkouwer
agrees. In defense of infant baptism, he notes, "This grace precedes all human
activity, and one can certainly see in infant baptism that the covenant is not a
matter of God and man facing each other as equal parties. The efficacy and
certainty of the promise certainly do not issue from human activity."[16]

I find this line of argumentation to be the most compelling case that can
be made for infant baptism, and I have no doubt that child dedication does
indeed carry such meanings. But baptism as a rite of union with Christ by
faith requires greater balance. True, grace is all encompassing and is the
dominant element in our relationship with Christ. But Luther's argument
reduces faith to near insignificance, which is unexpected given his role as the
great defender of justification by faith alone. I do think that the combina-
tion of infant baptism and a genuine confession of faith given later would
essentially constitute what baptism in the New Testament signifies, though
I would still find it ideal that the child, after receiving Christ as Lord and
Savior, undergoes believer's baptism.

If baptism is the rite of *union* with Christ, the Lord's Supper is the rite
of ongoing *communion*. Baptism ordinarily occurs once since it celebrates
a once-and-for-all union with Christ by faith. The Lord's Supper, which ordinarily follows baptism, is ongoing and repeated many times, because it is
the rite of ongoing communion with our Lord. The church is indeed a communion of saints, so there is something about the Lord's Supper that brings
to ritual expression who we are as the church. The Lord's Supper is anchored
in Christ's Last Supper with his disciples. The words of institution that Jesus
spoke at that meal are repeated every time we practice communion today. After
breaking the bread, Christ said, "This is my body, which is for you; do this
in remembrance of me." After offering the cup, he said, "This cup is the new
covenant in my blood; do this, whenever you drink it, in remembrance of me"
(1 Cor. 11:24–25). The bread (broken body) and the wine (spilled blood) are
not two separate things; they arguably signify the same thing, self-giving love
that is given unconditionally and thoroughly. To be more exact, they signify
the crucified and risen Christ bringing us to a deep awareness once again of
his self-giving for us and beckoning us to communion. It is fitting that we
invoke the Spirit as the one who works on us through the meal to bring about
the remembrance and communion.

15. See Jaroslav Pelikan, *Spirit versus Structure: Luther and the Institutions of the Church*
(London: Collins, 1968), 96–97.
16. G. C. Berkouwer, *The Sacraments: Luther and the Institutions of the Church* (London:
Collins, 1968), 184.

Communion has indeed become an important concept in overcoming past divisions over the meaning of the sacred meal. The Catholic Church has classically called Christ's presence in the bread and wine as coming through a **transubstantiation** of these elements. This teaching holds that when the sacred meal is consecrated, its inner substance is mysteriously transformed into the body of Christ and the inner substance of the wine into Christ's blood. Of course, the outward form of the meal remains bread and wine. More recent Catholic theology has tended to move more in the direction of explaining Christ's presence in personal rather than metaphysical (or substance) categories. Catholic theologian Karl Rahner, for example, views the elements (bread and wine) of the Lord's Supper as the "words" or proclamation through which Christ is really present to commune with us.[17] Some have called this approach to the Lord's Supper **transignification**, focusing on the sign value of the meal. As a hug makes one's love present to someone, so also the sign of the bread and wine makes Christ present to us.

Luther held to a view of the Lord's Supper called **consubstantiation**, meaning that the Lord's body is really present "with" the meal but not "as" the substance of the elements. Luther believed that the Lord's body is so deified in exaltation that it becomes universally present and may accompany the Lord's Supper wherever it is celebrated. He did not like the idea of the Lord's body *becoming* bread and wine, for that would place him at the disposal of the priests, who can distribute him at will. The idea that the Lord accompanies the elements seemed to Luther to preserve divine freedom.

John Calvin viewed the Lord's Supper as an event of the Holy Spirit by which we experience *elevation* to heavenly places to communion with Christ and to be nourished from his spiritual fullness. Rather than the Lord coming to us in the elements, the elements facilitate our access to Christ at the right hand of the Father. Swiss reformer Huldrych Zwingli also believed in the Spirit's involvement in the Lord's Supper, but he held to what may be termed a *memorial* view of the meal, since it accented the believer's *remembrance* of the Lord at the meal, a deep remembrance that takes us to the event of Christ's self-giving. The Anabaptists stressed the church's *discipleship* commitment during the meal to pick up their crosses and follow after Christ in life. Relatively recently, Geoffrey Wainwright has shifted the emphasis from the presence of Christ in the meal to the ultimate communion that we will have in Christ's presence, of which the meal grants us a foretaste.[18] The role of the

17. See Karl Rahner, "The Theology of the Symbol," in *Theological Investigations* (New York: Seabury, 1982), 4:221–52.

18. Geoffrey Wainwright, *Eucharist and Eschatology* (New York: Oxford University Press, 1981), 7–17.

Spirit is important to all these accents: divine embrace, elevated communion, remembrance, and hope. Also worth mentioning is the rite of footwashing that occurred historically after baptism as a preparation for the Lord's Supper. John Christopher Thomas argues persuasively that John 13 conveys the intention that this practice remain as part of the church's sacramental ordinances to extend the symbol of baptismal cleansing and set up the servant commitment implied in eucharistic communion.[19]

Ministry involves the entire church. Baptism is the ordination ceremony of every Christian for service. "From him the whole body, joined and held together by every supporting ligament, grows and builds itself up in love, as each part does its work" (Eph. 4:16). Using the universality of the ministry as our starting point, we can move from there to understand those who are ordained to ministries of leadership and oversight. If we start with the latter, we may be drawn to a clerical view of "the ministry," which consists of those who have a special ordination for leadership, while the "laity" takes a passive role. "Laypeople" become merely the ones to whom the ministry is directed. Church services are often arranged to foster this impression. This is not what the church is meant to be. It is rather an accommodation to consumer society, a church that has conformed to its cultural environment.

But there *are* people who receive ordination to function as leaders and to engage in oversight of congregations. They are "ministers of ministers," so to speak. Timothy, for example, was ordained under the laying on of hands by a "presbytery" or body of "elders" (or presbyters). Paul writes to Timothy, "Until I come, devote yourself to the public reading of Scripture, to preaching and to teaching. Do not neglect your gift, which was given you through prophecy when the body of elders laid their hands on you" (1 Tim. 4:13–14). The phrase "body of elders" in this text (πρεσβυτερίου, or *presbyteriou*) most likely refers to a board of pastoral leaders who led house churches (the predominant form of church in those days). The question becomes, Who is the "overseer" (ἐπίσκοπή, or *episkopē*) mentioned in the previous chapter, in 1 Timothy 3:1–2? Some think it refers to those who exercised oversight over regions or clusters of congregations, having authority over the elders who ordained Timothy, according to 1 Timothy 4:13–14. But that may be reading a later development back into the text. It is more likely that "overseer" is simply another term for "elder."

A century later, however, such a distinction did exist: the overseers were bishops who did indeed exercise oversight over regions of elders or presbyters,

19. John Christopher Thomas, *Footwashing in John 13 and the Johannine Community*, 2nd ed. (Cleveland, TN: CPT Press, 2014), esp. 150–91.

who functioned to pastor local churches with the assistance of deacons. The early structure of leadership included bishops, presbyters (elders/pastors), and deacons. This understanding of the evolution of ecclesiastical authority undermines the argument called **apostolic succession**—namely, that there was an unbroken chain of episcopal authority stretching from the apostles of Jesus to the modern-day bishops of the church. But even those who concede that such an unbroken chain cannot be justified may be quick to add that bishops do come into being as early as the second century, playing an important role in both the canonization of the Bible and the formation of early creeds. Is it the case that the church cannot do without this office? If so, one could shift the argument for succession to *irreversibility* when it comes to the office of the bishop—namely, we cannot revert to a time before bishops existed. They have proved to be indispensable to the church.

Catholic, Anglican, and Eastern Orthodox churches regard the office of the bishop as indeed essential to the church. Bishops link the church to the foundation of the apostles (Eph. 2:20) and secure the church's unity. Protestant churches (besides the Anglicans) may have bishops but would not typically regard them as essential (*esse*) to the life of the church; only Christ is essential. For them, bishops are for the good (*bene esse*) of the church. This approach to the church is no doubt connected to the fact that Protestantism regarded the bishops of the Catholic Church as largely having failed to sufficiently defend the faith of the church, leading the "exiled" Protestant churches to live (at least for a while) without bishops (or episcopal oversight). These churches still thrived as churches because Christ was among them in the presence of the Spirit, especially through the instrumentality of Word and sacrament. This has led most Protestants to say, as I just did, that the church is the church through the presence of Christ in the Spirit, through the instrumentality of proclamation and sacraments.

The Catholic Church views the church as a global society under the head of the Petrine office, or the office of the pope. Eastern Orthodox churches view the church rather as the local church, by which they mean a regional cluster of churches under the head of a single bishop. The Eastern churches cherish consensus among the bishops when it comes to matters of crucial importance to the church's unity, whereas the Catholic Church, though also valuing consensus, looks to a single head (the pope) as the ultimate source of guidance and the focal point of unity. Peter holds a place of honor in the Catholic Church as the first to hold the papal office, which is thus also called the Petrine office in his honor. Catholics regard Matthew 16:18 as key here: "I tell you that you are Peter, and on this rock I will build my church, and the gates of Hades will not overcome it." Peter's name literally means "rock"

(Πέτρος, or *Petros*). So when Jesus says "You are Peter, and on this rock I will build my church," the natural reading is that he is building his church on Peter's shoulders.

Protestant efforts to remove Peter entirely from this "rock" on which the church is built have not been entirely successful, in my view, as the Protestant New Testament scholar Oscar Cullmann has helped me to see.[20] But this building the church on Peter requires careful qualification from the context of the verse. First, Peter has just confessed Jesus as Messiah. "You are the Messiah, the Son of the living God" (Matt. 16:16). It seems clear that the "rock" signified by Peter's name was Peter, the one who genuinely confesses Christ as Messiah and Lord with the totality of his life. It is such a life that now functions as a living confession of Christ; *that* is the rock Christ will use as a foundation stone on which to begin building his church. Second, Peter is not alone in being such a rock. The binding and loosing that Peter will do as such a rock (v. 19) is opened to the other disciples as well only two chapters later (18:18). This binding and loosing may refer to binding the dark powers and liberating people from their hold. Ephesians 2:20 notes that the church is "built on the foundation of the apostles." Peter was perhaps "first among equals" (i.e., among the disciples) in serving such a foundational role in the life of the church. But he was first among *equals*. Moreover, Christ is the only true foundation; apostles stand out as "foundational," but they are not *the* foundation. Only Christ is that. But the apostles (including the twelve and perhaps Paul and James the brother of Jesus) are foundational because their Spirit-inspired preaching fed and guided the formation of the New Testament canon, and their message through the canon (rather than the office of the bishop) is *primarily* that which continues to guide the church in its apostolic identity and witness down through the centuries.

It is important to note before leaving this topic that the pope in Catholic theology is not in himself infallible. When he speaks under the influence of his gift from the chair of Peter, he may do so infallibly. Even if his judgment is not designated as such, it is still to be regarded as significant for the guidance of the church. Swiss Catholic theologian Hans Küng became quite controversial when he wrote his book *Infallible? An Inquiry* in rejection of infallibility with regard to the pope.[21] Recent Catholic theology, while not backing off from the supreme authority granted to the pope in the Catholic Church, has shifted the emphasis to the pope as a humble servant to the global church,

---

20. Oscar Cullmann, *Peter: Disciple, Apostle, Martyr* (Waco: Baylor University Press, 2011), 164–217.

21. He would apply this criticism to Scripture as well. See Hans Küng, *Infallible? An Inquiry* (San Francisco: Collins, 1971).

including non-Catholic Christians. Pope John Paul II's May 25, 1995, encyc-
lical, *Ut unum sint* (*That They May Be One*), served as the impetus for this
trend. While Protestants would not grant any one office or person that kind
of authority (that is, other than Christ), they can still appreciate, support,
and pray for the gospel leadership that comes from any high-profile Christian
leader.

Lastly, the church is also a mission. When Christ appears to the disciples on
the eve of his resurrection, his message is clear: "As the Father has sent me, I
am sending you" (John 20:21). The church, from its earliest beginnings in front
of the risen Christ, is made up of sent ones, those sent in the power of the
Spirit to be instruments of Christ's mission in the world. In Acts 1, the risen
Christ teaches his followers about the kingdom of God, which provokes the
question "Lord, are you at this time going to restore the kingdom to Israel?"
(v. 6; cf. vv. 1–5). Christ replies that it is not for them to know what the Father
has planned for the latter days. But their task until the end is to be witnesses
in the power of the Spirit to all nations, to the very ends of the earth (vv. 7–8).
In other words, the end will not come, Israel will not be restored to its Messiah, and the kingdom of God on earth will not be fulfilled until the mission
to the nations is accomplished. There's a lot to do!

Marks of the Church

One last point still worth mentioning has to do with the marks of the church.
The Nicene Creed, which affirms Christ's deity, also refers to the church as
"one, holy, catholic, and apostolic." That the church is one, meaning the
unity of the church, is the chief mark. This unity is not only to be experienced
within a local congregation, though it is to be experienced primarily there.
Paul tells us what undergirds this unity: "Make every effort to keep the unity
of the Spirit through the bond of peace. There is one body and one Spirit,
just as you were called to one hope when you were called; one Lord, one faith,
one baptism; one God and Father of all, who is over all and through all and
in all" (Eph. 4:3–6). The one God secures the unity of the church. The fact
that we are one body in one Spirit prohibits warring factions in the church.
The same may be said of Christ as one Lord and of the fact that there is only
one Father. There is also one hope, one faith, one baptism. In short, the God
who saves us is one, and the life that God grants us is one. The consequence of
this all is that we make "every effort" to keep the unity that the Spirit grants
us. It is as if unity is a precious gift that we are to cherish and preserve to the
best of our abilities. In the face of a possible division, we are compelled to

ask, "Have we done everything we can to preserve our unity?" In the 1964 Vatican II decree *Unitatis redintegratio*, the Catholic Church accepts non-Catholic Christians as "separated brethren," as Christians who are tied to the Catholic Church in important ways: "Though we believe them to be deficient in some respects, [they] have been by no means deprived of significance and importance in the mystery of salvation. For the Spirit of Christ has not refrained from using them as means of salvation which derive their efficacy from the very fullness of grace and truth entrusted to the Church."[22] Other church bodies have also taken important steps toward some degree of unity in the modern era. It is a new day. Since communion can be experienced on different levels (faith, ministry, mission), a meaningful degree of unity can be had even among divided churches.

Paul does not say that division is never warranted. If anyone in the church forsakes a point of faith that is essential to the gospel, such as the deity of Christ or salvation by grace, there is no longer "one faith" of which to speak. The key issue becomes whether a point of dispute is "church dividing." The ecumenical movement has addressed this issue. The term "ecumenical" comes from the Greek οἰκουμένη (or *oikoumenē*), which refers to the inhabited world. In the church world, it has to do with respecting the church's catholicity or universality, being willing to preserve widespread unity among all Christians and church families or denominations, beyond the boundaries of a local congregation. The ecumenical movement has dealt with the question of whether a point of doctrine is church dividing under the heading of the **hierarchy of truth**. All truths are important, but not all truths carry the same weight. A difference of opinion over tithing or footwashing would not, in my view, be weighty enough to be church dividing. Tolerance is to be exercised toward those who disagree. These kinds of issues would be low in significance in the hierarchy of truth. But an issue like the deity of Christ is very high in the hierarchy, since it has to do with the lordship of Christ and the legitimacy of regarding him as Savior and as an object of worship. A difference over that point would be church dividing in significance. But, second, there is also a hierarchy of truth when it comes to how a single doctrine is explained. Some explanations include points that are low in the hierarchy of truth that constitutes a given doctrine, whereas some are higher up. So with regard to the deity of Christ, all might legitimately say that Christ embodied divine love or was the "parable" of divine love in flesh. But is this explanation sufficient to capture what it means to call Christ "divine"? Such an explanation may

22. Second Vatican Council, *Unitatis redintegratio* (Rome: The Holy See, 1964), chap. 1, sec. 3.

be low on the list of points to make when explaining this doctrine, not high enough to preserve our unity around this doctrine. So a church's leadership might raise additional points that are even higher up in significance. They might mention that the Son of God is fully divine in "nature" and not just "function," being eternally *essential* to God. Or they might add that Christ is indispensable to God's self-giving and act of salvation. If a faction disagrees with all of this and only wants to stick with saying that Jesus reveals divine love in flesh, the leadership might point out that other figures may be said to reveal divine love as well. Such is not unique to Jesus! This point alone does not make Jesus indispensable to God or divine salvation. Christ could still feasibly be replaceable in the faith of the church. So just saying that everyone agrees with a doctrine is not enough. A church should specify which points in the hierarchy of explanations must be included for a certain doctrine. There should remain some flexibility as to how people choose to explain things, some room for creativity. But if there are points that need to be said, the church should spell these out, noting that at least the substance of these points should be i ncluded.

How is the unity of the global church to be understood? Croatian theologian Miroslav Volf has written a brilliant ecclesiology, *After Our Likeness*, which makes a strong case for local-church unity. Global unity in his view is unattainable in time. It is an eschatological goal that is only realizable in the communion of saints in eternity. Any effort to secure it now will result in overreach (an overly realized eschatology). Local churches are to remain "open" to each other as representatives of one body and willing, in different ways, to signify together their eschatological unity. But that is the most we can do outside of local-church unity.[23] Yet dare we be bolder than this? It is impossible to form a world church this side of eternity; Volf's warning should be heeded here. Yet can we not still make every effort to form visible alliances, expressing common faith and sharing in common life, so that the world will know that Christ is Lord among us all and that we are bound to each other in his love? A many-branched tree still has a visibly shared life! The unity that is a gift from God is also a challenge to be enhanced and preserved. Koinonia, or communion, exists on different levels (faith, worship, life witness, etc.). Are we doing what we can to experience at least a degree of koinonia in a way that the world can see? Are we meeting this challenge? In part, the credibility of our witness before the world depends on it.

23. Miroslav Volf, *After Our Likeness: The Church as the Image of the Trinity* (Grand Rapids: Eerdmans, 1997), 225–26.

FINAL REFLECTIONS

The church is a gift granted by the Father, through Christ, and in the outpouring of the Spirit. It is both local and global, both existing in time and headed for an eternal, eschatological fulfillment in a final communion of saints, around which the new creation will be formed. The church is the elect people who are adopted into the elect Christ, sharing in the benefits of his elect sonship through the Holy Spirit and by faith. Though the corporate election of Israel and the nations in Christ is ordained (predestined) by God, individual participation (or actualization) of it depends also on faith. The mission of the Spirit-empowered church is thus at the cutting edge of the expanding boundary of election in the world. The church proclaims the gospel as an instrument of the Word of the Father in flesh; the church partakes of the sacraments as occasions by which it partakes of Christ, the Sacrament of the Spirit to all flesh. We do not mediate God, but we are privileged to be instruments of God's self-mediation, witnesses through which and beyond which God acts in the world to save. All the models of the church are shown to be both a gift and a challenge, which must be taken up by the power of God among all Christians, bar none. This includes the unity of the church, for which we are to strive in our shared life and witness together. We all are Christ's varied family. Let us live this way.

TOPICS FOR REVIEW

1. What is election according to Calvin? To Arminius? To Barth?
2. What is election in Romans 9 and 11?
3. Choose one of the models of the church and thoroughly describe it.
4. Choose one church practice (e.g., proclamation, baptism, or the Lord's Supper) and thoroughly describe it.
5. Explain the issue of ministry in the New Testament for all members and for ordained ministers.
6. What are the roles of the bishop in the different churches and of the pope in the Catholic Church?
7. Thoroughly explain the issue of the church's unity.

6

FINAL PURPOSES

Eschatology literally means "the study of the end." But the term "the end" here does not mean "conclusion" but rather "telos" or "end" in the sense of ultimate purpose. Thus, I have titled this chapter "Final Purposes." Theologians used to call eschatology the study of the "end times." In speaking of God's final purposes for history, Christ did indeed speak of the "times or dates the Father has set by his own authority" (Acts 1:7). So there is such a thing as "end times." But Christ admonished his disciples not to fixate on when and how these "times" will come to their end or, better, how their fulfillment will occur in the arrival of God's kingdom on earth. He commanded the disciples to concentrate instead on bearing witness to all nations, to the very ends of the earth (v. 8). It has thus become apparent that eschatology is not fundamentally about mapping out end-time events or times but rather about hope and courageous witness in the midst of all circumstances. It is the conviction that God has final purposes in Christ and the outpouring of the Spirit that will indeed be fulfilled. The Spirit who is poured out in the latter days will bring the victory of Christ (and of the Father's love) to ultimate fulfillment by conforming all things to Christ's glorious image (2:17–21). So the emphasis on eschatology in theological discussion has shifted from a concern over "end times" to a living and active hope that permeates life in the present, concerning all that God is doing and will do to fulfill the kingdom of God on earth.

Faith is indeed oriented toward such a hope. "Now faith is confidence in what we hope for and assurance about what we do not see" (Heb. 11:1).

Rather than eschatology merely functioning as the last chapter of a systematic theology, it is really the burning hope that informs *all* areas of theology. It sets us at odds with the status quo and inspires action to change the present in hope for the **new creation** that God is going to bring to the earth (that he is already bringing in the work of the Spirit). As Jürgen Moltmann writes in his provocative classic *Theology of Hope*, "Christianity is eschatology, is hope, forward looking and forward moving, and therefore also revolutionizing and transforming the present. The eschatological is not one element *of* Christianity, but it is the medium of Christian faith as such, the key in which everything in it is set, the glow that suffuses everything here in the dawn of an expected new day."[1] He contrasts this radical vision of the biblical God with the Platonic God of the "eternal present," which tends to justify the status quo.[2] In response to this trend, Amos Yong has even written a systematic theology with eschatology as the *first* chapter![3] This is certainly one way of making the point.

When it comes to eschatology, the challenge we always face is that the final fulfillment of divine purposes for history has not yet happened. All that we have in the present moment is a "guarantee" in the form of a down payment in the life of the Spirit (2 Cor. 5:4–5), a mere glimpse of the exalted Christ through the eye of faith as if looking into a dim mirror (1 Cor. 13:12). We await the time when in resurrection we are "swallowed up by life" (2 Cor. 5:4) and the kingdom of God brings final mercy and justice to the earth. How can we imagine such things now? Anglican bishop and New Testament scholar N. T. Wright rightly notes that "all Christian language about the future is a set of signposts pointing into a mist."[4] By focusing theology on Pentecost, we can discuss the fulfillment of Christ's mission and look forward in hope to the ultimate fulfillment that is yet to come. We can make preliminary remarks based on that event in light of the totality of the scriptural message about what this end will consist of, but we admit all along the way that we are approaching one of the most uncertain and mysterious areas of theology. We rejoice at the down payment of the Spirit's presence and work in our lives and at the signposts of divine mercy and justice in the world. But the fullness yet to come is still outside of our grasp.

1. Jürgen Moltmann, *Theology of Hope: On the Ground and the Implications of a Christian Eschatology*, trans. James W. Leitch (New York: Harper & Row, 1967), 16 (emphasis original).
2. Moltmann, *Theology of Hope*, 29.
3. Amos Yong, *Renewing Christian Theology: Systematics for a Global Christianity* (Waco: Baylor University Press, 2014).
4. N. T. Wright, *Surprised by Hope: Rethinking Heaven, the Resurrection, and the Mission of the Church* (San Francisco: HarperOne, 2008), 132.

Christ and Death

Christ is the focal point of eschatology. Indeed, Paul tells us that "all things have been created in him and for him" (Col. 1:16). If all things are created "for him," it stands to reason that all things will find their fulfillment only in him. This is what the New Testament says in so many words. "When the times reach their fulfillment," Paul writes, God will "bring unity to all things in heaven and on earth under Christ" (Eph. 1:10). Eschatology is the victory of Jesus Christ in all of creation; it is not primarily about "end times" but about the ultimate purposes to be found and fulfilled in and through *him*. The raising and exaltation of the crucified Christ is the decisive event that inaugurates the raising and exaltation of all things in him. The Spirit is involved in the raising and exaltation of Christ (Rom. 1:4), and Christ's pouring forth of the Spirit at Pentecost will eventually grant the exalted Christ eschatological significance and fulfillment. Christ in the Spirit will, in the end, have the exalted church as his body extended by the renewal of all things in his image. All of creation in the Spirit will sing his praises as the Lord of all.

> Then I heard every creature in heaven and on earth and under the earth and on the sea, and all that is in them, saying:
>
> > "To him who sits on the throne and to the Lamb
> > be praise and honor and glory and power,
> > for ever and ever!" (Rev. 5:13)

In waiting for the coming kingdom of God, we are waiting first and foremost on *Christ*, not primarily on end times or on world peace or on human fulfillment, as important and joyous as these things are among Christ's benefits. Christianity is first and foremost a relationship with Christ; his benefits are secondary. Eschatology is caught up in knowing *him*: "I want to know Christ—yes, to know the power of his resurrection and participation in his sufferings, becoming like him in his death, and so, somehow, attaining to the resurrection from the dead" (Phil. 3:10–11).

Eschatology through Christ and in the Spirit is both individual (life after death) and corporate (resurrection and new heaven and new earth—what N. T. Wright calls life *after* life after death).[5] Of course, the two dimensions overlap since we participate in God's final purposes in Christ both as individuals and as a church. We will discuss life after death first. Life after death for the believer revolves around the departure from one's body so as to be with

5. Wright, *Surprised by Hope*, 197.

Christ. While Paul lay chained and imprisoned, he was not sure that he would make it out alive. He took comfort from the fact that fellow Christians were praying for his deliverance (Phil. 1:19). But he was ready to die if need be "so that now as always Christ will be exalted in my body, whether by life or by death" (v. 20). For Paul, life and death are simply two means by which he can bear witness to Christ and be conformed to his image: "For to me, to live is Christ and to die is gain" (v. 21). Dying is gain for Paul because at death he departs to be with Christ, "which is better by far" (v. 23). But since remaining in the flesh is for the betterment of those who need him, Paul writes, "It is more necessary for you that I remain in the body" (v. 24). For this reason, he strives to live on in the body.

This life certainly has its joys, though for some people hardships can seem overwhelming. Wishing for longevity has its place in the life of faith, but so does helping those who are less fortunate than we are. God wills that we should never live under the terror of death, for Christ has delivered us from it (Heb. 2:14).

> Where, O death, is your victory?
> Where, O death, is your sting? (1 Cor. 15:55)

Here Paul makes it clear that our victory over death is assured because we belong to the risen Christ. He also makes it clear that nothing, not even death, can separate us from Christ or from the love of God that binds us to him in the Spirit. "For I am convinced that neither death nor life, neither angels nor demons, neither the present nor the future, nor any powers, neither height nor depth, nor anything else in all creation, will be able to separate us from the love of God that is in Christ Jesus our Lord" (Rom. 8:38–39). As Paul writes elsewhere in Romans, "If we live, we live for the Lord; and if we die, we die for the Lord. So, whether we live or die, we belong to the Lord" (14:8). Christ's Spirit, granted to us by Christ, unites us to Christ and is also the guarantee that "he who raised Christ from the dead will also give life to your mortal bodies" (Rom. 8:11).

Life after death is life with Christ. It is also life in the communion of saints in and with Christ. We are his body. At death, we go to be with Christ in *heaven.* John 14:1–3 is the key text. Christ tells his disciples that one day he will claim them all at their point of death as his own. He will claim them for himself at his Father's "house," or heaven, where the Father's will is perfectly done and God's presence is perfectly felt (cf. Matt. 6:10). This is the space of the love between the Father and the Son (John 14:23), the space of the Spirit. John 14:1–3 tells us about Christ's claiming us as his own at our death: "Do not let your hearts be troubled. You believe in God; believe also in me. My Father's house has many rooms; if that were not so, would I have told you that I am going there to prepare a place for you? And if I go and prepare a place for you, I will come back and take you to be with me that you also may be where I am." Notice that heaven has as its chief and all-encompassing benefit being in the presence of Christ: "that you also may be where I am." The Father's house has "many rooms"—or, if you will, rooms to spare. God has indeed opened the divine embrace to the entire world (3:16). That embrace will never be filled, for there is infinite room for love in the wide-open spaces of triune communion. Heaven is thus not a literal house or cluster of houses but rather the presence of God, concentrated in a dimension of existence outside of our own and yet experienced to a degree by us in the Spirit. There is no way of reaching heaven by flying outward into space, even if we had the means of reaching the edge of the cosmos.

The term "rooms" or "dwelling places" in the original Greek (μοναί, or *monai*) was translated as *mansiones* (meaning "places for lodging") in the Latin (Vulgate) translation of the early Middle Ages. This translation influenced the King James Version, which misleadingly translated the Greek *monai* as "mansions," which, in turn, exercised a widespread influence on popular evangelicalism in America, even inspiring the well-known hymn "Mansion over the Hilltop," written in 1949 by Ira Stanphill (1914–93). Many then connected the idea of living in mansions in heaven with the costly stones said to decorate the heavenly city in Revelation 21:11–12. The end result was an imagined neighborhood of large mansions in sprawling estates near streets of gold and walls of rare gems. However, John 14 implies something different. The emphasis there is not on life in isolation from people, tucked away in wealthy estates built for privacy and self-indulgence, above all else. The emphasis of the original term for "rooms" (*monai*) is rather on communion and sharing of life. Living quarters for the vast majority of people in the ancient world were relatively small and clustered in living arrangements or dwelling places that facilitated a mutual sharing of life. Since populations were to a degree mobile, these living quarters were often viewed as temporal. The result is that Jesus's reference to rooms to spare in his presence accents communion and a sharing of life in God, which eventually are to give way to relocation in the new heaven and new earth. John beheld the heavenly city coming down from heaven to earth at the final end (Rev. 21:2).

Death in the Bible is not a friend to humanity, nor is it an automatic passage to a higher life with God. Christ conquered death, regarded as an *enemy* to humanity: "The last enemy to be destroyed is death" (1 Cor. 15:26). Death is a departure from both God and the body. Spiritual death is the departure of the soul from both living communion with God and the divine cause in the world. "We all, like sheep, have gone astray, each of us has turned to our own way" (Isa. 53:6). Physical death is the consequence of spiritual death, a departure of the soul from the body and a returning of the body to the dust from which it came (Gen. 3:19). Spiritual and physical death are inseparably linked, for physical decay and death are the outward manifestation of a spiritual alienation from God's immortal life. Christ thus overcame both spiritual condemnation and bodily corruption or decay in his resurrection, so as to restore us to God in soul and body (Acts 13:34–37). Salvation is of both soul and body. It is holistic, for soul and body, individuals and the communion of saints.

Communion with Christ remains the focal point of life after death, since it is his glory through the Spirit that shines in us and through us to one another. We are even now being conformed to his image: "And we all, who with unveiled faces contemplate the Lord's glory, are being transformed into his image with ever-increasing glory, which comes from the Lord" (2 Cor. 3:18). We bear his glory as we give of ourselves in self-sacrificial love like he did: "I have been crucified with Christ and I no longer live, but Christ lives in me. The life I now live in the body, I live by faith in the Son of God, who loved me and gave himself for me" (Gal. 2:20). This self-sacrificial giving is a dying to the self-centered self, which is condemned to death, and the rising up of the self in Christ, renewed by the Spirit. But this dying and rising of the self, foreshadowed in regeneration and signified in baptism, does not annihilate the self; it decenters and renews the self in the Spirit. All that we were created to be in the Spirit comes to fulfillment. The many tongues of Pentecost reveal an eschatology of embodied souls that reflect the crucified and risen Christ in many diverse ways. Otherness and difference are embraced as wonderful reflections of the Christ of Pentecost, who opens his life to many different contexts by pouring forth the Spirit upon all flesh. As Daniela Augustine writes, "The capacious polyphony of the eschaton vibrates in the many tongues of Pentecost's radical inclusion of and hospitality towards the other."[6] In the crucifixion and resurrection, Christ gives himself to redeem "persons from every tribe and language and people and nation" (Rev. 5:9), not to annihilate God-created differences but to redeem them in the diverse witness of the Spirit, whom he pours forth at Pentecost. We will all reflect the glory of Christ throughout eternity in a diversity of unique ways. God does not will the beauty with which God created us to ever be lost; he only

---

6. Daniela C. Augustine, *The Spirit and the Common Good: Shared Flourishing in the Image of God* (Grand Rapids: Eerdmans, 2019), 10.

wills it to be fulfilled in Christ, by whom we were created. Christ gave himself to flesh and poured forth the Spirit upon all flesh for this purpose, to be the Christ of the new creation.

Of course, our manifestation of Christ's self-giving love is still weak; we have only a foretaste of his transformative love in us, though we strive for greater conformity to Christ each day. Our fullness of life, which is yet to come, is still a mystery to us, still so out of reach, because we have not yet been revealed in full glory, bearing Christ's glorious image. Paul writes to believers that they are to keep their spiritual contemplation focused on Christ. He tells them why: "For you died, and your life is now hidden with Christ in God. When Christ, who is your life, appears, then you also will appear with him in glory" (Col. 3:3–4). On that day, the day of our resurrection, we will be taken up into the glory of divine love in such a full way that the sufferings of our life will not be worth mentioning (Rom. 8:18). All of creation awaits the revelation of the children of God in the glory of resurrection, for the renewal of all things will follow (v. 19).

The time in between our death and the resurrection is called the **intermediate state**. Some believe that the soul will experience a kind of slumber in Christ (called "soul sleep") until the resurrection awakens us, so that we could arise from our burial place in glorified bodies:

> But your dead will live, LORD;
>   their bodies will rise—
> let those who dwell in the dust
>   wake up and shout for joy—
> your dew is like the dew of the morning;
>   the earth will give birth to her dead. (Isa. 26:19)

Likewise, Paul writes about "those who sleep in death," that they will arise from the dead in response to the "voice of the archangel" and the "trumpet call of God" (1 Thess. 4:13, 16). Yet these verses are arguably poetic. Referring to death as "sleep" is a euphemism, a way of saying that death as an enemy loses its terror in the context of the Christian life and is likened instead to a blissful state awaiting a grand awakening. But it is hard to square a literal **soul sleep** at death with Paul's idea that death is a departure to be with Christ (Phil. 1:23). It doesn't seem that joining Christ at death refers to an entry into spiritual slumber. One may argue that it *seems* to the soul that resurrection occurs directly after death because the intermediate state is a period of slumber. But if the experience of rising directly after death were an illusion, how does one explain the appearance of the souls of Moses and Elijah "talking with Jesus"

at the time of his transfiguration (Matt. 17:3)? It would seem that the souls of
the saints are with Christ in heaven, in communion with him until his return,
at which point they come with him to the earth and arise from the earth with
glorified bodies. Since we were created from the dust of the earth and became
living souls by the Spirit (Gen. 2:7), is it not beautifully symbolic that we
should rise again at the end of time from that very same dust with glorified
bodies in the fullness of the Spirit? Since we (with Christ) are the firstfruits
of the new creation, is it not wonderfully symbolic that we rise in new bodies from the earth, knowing that the earth will itself be made new afterward
(Rom. 8:18–22)? Since our souls are connected as one family with all souls
in all times and places that are in Christ, is it not beautifully significant that
we all, from Adam and Eve to the last person on earth, rise together on that
final day? Hebrews 11:39–40 states of Old Testament saints: "These were all
commended for their faith, yet none of them received what had been promised,
since God had planned something better for us so that only together with us
would they be made perfect." Encouraged by such thoughts, we should run
"the race marked out for us, fixing our eyes on Jesus, the pioneer and perfecter
of faith. For the joy set before him he endured the cross, scorning its shame,
and sat down at the right hand of the throne of God" (12:1–2).

Christ and the New Heaven and New Earth

Christ is not only the Savior of individuals. He is also the one who inaugurates
the new creation. **Resurrection from the dead** and the new heaven and new
earth bring salvation to fulfillment. N. T. Wright declares that we look forward
to life after death in heaven but also life *after* life after death in resurrection and
new creation. The idea that salvation is fulfilled when the soul goes to heaven
at death is not biblical. Paul tells us that our adoption into Christ's family is
not finalized or fulfilled until the resurrection. According to Romans 8:15, we
are the children of God because we have the Spirit already in us, uniting us
to Christ. But note verse 23 of that chapter: "Not only so, but we ourselves,
who have the firstfruits of the Spirit, groan inwardly as we wait eagerly for
our adoption to sonship, the *redemption of our bodies*" (emphasis added).
Even though we *are* children of God, our adoption into Christ's family is
still something for which we are waiting! It is yet to be finalized or fulfilled.
When? At the "redemption of our bodies," or our resurrection from the dead.
Our union with Christ is not yet fulfilled, even in heaven. The reason is that
Christ is the one who was raised bodily in the fullness of the Spirit. As his
family, we are not yet in his image, not yet fulfilled by his benefits, until we

are raised by the Spirit *bodily* as well. No fulfillment without the risen body! The soul may be most essential to who we are, but the body is essential too.

Yet the resurrection of the children of God is not by itself the fulfillment of the kingdom of God. All of creation groans for liberty, implicitly waiting for the resurrection of the children of God (Rom. 8:22). All of creation was subjected to suffering, decay, and death "in hope that the creation itself will be liberated from its bondage to decay and brought into the freedom and glory of the children of God" (vv. 20–21). God wills not only resurrection but also a new heaven and new earth. God is the Creator who will remain faithful to the creation. Though humanity is elected in Christ in a way that is special, God wills to renew all things in the Son and in the Spirit. After all, it was by the Word and in the Spirit that all things were made to be God's dwelling place. "He stretches out the heavens like a canopy, and spreads them out like a tent to live in" (Isa. 40:22). And all of creation is meant to be the arena of God's glory, liberated from sin and death and reflective of God's pure and majestic glory (Isa. 6:3). Humanity should presently look at the heavens and hear its declaration of the glory of God (Ps. 19:1). Animals can show love and altruism; the beauty of countryside and bodies of water can strike one with awe. Even this creation, which is so subject to (and promotive of) chaos, destruction, and death, can also declare the glory of the Creator. We have no idea what it will all look like in the new heaven and new earth!

All this is a bold vision of faith, yet it is compelled by the eschatological vision of the new creation that Christ has inaugurated in his resurrection and will perfect in all of creation in the presence of the Spirit. In Revelation 1, John beholds a stunning vision of the exalted Christ:

> The hair on his head was white like wool, as white as snow, and his eyes were like blazing fire. His feet were like bronze glowing in a furnace, and his voice was like the sound of rushing waters. In his right hand he held seven stars, and coming out of his mouth was a sharp, double-edged sword. His face was like the sun shining in all its brilliance. When I saw him, I fell at his feet as though dead. Then he placed his right hand on me and said: "Do not be afraid. I am the First and the Last. I am the Living One; I was dead, and now look, I am alive for ever and ever! And I hold the keys of death and Hades." (vv. 14–18)

There are several connections here that indicate Christ's deity. His hair is white as wool, which resembles the Ancient of Days, or God the Father (Dan. 7:9). The voice having the sound of running waters is also indicative of God (cf. Ezek. 43:2). Christ as "the First and the Last" is most indicative of God. "I am the first and I am the last; apart from me there is no God" (Isa. 44:6).

The exalted Christ shines forth with the glory of the Father, for Christ is "the radiance of God's glory and the exact representation of his being" (Heb. 1:3). And Christ is revealed as such in the flesh as the risen and exalted Lord. He took on the weakness of human flesh so as to exalt all flesh with the Spirit and glory of God. He is the beginning of the new creation, the "firstborn from the dead" (Col. 1:18 ESV). When John beholds him, he beholds God's victory over the devil, sin, and death. He beholds God's victory not only for humanity but also for all of creation. When the devil and the antichrist show up later in the book of Revelation with their own displays of power (13:1–8), John and his readers know that these agents of evil are destined to lose; in fact, they've already lost. John beholds the exalted Christ. This is all that he needs to see. He falls at his feet in worship. There is no more fitting response than this (1:17).

Even though John sees the foundation for total victory when beholding the exalted Christ in Revelation 1, he also knows that this victory has yet to be actualized or perfected in all of creation. In the Spirit, this is sure to happen. But a witness is to go forth, and the actualization of victory has yet to be fulfilled. Revelation 21 describes it well. The entire passage is worth quoting in full:

> Then I saw "a new heaven and a new earth," for the first heaven and the first earth had passed away, and there was no longer any sea. I saw the Holy City, the new Jerusalem, coming down out of heaven from God, prepared as a bride beautifully dressed for her husband. And I heard a loud voice from the throne saying, "Look! God's dwelling place is now among the people, and he will dwell with them. They will be his people, and God himself will be with them and be their God. 'He will wipe every tear from their eyes. There will be no more death' or mourning or crying or pain, for the old order of things has passed away." He who was seated on the throne said, "I am making everything new!" Then he said, "Write this down, for these words are trustworthy and true." (vv. 1–5)

I hardly need to comment on this. This passage makes it clear that salvation, broadly conceived, is not an escape from creation to heaven. Salvation is rather new creation. The heavenly city comes down from heaven to earth, and the heaven and the earth are made new to accommodate it. In fact, God's reign, God's sovereign presence, is now concentrated on the earth as well, and heaven and earth are reconciled. This fulfills Christ's prayer: "Your kingdom come, your will be done, on earth as it is in heaven" (Matt. 6:10). All things are made new. God's predestined plan that all things be united under Christ (Eph. 1:10) is fulfilled. Salvation is not an escape from earth to heaven; it's bringing heaven to earth.

Of course, this final victory does not come without considerable resistance. Here we discuss the doctrine of **end-time tribulation**. As we near the end, evil rises up to take a last stand. Though evil and trial characterize the entire history of the church, the New Testament indicates that there will be a final conflict with evil as the Lord's return draws near. Revelation 6 tells us that war, famine, and death will be unleashed on the earth from the wrath of the nations (vv. 1–8). *God* is not the one who brings tribulation or *divine* wrath that initiates the final conflict. It's rather the anger of the *nations*. After there is so much killing, the innocent who have died cry out for justice (vv. 9–11). Only *then* does God pour forth wrath to stop the violence and to bring the kingdom of God to earth. People cry out, "Fall on us and hide us from the face of him who sits on the throne and from the wrath of the Lamb!" (v. 16). In the chapters that follow Revelation 6, we receive descriptions of God's wrath, which involves plagues. As God used plagues to free the children of Israel from Egyptian bondage, so God uses plagues in the book of Revelation to bring the powerful nations to their knees and to liberate the world from the destruction of evil. Revelation 11:18 makes this point exactly:

> The nations were angry,
>   and your wrath has come.
> The time has come for judging the dead,
>   and for rewarding your servants the prophets
> and your people who revere your name,
>   both great and small—
> and for destroying those who destroy the earth.

Notice that the end-time tribulation starts with the anger or wrath of the *nations*. But then *God's* wrath comes by way of response. And the goal? To stop those attempting to destroy the earth from doing so. The reason why the time of tribulation is so short (perhaps forty-two months [Rev. 13:5]) and the time of peace so long (according to Revelation 20, one thousand years) is that God is the God of peace and not war. God strikes out against the powerful nations to stop the killing and to save the earth. It is all to end in the reign of Christ over the nations of the world:

> The kingdom of the world has become
>   the kingdom of our Lord and of his Messiah,
>   and he will reign for ever and ever. (11:15)

What exactly will happen as the end draws near? The issue of tribulation signs has excited quite a bit of imagination and literary output in popular evangelical Bible teaching. Historical connections that contextualize the writing of Scripture are sometimes ignored in the process. For example, Jesus's Olivet Discourse in Luke 21 about the destruction of Jerusalem and the temple is often understood in popular expositions to be dealing entirely with the end time, overlooking the fact that Rome did overtake Jerusalem and destroy the temple in 70 CE, about forty years after Jesus predicted the temple's demise. Paying attention to this event, a number of evangelical scholars have interpreted verses 5–24 as referring to what Rome did in 70 CE and then the remainder of the verses in that chapter to the final days.[7] Prophecies about future tribulation in the Bible are also often treated as if they are a crystal ball that gives us a literal portrayal of all that will happen before Christ returns. Though we are to take what the Bible says about such matters with utmost seriousness, a great deal of its symbolism may be more geared to evoking an emotive or behavioral response than a scientifically literal one. Its purpose may be oriented more toward comfort or courage than satisfying intellectual curiosity about the future. The intent is to offer reassurance that even if evil were to rise up to the extent depicted here, God still reigns and victory is assured. We are to stand firm in the victory wherein Christ has made us free. This is not to deny the profound theological significance of what the Bible says about these things. But it is to say that we should exercise caution before we hold up our literal interpretations on every detail of the future with a certainty that is beyond dispute.

In the end, the nations are blessed. God wins. One wouldn't know that given what is revealed about the nations in Revelation 6. Though there are losses along the way, God's grace brings the nations to repentance. Notice this description of the heavenly city in the new heaven and new earth: "I did not see a temple in the city, because the Lord God Almighty and the Lamb are its temple. The city does not need the sun or the moon to shine on it, for the glory of God gives it light, and the Lamb is its lamp. The nations will walk by its light, and the kings of the earth will bring their splendor into it" (21:22–24).

The new creation is not only the victory of Christ's redeeming work but also the victory of the Spirit, who anointed Christ and is poured forth through him. This point is made particularly clear when it comes to the resurrection of Christ and the saints. Paul calls the risen body the "spiritual" body (πνευματικός, or *pneumatikos*), which is "heavenly" or immortal in contrast to the "natural" body (ψυχικός, or *psychikos*), which is of the earth or the

---

7. See, e.g., Norval Geldenhuys, *Commentary on the Gospel of Luke*, New International Commentary on the New Testament (Grand Rapids: Eerdmans, 1972), 522–45.

dust of the ground (enlivened by the Spirit, 1 Cor. 15:44–49). "Spiritual" body may not be the best translation here: to many a modern ear, it seems to be something not tangible or visible. But the body of the risen Christ, according to the New Testament, can be touched and clearly seen, even though it can seemingly enter a room while the door is locked (John 20:19). Christ was raised "according to the Spirit of holiness" (Rom. 1:4 ESV), and he appears afterward as a life-giving Spirit (1 Cor. 15:45). So the risen body of Jesus is at one with the Spirit. Christ arose in the fullness of the Spirit so as to pour forth the Spirit upon all flesh. By his Spirit, we will rise up as new creatures in him to share his love and justice in the world, rising at the end in bodies like his risen body to enjoy the perfect sanctity, freedom, and glory of the Spirit. Such is the new creation! As Paul phrases the matter, when we put on the new body in resurrection, we will be "swallowed up by life" (2 Cor. 5:4).

Controversy: Rapture and Millennium

A controversial issue within evangelical eschatology is the so-called **rapture**. In the time between the writing of the New Testament and the nineteenth century, there was no rapture doctrine as it is known today. This alone does not mean that the rapture is not biblical, but it has caused some to question it. The key biblical text in question is 1 Thessalonians 4:13–18:

> Brothers and sisters, we do not want you to be uninformed about those who sleep in death, so that you do not grieve like the rest of mankind, who have no hope. For we believe that Jesus died and rose again, and so we believe that God will bring with Jesus those who have fallen asleep in him. According to the Lord's word, we tell you that we who are still alive, who are left until the coming of the Lord, will certainly not precede those who have fallen asleep. For the Lord himself will come down from heaven, with a loud command, with the voice of the archangel and with the trumpet call of God, and the dead in Christ will rise first. After that, we who are still alive and are left will be caught up together with them in the clouds to meet the Lord in the air. And so we will be with the Lord forever. Therefore encourage one another with these words.

The overall thrust of this text is clear enough. Believers were grieving like those who have no hope. Grieving at the passing of a loved one is certainly normal, even for Christians. But grieving *as if there were no hope* requires a reminder of our hope and comfort. There is a difference between grieving *without hope* and grieving *in hope*. Jesus died and rose again! That makes all the difference in the world. And he will come again. When he does, all believers of all times and places who died will be raised to meet the Lord in the air—a grand reunion in the sky joined also by those who are still alive when the Lord returns. Those alive at Christ's return will be transformed immediately into immortal bodies and caught up to meet all those who were raised from the dead to welcome the Lord. The thrust of the text is to comfort the grieving, as the final line of the above text indicates. We are to recognize from the start that the "rapture," or being "caught up," is not the main point of the passage. This does not mean, though, that we should ignore it. This wording is still part of the text.

What some might consider a relatively incidental detail in the above text has become the major point for those who hold to the rapture doctrine. Paul speaks of the fact that those still alive will be "caught up" to meet the others in the sky. One could translate this "catching up" as "raptured." Nineteenth-century Plymouth Brethren minister John Nelson Darby (1800–1882) focused on this word; in fact, he made it the chief feature of the entire event. The passage for him is not even about Christ's return to earth. The entire passage indicates rather an event that *predates* the second coming of Christ, since it occurs prior to the final time of trial or tribulation and rescues Christians from that terrible time. The entire event is thus called "the rapture" because it delivers believers up so they avoid the final tribulation. It is to be conceded, I think, that the Thessalonian text quoted above does not say that the catching up is for the purpose of delivering us from tribulation. One must draw from other passages to make this point, which causes some to hold that the rapture doctrine is not especially strong or compelling. Texts elsewhere indicating that we are not destined for wrath (1 Thess. 5:9) are used to make this case. Whether or not such texts should serve as a lens for interpreting the purpose for the catching up in 1 Thessalonians 4 is part of the controversy surrounding the doctrine. Darby's doctrine came to be known as the **pretribulation rapture**, since it was believed to come prior to the tribulation, to save Christians from it. Though this doctrine does not garner widespread support among evangelical scholars, it does have broad support among pastors and laity within sectors of the evangelical movement.

To comment further on the Thessalonian text quoted above, I would like to note that Paul clearly states that his topic is indeed "the coming of the Lord" (v. 15). In this light, are pretribulation-rapture advocates asking us to await both a second and a *third* coming of the Lord—the second to rapture us away before the tribulation begins and the third when Christ returns to earth? A rapture-doctrine advocate could maintain that the Lord will return only *once* but in *two stages* (the rapture and then again, after the tribulation, to end the age). Others, though, may find that a seven-year gap between the rapture and the final return of Christ is too lengthy to represent a single event. But why separate them at all? The answer is to remove believers from tribulation.

Those who defend a pretribulation rapture commonly highlight two points. First, they argue that there seems to be a pattern in Scripture whereby God removes the faithful from a time of divine wrath, such as Noah and his family from the flood and Lot and his family from the wrath poured out on Sodom and Gomorrah. Second, they note that some texts indicate the Lord can come at any time, like a thief in the night (1 Thess. 5:2), whereas other texts imply that the Lord will come only after certain signs have been fulfilled (Luke 21:29–31). Rapture defenders argue that two future comings of the Lord might account for these two kinds of texts. The rapture is the event that can come at any time and will not follow signs, since it takes place *before* the end-time tribulation, whereas the final return takes place with signs preceding. Others may wonder whether or not two separate comings of the Lord are needed to deal with such an issue.

Arguably, in 1 Thessalonians 4:13–18, the resurrection of the saints is the more prominent issue of the text than our being caught up to join these raised saints. The resurrection itself is the major issue, since Paul is seeking to comfort those who were overly grieving their dead. None of this by itself nullifies Darby's rapture doctrine, but again, it leads us to wonder whether he has put the emphasis where it is warranted by the text. Regardless, we all in the text quoted above *do* meet the Lord in the air. Why is that? Scholars who don't hold to the rapture doctrine have noted that the Thessalonian text quoted above could easily be explained without presuming a pretribulation rapture separate from the Lord's final return to end the age. The Lord's return can be both immanent (it can happen at any moment) *and* preceded by signs, since one never knows precisely how history will reach its fulfillment. Moreover, even those who hold to the pretribulation rapture admit that there will be a "church" in the world during the time of trial consisting of Christians who are converted at that time. In fact, Revelation tells us that there will be a "great multitude" from every nation who will "come out of the great tribulation" (7:9, 14). If *they* are expected to weather this storm, why not the rest of the church? Won't their witness be needed the most at this time? Moreover, several evangelical New Testament scholars have suggested that the rising or catching up of believers to greet the Lord in the air could very well be for the purpose of welcoming him and escorting him to his reign on the earth, similar to the way that people of ancient societies would gather in the countryside to meet visiting dignitaries so as to escort them into their towns. As N. T. Wright remarks about 1 Thessalonians 4, "Paul conjures up images of an emperor visiting a colony or a province. The citizens go out to meet him in open country and then escort him to the city."[8] According to the Thessalonian text quoted above, the Lord returns with trumpet sounds and the voice of the archangel to announce his arrival, similar to the arrival of an emperor to a province. Believers are caught up to meet him in the air so as to escort him to his reign on the earth. Given the fact that a global *bodily* resurrection occurs at this time as well, it will be a public event. Some maintain that it will not be as secretive and mysterious as most pretribulation advocates assume!

The idea that the "rapture" occurs at the Lord's return after the tribulation is sometimes called the **post-tribulation** rapture theory, to distinguish it from the pretribulation rapture discussed above. Actually, the so-called post-tribulation theory is simply the idea that there is no rapture doctrine at all, merely the Lord's people greeting the Lord in the air upon his return so as to escort him to earth. Once the rapture becomes an element of Christ's final return to earth, it loses the spotlight that had previously been placed on it and becomes a relatively incidental feature of Christ's return to earth to reign. Then the text no longer presents a separate rapture: a rapture would not exist as an event of its own apart from everything else.

At any rate, the overall rapture issue is controversial and has been debated among evangelicals for quite some time. Reformed evangelicals tend to be skeptical of it, whereas non-Reformed Baptists and Pentecostals are more receptive. Even among Baptists and Pentecostals, scholars tend to be more critical of it than pastors and laity. I would encourage tolerance by both sides on this matter. Pretribulation-rapture advocates are fearful that a neglect of the rapture doctrine could lull the church into a spiritual slumber rather than encourage it to be watching and waiting at its post, passionately bearing witness while awaiting Christ's coming to rescue it from tribulation. The church's need to watch and wait is indeed a valid concern. On the other hand, those who do not hold to this rapture doctrine are concerned that people who do so could end up inadvertently encouraging an escapist mentality that urges Christians to yearn for an escape from this world and its trials rather than engage the world courageously with compassion and witness. This is a valid concern as well. Perhaps showing a sensitivity to one another's concerns can help us find unity amid our differences of opinion as to the precise series of events that will transpire during the Lord's return. We will certainly know when it happens! Let the Lord hold sway over this matter. I can hold with my church a belief that we will be delivered from the wrath to come (1 Thess. 5:9). Our overall task is to be vigilant in faithful witness until the day the Lord returns.

8. N. T. Wright, "Farewell to the Rapture," N. T. Wright Online, https://ntwrightpage.com /2016/07/12/farewell-to-the-rapture/.

Another controversial issue is the so-called **millennium**. Those who debate this issue focus on Revelation 20. Some texts seem to indicate that the new heaven and new earth will arrive at the moment the Lord returns: "But the day of the Lord will come like a thief. The heavens will disappear with a roar; the elements will be destroyed by fire, and the earth and everything done in it will be laid bare" (2 Pet. 3:10). The book of Revelation, however, seems to indicate that there will be an intermediate period between the Lord's return and the arrival of the new heaven and new earth, in which the Lord reigns on the earth. Revelation 19 describes the Lord's return. He will "strike down the nations" in order to rule over them (v. 15). This striking down cannot refer to annihilation, since there would then be nothing left over which to rule. Besides, the sword that the Lord will wield upon his return is not material; it is rather the word of truth, which comes "out of his mouth" (v. 15). The striking down is rather the devastating blow of penetrating truth that shatters the self-justifying lies and idols by which the nations have lived. The Lord's return will strike them down and humble them. The doctrine of Christ as the one who comes in judgment is not an outmoded doctrine but is quite relevant to every time and culture. It means that the lies by which nations and empires have deceived and oppressed so many people will be shattered and shown for what they are. These lies should be at least to some extent discerned and called out by the church's prophetic witness before the time of Christ's return. But the Lord's return will vindicate the witness of the righteous and grant that witness a decisive victory. This implies that a mass conversion may well happen at the time of the Lord's return: "All peoples on earth 'will mourn because of him'" (Rev. 1:7). The Greek term for "mourn" (κόπτω, or *koptō*) was sometimes used in the ancient world to describe a striking at one's chest in sorrow and lamentation, as if being devastated by this vindication of the truth. It could be that this is the moment Paul awaited, which would release Israel with finality from its hardening and bring it to the body of Christ: "But if their transgression means riches for the world, and their loss means riches for the Gentiles, how much greater riches will their full inclusion bring!" (Rom. 11:12).

All of this implies an inseparable connection between what happens at the Lord's return in Revelation 19 and the Lord's reign on earth that will last a thousand years, as described in chapter 20. In fact, this **millennial reign** ("millennial" describing a period of one thousand years) may indeed be a "second chance" for Israel and the nations.[9] They had been hardened and deceived

9. See John Christopher Thomas and Frank D. Macchia, *Revelation*, Two Horizons New Testament Commentary (Grand Rapids: Eerdmans, 2016), 351.

for so long; now the tempter is locked up (vv. 1–3), right after the Lord has revealed the truth of the kingdom of God in penetrating power at his return. The righteous dead are raised and reign with Christ (v. 6; cf. 5:10); especially noteworthy is the reign of the martyrs (20:4). The offer of grace is granted to the world under ideal conditions. The dark cloud of the tempter, who deceived so long, is now lifted under the blazing light of truth. But will those who yield to it remain? Not all. At the end of the thousand years, the tempter is released, and as hard as it is to imagine, some will yield to deception once more. There is a dividing of the ways, and those who are deceived seek to make war against those who remain true. Naturally, the Lord puts a swift and devastating end to the rebellion (vv. 7–10). The book of Revelation is not very optimistic about human nature, and neither should we be. If history has taught us anything, it's that a widespread deception will always gain a substantial following if it taps effectively into hidden biases, self-serving grievances, and fears. Even noble aspirations can be twisted and bent into the service of deceptive ends. A crafty deception plays to what people *want* to believe, even if such desires lie dormant for a very long time and are manifestly disputed by the evidence. If a lie gets enough press, a notable number of people will follow, simply because they are already prone to believe it. One can take the people out of the darkness, but it is a great deal more difficult to take the darkness out of the people.

Some have interpreted the millennium in Revelation 20 as referring to a literal one-thousand-year reign of Christ on earth before the new heaven and new earth arrive. This means the new heaven and new earth do not arrive immediately upon Christ's return. A thousand-year delay precedes it, with a kingdom presented as idyllic but still belonging to this age. The new heaven and new earth have not yet arrived. This view of Christ's return—called **premillennialism**, since it occurs *before* ("pre" or prior to) his thousand-year reign on earth—has raised a few questions. First, those who reign with Christ have been raised from the dead or otherwise transformed into immortal bodies. What about those converted at his return? If they, too, become immortal, how is it that there can be a falling away of a portion of humanity at the end of Christ's thousand-year reign (Rev. 20:7–10)? Or are they ushered into the kingdom of Christ in mortal bodies so that their newly formed faith forged at Christ's return can be tested, as it arguably is at the end of the thousand years when Satan is released? And is the thousand years a literal number? Second, what exactly is the purpose of this intermediate kingdom besides possibly being a second chance for Israel and the nations? Some view it as a "Sabbath rest" after evil has caused so much suffering on the earth for so long. And, third, what about 2 Peter 3:10, which implies that the new heaven and new earth will be introduced directly after Christ's second coming?

Because of such questions, premillennialism is not the only view of Revelation 20 among evangelicals. Some hold to a view called **amillennialism**, which is the belief that there is no literal thousand-year reign to speak of in between Christ's return and the introduction of the new heaven and new earth. The new heaven and new earth come directly upon Christ's return; Revelation chapter 21 follows directly after chapter 19. Chapter 20 is a pause in the narrative intended to summarize the entire story of Christ's victory and reign in the time leading up to his return. Jay Adams, for example, offers a clear defense of this view in his little book *The Time Is at Hand*.[10] He maintains that the kingdom described in Revelation 20 is a figurative description of the entire age of the church leading up to Christ's return. The major events of this reign follow the age of the church exactly. It starts with the binding of Satan, which Christ arguably does in his first coming; he has come to "bind" the strong man and spoil his ill-gotten goods (Matt. 12:29). After his resurrection, Christ then ascends to his throne to reign, and he is joined in his reign by notable saints in heaven, like the twenty-four elders that John beholds reigning with Christ in heaven (Rev. 4:4). At the end of the "thousand years" (or age of the church), there is a grand deception, a rebellion among the ungodly, an appearance of the Lord, and the final judgment and resurrection.

Adams challenges his readers to view these parallel scenes, the age of the church and the thousand-year reign in Revelation 20, as an indication that this chapter is replaying before our eyes the major events of the age of the church leading up to Christ's return. The events of Christ's reign are revealed after the description of Christ's return given in the previous chapter (chap. 19) as a summary of all that led up to that decisive victory. This view does solve a few theological difficulties, especially the implication elsewhere in the New Testament that the new heaven and new earth are introduced directly after Christ's return. The only difficulty with amillennialism is the fact that in Revelation 20 the millennial reign begins *after* the resurrection of those who reign with Christ: "They came to life and reigned with Christ a thousand years" (v. 4). This implies that the reign begins after the return of Christ. Adams regards this "coming to life" as figurative of their born-again experience, which allows them at death to reign with Christ from heaven. I find the reference to the saints "coming to life" to reign with Christ to be a resurrection which points to the premillennial coming of Christ. Again, we have a controversy in response to which I encourage toleration and dialogue.

Another view of the millennial reign of Revelation 20 that is no longer widely held is called **postmillennialism**. Popular among late nineteenth-century

10. Jay E. Adams, *The Time Is at Hand* (Memphis: Institute for Nouthetic Studies, 2021).

evangelicals and defended more recently by Calvinist theologian Loraine Boettner (1901–90), this view holds that the kingdom of God will be largely ushered in by the powerful witness of the church, so that Christ comes merely to perfect a kingdom that is already present.[11] Hence, Christ's return is called postmillennial because Christ comes *after* his millennial reign. This proposal is similar to the amillennial view except that it is more optimistic about the role of the church in ushering in the kingdom.

What interests many scholars is what views of the church are implied in these different views of the millennium. The premillennial view is not very optimistic about the role of the church in the coming of the kingdom of God to earth. Christ brings the kingdom in its entirety only after devastating the resistance of the nations through the sword of truth and purging the earth of an evil that would have consumed it. Both amillennial and postmillennial views open the door for a more robust and formative role for the church's witness in the advent of Christ's reign on earth. If premillennialism warns us against unrealistic utopian dreams, the other views encourage optimism. Optimism has a place. Evangelical eschatology tends to leave little encouragement for young people to enter science, the arts, politics, and social justice with the dream of making a tangible and notable difference in the world. It leaves little encouragement for those who dare to dream big dreams about what the Spirit can do through empowered witness to occasion signs in our world of the new creation yet to come.

Physicist Michio Kaku dreams of a future "Type III" civilization brought on by scientific advances in which people will wield enormous power for good: "They have exhausted the power of a single star and have reached for other star systems. No natural catastrophe known to science is capable of destroying a Type III civilization. Faced with a neighboring supernova, it would have several alternatives, such as altering the evolution of a dying red giant star which is about to explode, or leaving this particular star system and terraforming a nearby planetary system."[12] Can humanity ever reach this stage of development? Look how far we've come over the millennia we've occupied this earth. Yet premillennialism offers a note of caution. With great power comes great dangers. History has taught us that with every advent of the good, evil is not far behind.

11. Loraine Boettner, *The Millennium*, rev. ed. (Philipsburg, NJ: Presbyterian & Reformed, 1991).
12. Michio Kaku, "The Physics of Extraterrestrial Civilizations. How Advanced Could They Possibly Be?" Official Website of Dr. Michio Kaku, https://mkaku.org/home/articles/the-physics-of-extraterrestrial-civilizations.

The goal of the kingdom of God on earth, however, goes even beyond Kaku's dream of a Type III civilization. Unimaginably beyond. The new heaven and new earth will reflect the glory of the risen Christ, for "our present sufferings are not worth comparing with the glory that will be revealed in us" (Rom. 8:18). In fact, no natural bridge exists from this natural existence to the supernatural and immortal existence of resurrection and the new heaven and new earth. We cannot evolve from one to the other. Paul makes this point clear:

> I declare to you, brothers and sisters, that flesh and blood cannot inherit the kingdom of God, nor does the perishable inherit the imperishable. Listen, I tell you a mystery: We will not all sleep, but we will all be changed—in a flash, in the twinkling of an eye, at the last trumpet. For the trumpet will sound, the dead will be raised imperishable, and we will be changed. For the perishable must clothe itself with the imperishable, and the mortal with immortality. When the perishable has been clothed with the imperishable, and the mortal with immortality, then the saying that is written will come true: "Death has been swallowed up in victory." (1 Cor. 15:50–54)

The bridge from natural creation to the new creation is the victory of Christ's death and resurrection over sin and death and the Spirit poured out from him, offering us all the down payment of immortality in our souls. We groan for the ultimate liberty of the kingdom of God in the fullness of the Spirit, which characterizes immortal existence conformed to the image of the risen Christ (Rom. 8:22). But it will not arrive until that which is old is radically transformed into something higher, the new heaven and new earth. "But the day of the Lord will come like a thief. The heavens will disappear with a roar; the elements will be destroyed by fire, and the earth and everything done in it will be laid bare" (2 Pet. 3:10). The heavens and earth are being refined like gold, sanctified for God's presence.

What Lies Beyond? And for Whom?

What about human souls? How are they prepared for heaven and the new creation? The Catholic answer is **purgatory**. A person not only goes through a process of purgation in this life: purgation continues after death. The soul journeys through a path of purgation after death in preparation for an eternity with God. The key text used to support this is 1 Corinthians 3:11–15:

> For no one can lay any foundation other than the one already laid, which is Jesus Christ. If anyone builds on this foundation using gold, silver, costly

stones, wood, hay or straw, their work will be shown for what it is, because the Day will bring it to light. It will be revealed with fire, and the fire will test the quality of each person's work. If what has been built survives, the builder will receive a reward. If it is burned up, the builder will suffer loss but yet will be saved—even though only as one escaping through the flames.

This text seems to refer to the "building" being constructed by those involved in the work of God. God's judgment will test the work, rewarding that which is built on Christ, the foundation, and burning up that which is not. The person will be saved but only through the flames of God's judgment. Here God's judgment is unquestionably purgative. It burns up what is corrupt. The Christian worker is saved, "escaping through the flames." Judgment in this case does not damn the person but rather represents escape from damnation. This divine judgment is redemptive. If one personalizes the above text as though it is referring to individual salvation, purgatory would be a legitimate interpretation. But the context of the passage indicates something else. Paul wrote of working in the church to build up the body of Christ. "For we are co-workers in God's service; you are God's field, God's building" (v. 9). The work being tested by judgment is the work in the labor of God's church. Personal sanctification is not the issue.

Yet are there good theological reasons for some version of a sanctifying journey from death to heaven? Though the atonement covers all of our sins, there is still a healing and sanctifying process that God deems important in our journey *in this life* toward heaven. Why should the healing process stop at death? Most Protestants assume that God instantaneously perfects the soul at death. But as evangelical theologian John Stackhouse has asked, "If sanctification is only gradual and difficult in this life, why do we expect that it will be different in the life to come?"[13] This doctrine of purgatory has indeed been misused historically and elaborated on in erroneous ways. But can it still play a role in one's eschatology? Stackhouse supports it so long as it is separated from any idea of its completing satisfaction for our sin, which belongs to the work of Christ alone, or from the idea that we can pray for the dead or contribute to their sanctifying journey to God after death.[14]

It is also important to address the destiny of the unsaved. The parable of the rich man and Lazarus depicts the rich man as suffering in torment (Luke 16:19–31). It is difficult to know how much theology one is meant to take from a parable, since the possibility existed that Jesus used a commonly

---

13. John G. Stackhouse Jr., "Protestants and Purgatory: The Hard Work of Sanctification," *Christian Century*, January 11, 2014, 26.
14. Stackhouse, "Protestants and Purgatory," 26–29.

known folktale to make a point—in this case, the folly of wasting one's life on riches while squandering the possibility in this life of deciding *for life* as God intended it. The suggestion that other details of the parable are intended to teach eschatology as well is open to question. In Revelation 20, the final judgment leads to the devil, along with death and Hades themselves, being thrown into the "lake of fire," along with those who follow them there (vv. 10, 14). The description of the event is obviously symbolic, for how can death and Hades literally be thrown into a lake of fire? But the meaning is still clear. The lake of fire is symbolic of God's final judgment. The purpose of hell is obviously not meant for humanity. It is meant to rid humanity once and for all of their tormentors—the devil, death, and Hades. In this light, it must be maintained that, while on the cross, Christ descended into the depths of human alienation from God, including all the torment that comes with it. The psalmist claims that even if he flees from God into Sheol, the realm of the dead, "you are there" (Ps. 139:8). And God was there, on a cross. Christ arguably took upon himself the depths of hell so that humanity did not have to endure it. That a portion of humanity decides to flee from God down into the depths of alienation and despair is difficult to fathom but is apparently possible.

C. S. Lewis, in his book *The Problem of Pain*, proposes that the "lock" on the "door" to hell is on the inside; humanity locks itself away from God.[15] One may add, as Paul does in Romans 1:24–28, that God "hands them over" to the destructive path of their choosing. This is not meant to diminish in any way the seriousness of the divine judgment. But bear in mind that God handed the beloved Son over to the same fate in order to save all of humanity (4:25). What about those who lock themselves away from God? Some hold that God's ultimate victory, in which God will be "all in all" (1 Cor. 15:28), precludes an eternal punishment that excludes divine love. Some thus hold that those who choose once and for all to flee from God will be annihilated, which is described as the "second death," beyond the death of the body (Rev. 20:6).

Others support some form of **universalism**, holding that the defeat of hell at the cross, plus the fact that God created us for Godself, will ultimately lead all of humanity to the household of the Father, even if that path is marked by judgment and suffering.[16] Every tongue will confess Christ as Lord (Phil. 2:11). The book of Revelation does speak of the smoke of eternal torment (14:11), but some note that it also speaks of the fact that the gates of the new

---

15. C. S. Lewis, *The Problem of Pain*, rev. ed. (San Francisco: HarperOne, 2015), 130.

16. See Bradley Jersak, *Her Gates Will Never Be Shut: Hope, Hell, and the New Jerusalem* (Eugene, OR: Wipf & Stock, 2009); David Bentley Hart, *That All Shall Be Saved: Heaven, Hell, and Universal Salvation* (New Haven: Yale University Press), 2019.

Jerusalem never close (21:25) and that those who wash their robes by God's grace may enter in. Do they come from those who do evil on the outside, in the lake of fiery judgment (22:14–15)? John Hick argues that references to eternal punishment in the Bible are relatively few in number and hypothetical, depicting what would be the case without the intervention of divine grace.[17] We are in the realm of mystery here. In my view, one cannot read Scripture without accepting the prospect of eternal loss by those who flee the presence of God without yielding to grace.

There is no question that Christ is the only way to God. Christ says, "I am the way and the truth and the life. No one comes to the Father except through me" (John 14:6). There is no way to God except by way of Christ and his atoning death and resurrection—no way to the regenerating and sanctifying life of the Spirit except through Christ. The **exclusivist** position has rightly defended this point. The **pluralist** option, which defends a plurality of ways to God that are not reliant on Christ, fails to grant Christ adequate glory as the divine Son in flesh who alone redeems humanity and pours forth the Spirit to sanctify and glorify them. He is alone the atonement for humanity. Some theologians, however, believe that the saving light and grace of Christ exceeds the boundaries of the church and its mission. Christ's grace touches all people in some way and lures them to reach out to God and receive all things as a gift for which to be grateful. The view is that they can end up yielding to the love of God above all else and can be included in the saving work of Christ, even before they understand the gospel intellectually. They must still be brought into the full teaching of the gospel so as to secure them in the faith and guard them against the pitfalls of heresy. How vast this inclusivism can become is thought to be hidden in the mystery of God. The issue touches on eschatology. This view may be called **inclusivism**. The evangelist Billy Graham (1918–2018) is an example of a prominent evangelical who holds this position.[18] One must consider here Paul's assumption that acceptance of the gospel is necessary to salvation (Rom. 10:14–15).

Postscript: The Apocalyptic and the Prophetic

The term **apocalyptic** literally means something mysterious and transcendent that is unveiled or revealed. In discussions of eschatology, it is commonly used

17. John Hick, *Death and Eternal Life* (Louisville: Westminster John Knox, 1994), 243–50.
18. See "Robert Schuller and Billy Graham Speaking Wide Acceptance," YouTube video, 1:03, September 23, 2007, https://www.youtube.com/watch?v=TNCnxA91fHE&ab_channel =SacisutaDasa.

to mean an approach to the future that views it as transcendent, beyond the reach of rational thought or speech. It is sometimes contrasted with the term **prophetic**, which may refer to a possible historical future that, though also possibly fantastic in nature, is at least imaginable by us and part of our historical framework and thought. The prophetic impulse attempts to change the world into a more just and loving future. By contrast, the apocalyptic trend views the ultimate future as unattainable by human effort. It is beyond what we can build or imagine, a future created through God's supernatural intervention alone.

History tends to be viewed in apocalyptic literature as doomed for failure and divine judgment; all efforts to build a better future are shown to have been largely futile. One recalls Daniel's vision of a statue (which seems to resemble an idol) representing the empires of the world, which are signified by weaker materials the more one descends from the top to the bottom—as if to say that world history is decaying within, prone to collapse under the weight of its own self-destructive lies and evil behavior (Dan. 2:31–45). Nevertheless, the kingdom of God will strike the statue at its base to bring it down (v. 45). Those who work with a more prophetic eschatological vision, however, are prone to criticize apocalyptic eschatology as escapist and even deterministic, as if the future is predestined to fail so that God can usher in the kingdom. The prophetic vision opens the future to human participation and calls us to a liberating and more just future. Even if prophetic realism cautions that the way ahead will face stiff and persistent resistance from corporate power, the prophetic vision still encourages bold action to realize in history God's liberating purposes for creation. Apocalypticism looks to an unimaginable future beyond history that only God can usher in supernaturally, whereas propheticism looks to a realization of God's liberating purposes in history. Jewish philosopher Martin Buber (1878–1965) shared the prophetic criticism of apocalypticism and criticized both Jesus and the New Testament for taking this approach to the future and encouraging it to flourish.[19]

Much of the eschatology that we've discussed from the book of Revelation is in large measure apocalyptic in nature. At the very least, it has been interpreted this way within popular evangelical treatises on eschatology. But a more prophetic tradition also lies in the eschatology of the Bible. Jesus, under the anointing of the Holy Spirit, proclaimed the year of the Lord's favor to the oppressed, the sick, and the outcast. He challenged the way in which the Jewish leadership and their institutional religious and civil administration excluded and marginalized those who desperately needed their help. Christ healed those

19. Martin Buber, "Prophecy, Apocalyptic, and Historical Hour," *Union Seminary Quarterly Review*, March 1, 1957, 9–21.

who were sick and invited others to his table fellowship to help them discover their God-given humanity. He brought them the gospel so they could receive the Holy Spirit and start on their path toward salvation, including life everlasting. There is in Jesus's ministry a wonderful coming together of the prophetic and the apocalyptic. He undermined evil systems and modeled how the kingdom of God inaugurates a different way to treat those in need, a different community called the church, which will be both the sign of the coming kingdom and its instrument in the world. But he also granted them the future possibility of eternal life so that they could one day overcome death itself and rise from the dead into a realm of existence currently beyond the grasp of our imaginations.

In fact, the apocalyptic and the prophetic overlap and need each other. The apocalyptic prevents us from clinging to the status quo, to this world as we know it, as though this is all there is or could ever be. It prevents us from deceiving ourselves into thinking that our ultimate future is within our hands, as if we can create that which will ultimately fulfill us. The apocalyptic points us to a glorious, transcendent level of existence in God that far exceeds this world and its history, proceeds far beyond what we can create. Our only access to it is through resurrection. Yet the prophetic reminds us that our participation in the betterment of this world and this history under the power of the Spirit matters. It matters so much that it will have an influence on the transcendent future that God will supernaturally usher in and usher us into. As we noted earlier, there is indeed no natural path from this history to eternal glory. But we will in eternal glory remember, celebrate, and fulfill all that we graciously do in the here and now. Apocalyptic assures us that all forms of life that have been thrown into the ash heap of natural history, all those whom our greatest works were not able to help or rescue, can still be taken up in the new creation. All those babies or small children who died far too young will know life eternal in God and the communion of the saints. None of them will be forgotten. This shows us, in part, the need for eschatology as the work of God beyond that which human history can produce. No natural, historical future—no matter how advanced or wonderful—can ever grant justice for the abandoned or forgotten of history. Only the ultimate future that God will usher in can fulfill it.

FINAL REFLECTIONS

Eschatology is about God's final purposes for creation. It's about life after death in heaven, but it is also about life *after* life after death in the resurrection of the dead and the new creation. This point causes us to look to Christ's death and resurrection as the decisive event of eschatology, the climactic inauguration of the new creation. Eschatology is sharing in Christ, being conformed to him. Eschatology is also life in the Spirit as poured forth from the risen Christ, for it is in the Spirit that Christ opens his life to history, to all nations in all of their diversity, to all times and places, so that they can be partakers in his glory. His glory is reflected in a diverse array of ways through many cultures and contexts. We will all in resurrection reflect the glory of Christ in many diversely unique ways throughout eternity. Christ poured forth the Spirit so as to be the Christ of the diversely arrayed new creation. Eschatology is not fundamentally about "end times" but rather about hope in Christ that overcomes all opposition and pervades all topics related to theology. It has to do with final purposes in Christ that cause us to transcend the status quo and move forward in the direction of his mercy and justice in the world.

Heaven is focused on being in communion together in and through Christ. But even heaven, as glorious as it is, is not the ultimate fulfillment of salvation. Salvation involves resurrection, for salvation is to be realized in body and soul, communally and individually. Resurrection is the ultimate vindication of God as Creator and Redeemer and of our embodied witness throughout history. It is the ultimate realization of our conformity to Christ and of life in the fullness of the Spirit. The new heaven and new earth will be sanctified to receive the heavenly city; this is the event by which heaven and earth are reconciled and God's will is done on earth as it is always done in heaven. The intermediate state of the soul in heaven still yearns for the resurrection. Ample biblical evidence suggests that the soul is not in a slumber while awaiting resurrection. The souls return with Christ at his second coming, returning to the earth so as to rise from the dust in glorified bodies to meet Christ in the air. This symbolism is rich, since Adam was originally created from the dust. Our rising in glorified bodies from the dust represents a grand fulfillment and the beginning of the making of all things new.

The controversies of evangelical eschatology involve the rapture doctrine and the millennium. The rapture doctrine focuses on the "catching up" of risen and transformed saints in the air to meet Christ, as reported in 1 Thessalonians 4:17. The pretribulation-rapture doctrine assumes that this text does not refer to the second coming of Christ to earth, but rather to an event that precedes end-time tribulation so as to deliver us from it. The other prominent view on this matter is that of a post-tribulation rapture, which assumes that Christ will only come again once, after the end-time tribulation. Christ will come again to fulfill the kingdom of God on earth. This position is called a post-tribulation-rapture view, when in reality it simply refuses to make the "rapture" an event in its own right apart from Christ's return to earth. In a sense, there is in this view no rapture doctrine, only a welcoming of Christ by the saints at his return.

The millennial doctrine is also controversial. The premillennial view of Christ's coming assumes that Christ will come again before ("pre") the millennial (one-thousand-year) reign on earth. The key text here is Revelation 20. After Christ returns in Revelation 19, chapter 20 indicates, for some, that Christ brings a thousand-year reign on earth, granting Israel and the nations another chance and perhaps also giving the earth a Sabbath rest before the new heaven and new earth arrive. But difficult questions remain. Are those who are converted at Christ's return transformed into glorified bodies? Is the millennial reign literally one thousand years long? Why does 2 Peter 3:10 indicate that the universe will be radically transformed at Christ's return? For this reason, some hold that Revelation 20 is symbolic of Christ's reign from heaven during the age of the church. This view is called amillennialism because it rejects the idea that there is an intermediate kingdom on earth (a millennium) in between Christ's return and the new heaven and new earth. Postmillennialism also holds that there is no intermediate kingdom in between Christ's return and the new heaven and new earth, because the church is thought to have basically fulfilled the kingdom through its witness prior to Christ's coming. The difference is that the church's witness is thought to be the agent of the kingdom's fulfillment. While premillennialism stresses the supernatural fulfillment of the kingdom as an act of God alone, postmillennialism accents the power of the church's witness to be the instrument of this fulfillment. Amillennialism looks to the reign of Christ from heaven as the focus of the church's vision and worship. Wherever one lands with this doctrine, the accents of the other views are worth holding on to.

Similarly, apocalyptic eschatology looks to a future ushered in by God alone, since it is unimaginably transcendent, beyond anything that resembles this present history. History will decline and fail; the kingdom will come in fullness to rescue believers from it. The prophetic vision highlights the mercy and justice of the kingdom of God as worked out in history. The church is urged to be an instrument of its fulfillment. The prophetic tradition does not necessarily deny a transcendent fulfillment that exceeds history as we know it; neither does it fail to see that the kingdom comes by grace. The fact is that the two visions are intertwined in Scripture; they need each other. The balance of our hope depends on it—a hope that is both dependent on grace alone and willing to obey as an instrument of the kingdom of God with courage and resolve.

TOPICS FOR REVIEW

1. What is life after death in heaven, according to John 14:1–3?
2. What is death in the Bible?
3. What is the intermediate state and its version in the doctrine of soul sleep? How does this chapter respond to soul sleep? What evidence is used against it?
4. Describe what the Bible teaches about the resurrection of the dead.
5. Describe the issue of end-time tribulation in Revelation 6 (and 11:18) and Luke 21:5–24.
6. Discuss the rapture issue and its pretribulation and post-tribulation views. Which is your view? Why?
7. Summarize the issue of the millennium, as covered in this chapter.

THE BOTTOM LINE

Theology is ultimately the wisdom that is gained in declaring the wonders of God and the wonders of God's love poured out into the world. And like all wisdom, theology has a path to take. Theology follows after the divine Son sent into flesh by the Father, who so loved the world (John 3:16). Theology follows the Christ who conquered sin and death and opened humanity to the sanctifying Spirit and the new creation. Theology follows the path of the cross, of divine self-giving love, to its decisive victory at the resurrection. Theologians look from there to theology's birthplace at the event of the risen Christ pouring forth the Spirit upon all flesh. This is the event of divine overflowing, of penetration into the depths of the soul, of expanse throughout many contexts, in reach beyond the bounds of nature and history. Christian theology was born at the moment of this overflowing love as a gift to the global church.

From there, theology follows the declaration of God's wonders in praise and witness among the people of God. Theology guides the path that they take of the crucified and risen life. God cannot be known apart from this path. The wisdom of theology is precisely the wisdom that is devoted to this path above all else. "Whoever does not love does not know God" (1 John 4:8). What motivates and guides theology is expressed powerfully by Paul: "For Christ's love compels us, because we are convinced that one died for all, and therefore all died. And he died for all, that those who live should no longer live for themselves but for him who died for them and was raised again" (2 Cor. 5:14–15). There is no other path for theology than this.

I cannot stress this point enough: theology is born out of loving God above all else, praising and adoring God for God's own sake. Theology comes into being in the cradle of the divine embrace, and its vocation is discovered in the goal of catching a glimpse of the divine glory. Theologians speak ultimately with God as the sole audience in mind, wishing above all else to please God.

They know that they cannot fully grasp the divine mystery, nor do they try, for the object of such manipulation would no longer be God but rather an idol. Theologians wish to join the worship of the church, which respects the mystery and rejoices at the goodness of God that has been revealed and that is yet to be revealed. Theology is driven by a hope that has courage, that attempts to be free from the shackles of a self-serving status quo. It is devoted to the kingdom of God that is coming and is yet to come. Theology declares the wonders of God to and with the saints and for the world. In declaring the wonders of God, theologians discover the beginning and the end of their gift and their craft. Of course, all giftings in the body of Christ begin and end at this place, and this is the point. Theologians share the worship and mission of the people of God and view themselves as one gift among others, wishing to edify the entire body of Christ, just like everyone else. Paul writes that "knowledge puffs up while love builds up" (1 Cor. 8:1). Theologians need to bear this in mind.

Within this church context, theologians explore the unique features of their gift so as to edify the body of Christ. Their task is to academically reflect on the grand truths of revelation as given to us in Scripture and the historic faith of the church. Theologians study texts with the help of disciplines like history, ancient languages, literary criticism, philosophy, and sociology. They explore the many issues that arise from the discipline of theology itself, with a zeal for truth and a respect for diversity. Differences of opinion that are not church dividing are accepted as par for the course; yet theology seeks to accent common ground among such differences.

Theologians speak to different contexts and learn from one another as they do so. Guided by love for God and others, theologians are willing to accept the "other," to embrace and respect God-given differences. Theological discourse that ignores or denigrates such differences does not follow the path of love or its social expression, which is justice. Theology in service to love and justice wants to listen especially to those voices that society has marginalized. How can theology effectively resist idolatry without this? How can the love for God and neighbor that drives theology ever flourish without this? If theology is ever to follow the path of the cross, it will not neglect listening to the voices that speak from suffering. It will be sure to attend to the questions that they ask. It will seek answers in service especially to them. And when theology reaches its limits, it will observe holy silence. It will not cheapen the hard questions of others with superficial answers. It will revere God in all of the mystery that surrounds God's loving purposes for the world. It will not be afraid to explore, to ask, or to speak. But it will also wait patiently for greater wisdom, knowing full well that this patience will follow the theological path all the way to the end.

And what a glorious end this will be.

RECOMMENDED RESOURCES

Barth, Karl. *Evangelical Theology: An Introduction*. Grand Rapids: Eerdmans, 1992.

Cone, James H. *The God of the Oppressed*. Maryknoll, NY: Orbis Books, 1975.

Dunn, James D. G. *Baptism in the Holy Spirit: A Re-examination of the New Testament Teaching on the Gift of the Spirit in Relation to Pentecostalism Today*. London: SCM, 1970.

Kärkkäinen, Veli-Matti, ed. *A Constructive Christian Theology for the Pluralistic World*. 5 vols. Grand Rapids: Eerdmans, 2013–2017.

Koyama, Kosuke. *Water Buffalo Theology*. Maryknoll, NY: Orbis Books, 1999.

Macchia, Frank D. *Jesus the Spirit Baptizer: Christology in Light of Pentecost*. Grand Rapids: Eerdmans, 2018.

———. *The Spirit-Baptized Church: A Dogmatic Inquiry*. T&T Clark Systematic Pentecostal and Charismatic Theology. New York: Bloomsbury T&T Clark, 2020.

———. *Tongues of Fire: A Systematic Theology of the Christian Faith*. Eugene, OR: Cascade Books, 2023.

———. *The Trinity, Practically Speaking*. Downers Grove, IL: IVP Books, 2010.

Moltmann, Jürgen. *The Trinity and the Kingdom: The Doctrine of God*. Translated by Margaret Kohl. Minneapolis: Fortress, 1993.

Olson, Roger E. *The Mosaic of Christian Belief: Twenty Centuries of Unity and Diversity*. Downers Grove, IL: IVP Academic, 2016.

———. *The Story of Christian Theology: Twenty Centuries of Tradition and Reform*. Downers Grove, IL: IVP Academic, 2009.

Pannenberg, Wolfhart. *Systematic Theology*. Translated by Geoffrey W. Bromiley. 3 vols. Grand Rapids: Eerdmans, 1991–1998.

Pelikan, Jaroslav. *The Christian Tradition: A History of the Development of Doctrine*. 5 vols. Chicago: University of Chicago Press, 1971–1990.

Sonderegger, Katherine. *Systematic Theology*. 2 vols. Minneapolis: Fortress, 2015.

Spencer, Aída Besançon. *Beyond the Curse: Women Called to Ministry*. Grand Rapids: Baker, 1985.

Tyra, Gary. *A Missional Orthodoxy: Theology and Ministry in a Post-Christian Context*. Downers Grove, IL: IVP Academic, 2013.

Vondey, Wolfgang, ed. *Routledge Handbook of Pentecostal Theology*. Routledge Handbooks in Theology. New York: Routledge, 2022.

Wright, N. T. *Surprised by Hope: Rethinking Heaven, the Resurrection, and the Mission of the Church*. San Francisco: HarperOne, 2008.

Yong, Amos. *Renewing Christian Theology: Systematics for a Global Christianity*. Waco: Baylor University Press, 2014.

AUTHOR INDEX

SCRIPTURE INDEX